THE ORIGINS
AND PREHISTORY
of
LANGUAGE

THE ORIGINS
AND PREHISTORY
of
LANGUAGE

by

G. RÉVÉSZ
*late Professor of Psychology at
the University of Amsterdam*

Translated from
the German by

J. BUTLER

GREENWOOD PRESS, PUBLISHERS
WESTPORT, CONNECTICUT

Copyright 1956 by Philosophical Library

Reprinted with the permission
of Philosophical Library, Inc., New York

First Greenwood Reprinting 1970

Library of Congress Catalogue Card Number 78-138128

SBN 8371-4167-2

Printed in the United States of America

PREFACE

THIS book presents a theory of the origins and prehistory of language, together with a new functional theory based on living language. It is introduced by a critique of the principal theories now current on the subject of linguistic origins.

The core of this psychological and philosophical discussion is contained in three earlier publications. Two of them appeared in 1941 and 1942 in Volumes 44 and 45 of the *Proceedings der K. Nederlandsche Akademie van Wetenschappen*, Amsterdam, under the titles 'Die menschlichen Kommunikationsformen und die sog. Tiersprache' and 'Das Problem des Ursprungs der Sprache'. The third, 'De l'origine du langage', was represented at the memorial meeting in commemoration of the birth of Ribot, and is published in the memorial volume, *Centenaire de Th. Ribot* (1939). Compared with these earlier publications, the present work embodies important changes. It combines my functional theory and my views of the prehistory and proto-history of language into a unified theory. But the earlier works are not entirely superseded by the wider scope and improved method of the present one; in particular my discussion of the forms of communication and the so-called animal languages (which are here treated only incidentally) may be regarded as complementary to the present work.

In this book we examine the problem of the prehistory of language as a whole, and the methodological viewpoints employed in studying it. We also consider the significance of language in the general development of human expression and activity. It is not intended to trace the evolution of language (that inexhaustible quarry of information regarding the workings of the human mind) through its entire course, but only up to the point which is marked by the beginning of the known historical existence of our language systems.

Our efforts toward the attainment of an understanding of the prehistory and proto-history of language will not be in vain if they help to clarify the relations between man's mind and his means of expression, and to keep alive an active interest in the study of language.

It is a pleasure to express my gratitude to my colleagues in different places for the interest with which they have followed the development of my ideas on linguistic psychology. I also wish to thank Mr. J. Butler for undertaking the English translation; and my colleague Professor John Cohen for reading the manuscript and for his interest and assistance in the publication of the English edition of this work.

THE AUTHOR.

Amsterdam, October 1954.

CONTENTS

I

INTRODUCTION

LANGUAGE is the most wonderful creation of the mind of man. Its origin is hidden in the distant darkness of an irrecoverable antiquity. Sheer lack of empirical evidence prevents our attaining any direct knowledge of the mental constitution of earliest man; we are similarly barred from any direct knowledge of the first beginnings of language.

We are nevertheless driven by our thirst for knowledge and by our interest in history to face the question: how did language originate? We are never content with knowledge of things as they exist; we want to know how they have come about. We wish to know the causes and beginnings of all things—the *archê geneseos*; we want to know what forces have been operative in the creation of new things and how they originally took shape.

This quest for origins is deeply rooted in man's striving for understanding. Its first impulse was derived not from scientific research but from meditations on the cosmos and man's relation to it. As long as man's faith in a higher dispensation was firm, as long as he remained convinced of the divine nature of the world, he referred the question of origins to the sphere of myth by invoking divinities. Gods were held responsible for the formation of the world; man could employ only such means as the gods put at his disposal. As Prometheus stole fire from Olympus, so had man acquired speech and writing from the gods themselves.

When this theological orientation had lost its hold on men's minds, inquiring spirits were stimulated to attempt to unveil the entire history of language, in the hope of obtaining a clear and consistent view of its remote and mysterious origin. The conviction arose that it would be possible to reconstruct the individual stages of the development of language and to identify the ultimate source of its earliest manifestations. Even after many fruitless attempts, the hope survived that linguistic development could be traced back to its antecedent forms—that is, to states embodying some of the basic elements of language but lacking in other essentials.

These efforts culminated in a variety of theories, such as the invention theory, which conceived of language as a creative act of man, and the accident theory, in which the origin of language was ascribed to happy chance. The doctrine of evolution prompted a series of genetic theories which sought to reconstruct the earliest beginnings of language and to supply the missing stages with the aid of material derived from child and animal psychology. There has even been discussion of the idea that the problem is fundamentally incapable of solution; though this view has scarcely been subjected to serious examination.

Since none of these theories found general acceptance, the problem of origins continued to be a subject of controversy. Great minds took part in it; many promising theories were propounded and much critical debate raged; but a generally satisfactory conclusion could not be reached. Gradually the debate died out, less from the conviction that the right answer had been found than from the feeling that the limit of useful speculation had been reached.

In view of the lack of success in previous enquiry it may seem rash to return to the same old problem and to attempt anew a task which so many eminent investigators have found fruitless. Indeed, it seemed to me at an earlier stage of my research that the hypotheses hitherto proposed were all so dubious that it was scientifically justifiable, in view of the special place of man in the organic world, to declare the problem insoluble. I took this view because linguistic history and psychology were unable to offer even a partially acceptable starting-point for reconstructing the forms of communication immediately antecedent to human speech; still less did they provide clues to the understanding of early man's latent tendencies toward language.[1]

Despite the approval bestowed on these arguments by psychologists and philologists, such a negative conclusion seemed to me unsatisfactory. I became convinced that although my scepticism concerning the problem of origins was justified to some extent, it was premature to insist that it could not be solved. Though I regard the gulf that separates human speech from animal communication as unbridgeable, I do not see any sufficient reason for abandoning the idea of a more or less continuous biological evolution. I therefore began to consider the principles of evolution with a view to discovering whether expressions and tendencies could not be found in modern man which might point to a prelinguistic stage or an archaic form of communication, and which might serve as the starting-point for a theory of linguistic evolution. In this manner I hit upon a basic principle indicating a way of arranging human and animal forms of communication in a developmental sequence that would be valid from the point of view of psychology. It proved to be possible to set up a series of gradually differentiated stages leading from the most primitive forms of contact to language in its present developed form. The evolutionary point of view adopted is one which establishes a link between language and prelinguistic forms of contact, without prejudice to the uniqueness and autonomy of language.

There can be no doubt that my new approach represents a scientific advance compared with the old.[2] My earlier view that the problem of linguistic origins is insoluble could have nothing to contribute to linguistic theory; but my contact theory offers new and fruitful points of departure not only for linguistic psychology and general linguistic science but for the prehistory of mankind and for comparative psychology.

In the first part of this work I delimit the problem of origins

---

1 G. Révész, 'De l'Origine du Langage', *Centenaire de Th. Ribot, Seance commémorative à la Sorbonne*, 1939.

2 See my publications in the *Proceedings K. Ned. Akademie van Wetenschappen* for the years, 1940, 1941, and 1942 (Vols. XLIII, XLIV and XLV).

and state the principles to be kept in mind in discussing it. I then examine critically most of the theories of origin now current, and demonstrate that none of them is tenable. The section dealing with psychological evolution is introduced by a discussion of the functions of language, which are considered from a point of view that is new to psychology and linguistics. These functions play a decisive role in establishing the stages by which language developed from its earliest to its most advanced form.

Following this section of the work there is a change in our approach to the problem under consideration. In turning from the discussion of the views of others to the exposition of my own theory, instead of taking language itself as the starting-point I begin with a more general phenomenon, the forms of contact or communication employed by living creatures; of which language is only one. In identifying its antecedent forms we will not arbitrarily postulate elements of language such as expressive sounds, expressive gestures, or interjections, as is done in the well-known phylogenetic and ontogenetic doctrines of linguistic origins. On the contrary: the forms through which communication is accomplished and the stimuli which give rise to them will be precisely defined according to a basic principle of selection which embraces all the modes of communication. In this way we arrive at a biologically founded version of the development of communication which takes the idea of evolution into account without being dominated by it. This becomes the basis of a new theory, the contact theory, which illuminates the entire field of communications, including language. The results of our enquiry will depend on the validity and comprehensiveness of these guiding principles.

II

THE PROBLEM OF ORIGINS

STUDY of the human and the animal worlds reveals a striking phenomenon which has an important bearing on the basic problem of anthropology. Animals now living on the earth have existed in their present form for many thousands, probably even hundreds of thousands of years. During this time their instincts, emotions, needs, and patterns of behaviour, their individual capacities and their forms of social life have not shown the slightest change. The elephant roaming the jungles of Tertiary times behaved exactly like present-day elephants; it used its trunk for grasping, groping or drinking, and employed its tusks for tearing off bark or uprooting the soil, just as elephants do now. In prehistoric times the bees were just as suitably organized and regimented in their economy, and just as ferocious in pursuit of their enemies, as they are at present. In ancient times the young ass frolicked as gaily and comically as today; and crocodiles do not seem to have gained at all in amiability since the days of Leviathan.

This immutability in the way of life of animals can be explained by the fact that they are completely bound by their environment. Submitting wholly to the forces of nature, they have no choice but to adapt themselves to their physical surroundings. Governed entirely by instincts, they obey a conservative principle that protects whatever exists and resists any change. The animal can alter nothing in its circumstances of life or ways of behaviour through its own initiative; only natural events or changes of environment, such as domestication, capture, geographical change, can compel it to modify its habitual responses. Even animals which have been improved by cross-breeding retain most of the characteristics of wild creatures of their kind.

During this same long period, man has been caught up in a process of ceaseless change. In the course of it he has experienced a mental and moral evolution that has completely recast his individual and collective experiences and outlook, capacities and way of life.

Stone Age man started off with a very different culture and a much more primitive mental constitution than modern man. But he challenged nature, and emancipated himself from subjection to natural circumstances. He evolved new needs, and developed his talent for invention in order to satisfy them. It was in socially striving to appease these vital new needs that he discovered the use of fire for food preparation, learned to practise livestock-raising, agriculture and handicrafts, produced art, evolved religion and law, and created forms of social order. By refusing to submit completely to the dictates of nature and tradition, he won intellectual and moral freedom. He thereby attained the possibility of self-development, a possibility which he put to abundant use in the subsequent course of history. Thus the formerly dominant conservative principle gave way to greater elasticity. Biologically determined instinctive forces yielded to reason; the compulsion of the instincts gave way to freedom of decision.

If we now ask, 'What is it that separates man eternally from the beasts?' the answer can only be what, before the ascendance of evolutionary thought, was recognized as the only valid answer; *reason*. Though it may be difficult to define the concept of reason without ambiguity, it is easy to specify an unmistakable sign of its presence: *language*. It is language, the medium of mutual understanding, with its close relationship to thinking and its cultural and social importance, that makes man human, and fundamentally distinguishes him from the animals.

'In the beginning was the Word', the Logos, reason, the creative idea. Human existence begins with language. As Wilhelm von Humboldt says: man is only man because of language; he had to be human to invent language. The formula: *no language without man, no man without language,* lends a special interest to the question of the origins of language, and furnishes a clearly-defined starting-point for research.

This formula is not only a definition of man; to my mind it is the only acceptable standpoint from which man and language can be studied in their specifically anthropological sense. From an anthropological point of view man cannot be imagined except as a thinking and speaking being; for only the notion of a being capable of speech and thought is compatible with the empirical content of the concept of man. If we do not adhere strictly to an anthropological approach in this connexion, especially in dealing with genetic problems, we shall unavoidably become entangled in contradictions.[1]

A fictitious example may best illustrate the difficulties that would arise through failure to follow an anthropological method.

An expedition sets out to make a thorough study of the most primitive people on earth, the pygmies. Let us suppose that in searching for hitherto unknown primitive tribes the expedition stumbles unexpectedly upon some man-like creatures who differ from the pygmies only in that they do not employ language in their social intercourse. They make emotional sounds somewhat like the apes; but they have nothing that can be called a language, either of sounds or of gestures. On the ground of their external similarity to the pygmies, it is decided, with some misgivings, to regard these creatures as human despite their lack of language, and to consider them to be closely related to the hypothetical speechless primitive men, the *homines alali*. Should it then be discovered that these creatures wear self-made coverings, to be sure of the most primitive sort, to protect themselves from the weather or, from feelings of modesty, to cover parts of their bodies, this discovery would confirm the impression that they

---

1 Similar ideas have been expressed by W. von Humboldt in his study *Über das vergleichende Sprachstudium* (1820) and H. Delacroix in *Le Langage et la Pensée* (1930, pp. 218 ff.) Ernest Renan also shared this view; he once expressed himself as follows: 'C'est donc un rêve d'imaginer un premier état où l'homme ne parle pas, suivi d'un autre état où il conquit l'usage de la parole. L'homme est naturellement parlant, comme il est naturellement pensant' (*De l'Origine du Langage*, Paris, 1859).

were human beings. We pass over the fact that in classifying these problematical creatures we have attributed greater importance to clothing than to speech.

If on closer examination it should then prove that these 'pygmies' possess a fine long tail, which they use in climbing and jumping just like gibbons, our observers would be in a dilemma. Should they continue to regard these creatures as human, or should they assign them, on account of external somatic features that occur only in animals, to the animal world? Probably they would prefer the latter view.

Stimulated by this discovery, the expedition pushes further into the interior, and behold, they encounter similar pygmy-like beings, likewise equipped with long tails—but who can talk. It is even found that individual European words occur in their vocabulary, so that conversation with these arboreal creatures is possible to some degree. Despite their tails, despite their complete nakedness and their ape-like behaviour, one would feel compelled to call them human.

With the speechless 'pygmies' we employed somatic characteristics as the criterion of classification; the decision depending upon whether the creatures resembled men or apes more closely. With the creatures that resembled animals but talked, an anthropological trait, language, was selected as the basis of classification. Thus, in dealing with creatures gifted with speech an *anthropological* characteristic was used to determine the species; if they lacked speech, their assignment depended upon *biological* traits. Such dilemmas and methodological inconsistencies are avoided if we adhere to the proposition stated above, which is well founded empirically as well as logically: namely, that humanity is inseparably associated with language.

In fables animals are provided with human minds, just because they have the power of speech. All manner of human qualities, capacities and emotions are ascribed to them without falling into obvious contradictions. They appear simply as humans in animal form, and represent much nobler creatures than would human beings with bestial characteristics.

To avoid straying into dead ends during the course of our investigation we must not only postulate an inseparable bond between man and language; we must also, at the very beginning, define precisely the fundamental concepts involved in the evolution of language.

Truly reflective minds will not care to rest content with the view that the 'first' man was capable of understanding 'the language of God' and could communicate his wishes and thoughts by means of speech or speech-related gestures from the very beginning. It may be assumed that language has a prehistory, including stages in which the progenitors of present-day man employed means of expression which preceded true speech. We must seek to recover or reconstruct these prelinguistic stages, which must have begun several hundred thousand years ago and have lasted to the point of time when true language began.

Our thought is so strongly under the influence of the idea of continuous evolution that our knowledge of so advanced a cultural phenomenon as language can only be regarded as incomplete until we have found a sufficient explanation of its origin and a plausible conception of the sources from which it developed. But the problem must be formulated accurately before it can be solved. In particular we must state exactly what is meant by the concept of origin; from which our present task arises.

In speaking of the origin of a phenomenon or a function either of two different things can be meant. On the one hand we may be referring to the *form* in which the phenomenon or function first appears in the course of its development. Alternatively, we may have in mind its *antecedent state*; that is to say, the unformed material out of which, by a process of formation or mutation, the phenomenon or function arises. To employ Aristotle's illustration of the statue and its raw material in a slightly altered sense: the original lump of clay represents the statue's antecedent state, but not its initial form. The assumption of form by the material we describe as the *origin*. The most primitive expression of the form which yet contains all the essential criteria by which the kind may be distinguished we call the initial, earliest, or most primitive

B

form. This then develops or becomes modified into higher, more differentiated forms.

On the basis of these definitions we can divide the entire course of the evolution of language into three phases. The first of these we may call the *prehistory* of language; which includes the preparatory stages antecedent to true language. The second is the *early history*, or proto-history, of language; its aim is to reconstruct the earliest stages of language from the beginning of spoken and gestural communication to the hypothetical initial form of language. The third is the *historical stage* proper; it describes the evolution of our present language systems and establishes the laws of their development. Thus we have the framework of a *three-phase theory* on the basis of a division into evolutionary stages.

We must next consider how one distinguishes, from a logical standpoint, between an antecedent state and an initial stage, and between an original and a more advanced stage of development.

The existence of the same form at various stages of differentiation logically implies that we are dealing with a single kind or species in different degrees of specialization. This applies, for example, in comparing the language of children with that of adults; in comparing different stages in the evolution of one and the same language; or in respect of primitive languages, to the extent that these may be regarded as ancestral forms of more mature languages. If, on the other hand, two stages of development are not linked by community of kind, the emergence of one from the other signifies a change in kind. In this case we designate the chronologically anterior stage as the antecedent stage of the later, more differentiated phenomenon or function.

Thus the first condition for regarding a higher form as a derivative of a lower is the presence of common specific characteristics. The common factor can be similarity of form, of structure, or of purpose. The last case occurs whenever the common characteristic denoting the species presupposes the existence of a common basic tendency. This basic tendency can be manifested in various ways; such as in a specific striving or in the gradual development of a basic function or of a partial function of a particular kind. If such a tendency is discoverable, we are justified in assuming an evolutionary sequence, in the sense that the differentiated form has emerged as a result of the modification of the less differentiated one. This can be demonstrated more easily if other common characteristics are also found. No rule can be given for deciding when only one distinguishing trait need be identified and when more than one are necessary; it depends on the field with which we are concerned, the nature of the anterior form, and what sort of transitional forms occur between the primitive and the fully developed forms. If corresponding characteristics or unambiguous criteria are lacking, the derivation cannot be convincingly demonstrated.

This applies not only to the psychical and intellectual functions but to expressions and values of a social or cultural nature as well. Music could only be derived from forms of expression that already possessed the constituent characteristics of music. Similarly forms of human society can only have developed out of associations previously possessing those constituent social elements or forces which are essential to all forms of human society.

In determining the common characteristics of a species the methodological rule to be followed is the same as in any definition of species; namely, to proceed step by step and not by leaps and bounds, so that the points of transition may not be overlooked. In a sense the study of an evolutionary process reverses the procedure followed in definition. The latter proceeds from the species by way of specifying the lowest varieties; while the study of evolution traces the forms of the phenomenon or function under study by means of generalizing to the highest—that is, to the least specific—variety within the species, in order to identify the point at which the transition to a new species occurs.

It is very important to distinguish clearly between the initial stage of a phenomenon or function and the antecedent stage. An antecedent stage does not possess the distinctive criteria of the species; an initial stage does possess some of them. There is admittedly a subjective element involved in deciding what is to be recognized as the essential or the important criteria in distinguishing different species. But once the criteria of a group of phenomena have been carefully established it will be possible to decide in every case whether an initial stage or an antecedent one is involved. The difficulties that occasionally arise in a decision of this kind can be overcome if the distinction between the two is kept clearly in mind so that confusion is impossible. For example, the mating calls of animals belong at the most to the antecedent stage, but not to the initial stage of language. The mating call cannot belong to the initial stage because it lacks all the specific criteria which distinguish language from other forms of communication; it has neither the basic function, the symbolic nature, the articulation, the intonation, nor the grammatical structure of language. On the other hand, mating calls can be regarded as an antecedent form in the evolution of language, because it can be shown that they owe their origin to the same basic tendency as all the higher forms of communication, language included.

In doubtful cases a teleological criterion may be used. If, that is to say, two early forms of a phenomenon have the same *purpose*, it is generally justifiable to regard the more primitive form as the earlier in psychological development. But one must then determine to what extent the actual nature of the particular form logically justifies its inclusion as a member of the evolutionary sequence. From this standpoint we will be disposed to accept the mating call as an antecedent form in the evolution of language, provided it serves the same needs and pursues the same purposes as human speech.

On the other hand, it would not be permissible to put mere expressive sounds in the sequence of evolution of communication as an antecedent stage of language. Despite their resemblance to interjections in form, their purpose—the relief of inner tension— is not the same as language. This is also true of imitative sounds. The fact that there are formal resemblances, external similarities, between such sounds and the words they imitate is not sufficient to determine whether or not the capacity to imitate sounds can be regarded as an antecedent stage of language. This can only be decided after looking more deeply to ascertain whether or not the two activities are linked by a common tendency or purpose. From this standpoint we find that there is no inner connexion between imitative sounds and words, or between the impulse to imitate and the impulse to speak. Consequently we do not associate the imitation of sounds with the prehistory of language.[1]

In the study of linguistic origins these methodological requirements have been greatly neglected, chiefly because no one has properly understood what to look for. No distinction has been made between, on the one hand, forms of expression which played an important part in language formation but which cannot be regarded as verbal forms themselves, and, on the other, forms which actually represent the earliest stage of true language. Some theories, such as the imitation theory and the gesture theory, pertain to the antecedent stage of language; while others—for example, those based on ethnology and child psychology— appertain to primitive language proper. The same criticism applies to the evolutionary theories of the comparative philologists, such as Schleicher[2] and Jespersen,[3] who attempt to derive the higher types of language from lower ones (for example, the inflectional languages from the agglutinating ones) but who make no attempt to reconstruct the antecedent prelinguistic stages.

The task of identifying the forms of expression which immediately preceded language is a difficult one; the farther back one reaches, the more hypothetical and arbitrary these stages must be. This is not only true of language but of all human functions and capacities. In seeking to reconstruct a basic function of the human

1 A view similar to ours is held by Hönigswald, who maintains that previous investigation into the problem of origins has failed mainly because of the absence of a clear and consistent methodological approach. He believes that the origin of language can be discovered through the study of its ultimate causes (*Philosophie der Sprache*, 1937, p. 21). My own opinion is that the ultimate cause of the development of language is to be sought in the tendency to create a community of mutual comprehension through linguistic means.

2 A. Schleicher, *Über die Bedeutung der Sprache für die Naturgeschichte des Menschen*, 1865; *Darwinism Tested by the Science of Language* (1865).

3 O. Jespersen, *Progress in Language* (1894).

mind one must therefore proceed with caution, and with full consciousness that there is nothing but inference and analogy to build upon. One must not be deceived by mere resemblances, nor attempt to derive an advanced state from a more primitive one unless there are demonstrable similarities, and until one has carefully considered whether the principles and conditions stated above have been satisfied.

Special care must be taken in dealing with evolutionary problems extending far beyond the bounds of empirical knowledge and tradition. A critical attitude and a sense of historical development are necessary in order to preserve a proper balance between experience and theory. All this applies especially to language. Although no other cultural possession of man allows of such exact determination of the conditions of its later development, there is perhaps no other cultural element that offers so few facts about its origin.[1]

The monuments and artifacts of the prehistoric period that throw light on the development of mankind in antiquity tell us nothing concerning language. We are forced to rely on reconstruction of the prelinguistic condition of early men from expressions manifested by recent man. In so doing, we proceed from the assumption that present-day man still uses archaic forms of expression in his social intercourse which he has carried over from his 'prelinguistic' period. We will discuss later how these primary expressions can be evaluated from the point of view of evolution and whether they can be pursued even further back into the animal period.[2]

To establish the relationship between language and prelinguistic forms of communication and arrange them under a common heading we need to find a more general concept which will

[1] H. Paul, *Prinzipien der Sprachgeschichte* (1920), p. 4.

[2] Applying similar considerations to the study of artistic creation, one comes to the conclusion that the problem of origins in art could only be solved if the utilitarian forms of the products of primitive cultures could be clearly distinguished from the purely artistic forms. But it appears that even with primitive pottery, representing the purest products of automatic manual activity, the practical intention cannot be distinguished from the artistic.

include all the forms of communication, linguistic and non-linguistic, serving the same purpose; we cannot stretch the concept of language to include forms of expression which are not of the same nature as language. For this more general concept we choose the name *communication*, embracing all forms of utterance serving the purpose of mutual understanding.

For the sake of completeness we must consider the broader meaning of the word 'origin'. It is sometimes employed to designate those forces, internal or external, that bring a thing, a function, or a phenomenon into existence. It is commonly employed in connexion with the problem of life; in this sense Driesch uses the Aristotelian concept of entelechy,[1] Bergson that of élan vital,[2] Schopenhauer that of the Will,[3] Darwin that of the instinctive struggle for existence,[4] Freud that of the sexual instinct,[5] etc. The same conception of origin is implied when the physicist sees the ultimate cause of light in electromagnetic waves; when the student of aesthetics attributes the origin of artistic activity to an inner urge to create and organize forms; when the linguistic scientist attributes the origin of speech to the tendency to communicate or to God's gift. A satisfactory theory of the origin of language must provide an explanation of the forces that produced and gave form to speech, as well as an account of the antecedent and early forms of language, that is reasonable, logical, and sound from the point of view of evolutionary principles. We hope to show that the theory of origins which we have developed —the contact theory—fully meets these requirements.

These theoretical and methodological considerations are a necessary introduction to a critical analysis of the theories of linguistic origins and development. Now, in accordance with what has been said above, we must set forth a provisional definition of language; then establish on the basis of an analysis of speech

---

1 H. Driesch, *Der Vitalismus als Geschichte und als Lehre* (1905) and *Philosophie des Organischen* (1908).

2 H. Bergson, *L'évolution créatrice* (1910).

3 A. Schopenhauer, *Die Welt als Wille und Vorstellung* (1819).

4 C. Darwin, *The Expression of the Emotions in Man and Animals* (1892).

5 S. Freud, *Vorlesungen zur Einführung in die Psychoanalyse, Ges. Schriften*, VII (1924).

activity the essential criteria of language; and finally use these criteria to arrive at a final definition.[1]

Provisionally we wish to define as the basic function of language *the utterance or communication of words or groups of words for the purpose of mutual understanding.*[2]

For the psychologist the communicative function of language, which aims at the production of social contact between people, is primary; the fact that thought is expressed in the form of internal monologue presupposes the prior development of external speech activity. The fact that talking to oneself aloud is regarded as eccentric proves sufficiently that the basic objective of language is the communication of experiences and information to others. It is the goal of theories of origin to show how this communicative function of language has gradually developed out of more primitive forms of contact.

[1] For the final definition see below, pp. 124 ff.; where my views are also stated regarding the general principles to be observed in definition.

[2] From this point of view it seems curious that Piaget should regard the language of children up to the age of seven as essentially egocentric (*Le Langage et la Pensée*, 1923). It is hard to believe that in a period in which the seven-year-old child can already connect cause and effect without error, recognize regularities in nature, and use analogies as a method of thought, he can do no better than to use speech chiefly as monologue in play.

III

THEORIES OF ORIGINS

(A) INTRODUCTION

In the exposition of linguistic theories the systematic treatment of those dealing with origins has hitherto been neglected. No one has even called attention to the great diversity of viewpoints adopted in attempting to solve this problem.

It was Wundt who paved the way for the classification of theories of origins.[1] He distinguished between theories of invention and imitation, a theory of miraculous origin, and an evolutionary theory. This classification cannot be justified either from a historical or from a systematic standpoint. Scarcely more suitable is the classification proposed by Rudolf Eisler, who divided them into theological, inventive, and psychogenetic theories of origin. In the first group language is regarded as a direct gift of God; in the second, as the invention of gifted individuals; in the third group a variety of factors are held to be responsible for its origin, such as imitation, expressive gestures, interjections, or the communicative impulse.[2]

Another possible approach would be to classify the theories of origin on the basis of nativism and empiricism; most of the older scholars having continually emphasized these epistemological viewpoints. Here we need only mention the controversy between the nativists (Humboldt, Heyse, Renan, Adelung, Lennep, Lazarus, Steinthal, M. Mueller, Wundt) and the empiricists (Condillac, Tiedemann, Darwin, Spencer, L. Geiger, Taylor, Carus, Michelet, Madvig, Marty). Study of the theories from

[1] W. Wundt, *Die Sprache*, II (1912).
[2] R. Eisler, *Wörterbuch der philosophischen Begriffe*, III (1930), p. 142.

this standpoint leads to the conclusion that they do not really accept the consequences of the principles on which they are based. They oscillate between the two theoretical opposites, and really differ only in that they assign different roles to the nativistic and empirical factors in the origin and development of language. Consequently, these theories of cognition cannot serve as a useful basis for the classification of the theories of origin.[1]

A different division of the theories is reached by contrasting the teleological view of the basis and development of language with the views which emphasize naturalistic, unconscious, deterministic aspects. A classification of this kind also proves unsuitable; important as these headings are in other respects, not all of the theories will fit under them, as we shall show in detail in Chapter IV.

In the exposition and criticism of these theories, based as they are on diverse points of view, I think it best to distinguish between *biological* and *anthropological* hypotheses. A theory deriving human speech from animal reactions and patterns of behaviour, and placing the antecedent stages of language in the animal world, may be called a biological theory. An anthropological theory assumes, on the contrary, that even in its antecedent forms language is a product of the human mind; that at some stage of his development man was impelled by social and material circumstances to use his mental powers to create a special mode of communication, finding its most adequate means of expression in spoken language.[2]

Looking at language from the evolutionary point of view, the biologically-minded theorists stress the prehistoric phase of language, and envisage its gradual development from a biologically rooted non-linguistic mode of communication. This obviously calls for special attention to the modes of expression used by higher animals and by children in their prelinguistic stages. This

---

[1] Cf. the discussion on pp. 64 ff.

[2] Both these types appear in Greek philosophy, especially among the Sophists, who debated whether human language owes its origin to nature (*physei*) or human invention (*thesei*).

approach must rely on an ostensible relationship between forms of communication used by animals ('animal languages') and spoken or gestural human language, and emphasizes the parallels between ontogenetic and phylogenetic development in language.

For the proponents of anthropological linguistic theories, on the other hand, the prehistory of language is not a problem at all. Their research begins with, and is confined to, human language. In their view the question of origins has nothing at all to do with hypothetical early forms of *communication*, but only with early forms of *language*. They are concerned, that is to say, only with phenomena exhibiting elements and functions found in fully developed language, and that can be regarded on psychological and linguistic grounds as having been constituents of language from its very beginning. Such theories are mainly concerned with recorded linguistic material and the languages of primitive peoples. Their evidence largely derives from the present, only exceptionally going back several millennia; and this is a very small time-span compared with the period in which the various modes of communication have existed. When the proponents of these theories do speculate on the earliest forms of expression and communication they unjustifiably overstep the bounds of their proper field of research, and lose sight of their goal. They artificially connect two quite different fields of study using dissimilar materials and methods. It is in this way that certain ideas enter linguistic science and win unmerited acceptance.

The objection to these theories, and especially the biological ones, is their assumption of an original speechless state of humanity. This assumption can have two different meanings. The first assumes a *Homo alalus* as a *fiction*. This is scientifically defensible only if it can be shown to be profitable for future research. Here the concept of *Homo alalus* serves only as a sort of *working* hypothesis, and disregards the question whether there ever really was a speechless state in human prehistory. The other standpoint gives *Homo alalus* the character of a *hypothesis*, and does not exclude the possibility of there having actually been a period of prehistoric times when man's expression of his emotions and desires was like that of the higher animals, and of language having gradually developed out of such primitive modes of expression. Such a hypothesis is unprovable, and depends in any case on the definition of 'man'. If language is regarded as the most important characteristic of humanity, and if the two are inseparably associated, the hypothesis of primitive man without language is quite meaningless. For man without language was, by definition, not yet man; it would not make sense to have linguistic development beginning at a stage prior to the existence of language. From this standpoint a division of language into two parts, one of which is anterior to language, is obviously absurd. Postulating a prelinguistic stage of linguistic development leads to misunderstandings and to ideas that are fatal to research, such as the idea of primitive man without language. Linguistic evolution can only begin where language has manifested itself, when the first impulse to assertion and communication appears in its very simplest forms.

To facilitate our exposition of a new theory of linguistic origins it will be appropriate to survey the most important existing theories on this subject. In so doing we shall show that all of them have such flaws in their premises and approach, and even in their logic and content, that they do not appear to fulfil the conditions required of an evolutionary theory.

(B) BIOLOGICAL THEORIES

I. THE THEORY OF EXPRESSIVE GESTURES AND SOUNDS

It is not surprising that from the very beginning of the theoretical study of linguistic origins efforts have been made to derive language from expressive gestures and sounds, which are biological in origin and characteristic of all the more highly organized living beings.[1]

[1] The derivation of language from the emotions, that state of excitement which is common to men and animals, is already met with in Epicurus. E. Cassirer, *Philosophie der symbolischen Formen*, I (1923), p. 89.

According to this theory, language is unique in character and clearly distinguishable from spontaneous expressive gestures and sounds, but it is nevertheless a means of expressing experience. Thus both speech and gesture-language can be derived from expressive gestures. In view of the fact that the act of speech is supported and supplemented by spontaneous modes of expression and the further fact that ontogenetically the spontaneous emotional reactions of children gradually change into deliberate speech sounds and gestures, it is comprehensible that the spontaneous modes of expression should be regarded phylogenetically as the forerunner of language. This explains the prominence of the theory of expressive reactions among theories of origins and the wide acceptance it has attained. (Compare Condillac,[1] Wundt,[2] Darwin,[3] Spencer,[4] Höffding,[5] Madvig,[6] Ziehen,[7] Bechterew,[8] Jerusalem,[9] and also O. Jespersen.[10])

Seen from this standpoint, it is not surprising that in formulating theories of expression special weight has been placed upon the alleged external similarity of expressive sounds to elements of speech. But it has escaped the notice of these theorists that the similarities are only apparent and based on superficial observation and careless definition. Descartes warned us three hundred years ago not to identify expressive sounds with speech sounds or words. In his famous work on scientific method he declares:

'Et il ne doit pas confondre les paroles avec les mouvements naturels qui témoignent les passions, et peuvent être imités par des machines aussi bien que par les animaux; ni penser, comme quelques anciens, que les bêtes parlent, bien que nous n'entendions pas leur langage.'[11]

---

[1] E. B. Condillac, *Sur l'origine des connaissances humaines* (1746), I, p. 1.
[2] W. Wundt, *Die Sprache* (1911), I, pp. 43 ff.
[3] C. Darwin, *The Expression of the Emotions in Man and Animals* (1892).
[4] H. Spencer, *Principles of Psychology* (London, 1899).
[5] H. Höffding, *Psychologie* (1912), p. 212.
[6] L. Madvig, *Om Sprogets Väsen, Udvikling og Liv* (Copenhagen, 1842).
[7] Th. Ziehen, *Leitfaden der physiologischen Psychologie* (1898), p. 238.
[8] W. Bechterew, *Objektive Psychologie* (1913), p. 379.
[9] W. Jerusalem, *Lehrbuch der Psychologie* (1907).
[10] O. Jespersen, *Sprogets Oprindelse* (1882).
[11] R. Descartes, *Discours de la méthode* (Leiden, 1637), p. 58.

Herder too, in his well-known work on the origin of language, pointing to the essential difference between phonetic expression and words, says:

> But I cannot conceal my astonishment at the fact that philosophers, that is people who seek clear concepts, can have arrived at the idea that the origin of human language is to be found in these emotional cries; for are they not obviously something quite different? All animals, even the mute fish, express their feelings by sounds; but not even the most highly developed animals have so much as the beginnings of true human speech. However formed and refined and organized these sounds may be, if the intelligence to use them purposefully is lacking, I do not see how, in accordance with the previously-mentioned law of nature, they ever become deliberate human speech. Children produce emotional sounds like animals; but is the language they learn from human beings not an entirely different language?[1]

If more attention had been paid to the statements of these philosophers, and if it had been recognized that the problem is first and foremost anthropological, depending for its solution not on biological experiences but on psychological considerations and on the contrast in the nature of the two phonetic phenomena, so much effort would not have been wasted in defending and attacking the expressive sounds and gestures theory. (This observation is not limited to this theory alone but applies in greater or less degree to most of the doctrines which are to be discussed here.[2])

The outward similarity stressed by advocates of the expressive theory applies to the mere acoustic phenomenon, and not to

[1] J. G. Herder, *Ursprung der Sprache* (1772), p. 24.

[2] It is time that we emancipated ourselves from the erroneous idea that scientific truth, in the arts especially, is a function of time. We ought to cease thinking that things are important merely because they are new. Study of the original works of great thinkers is always stimulating and instructive. I have noticed that even highly estimable comparative philologists of the younger generation have not read, for example, von Humboldt's works on the philosophy of language, regarding them merely as historical documents in comparative philology. If trouble is taken to study these and similar works thoroughly, they will be found not only stimulating and intellectually refreshing but inspiring by virtue of the scientific ardour and modesty of spirit displayed by their authors.

those spoken sounds whose phonological, morphological and semasiological content is determined by an inner linguistic sense. It is, of course, true that all expressive sounds, cries as well as words, are vocal, and as such have certain purely auditory qualities in common. But the vocal organ and its physiological function of producing sounds are all that emotional cries and speech have in common. The total character and the intention of the sounds produced are fundamentally different in each case. It would be analogous to seek to derive gesture from the grasping movement; for here too the external similarity applies only to the organ (arm and hand) and to the movement as such, but not to the form of the movement, which derives its character from the intention.[1]

If we refuse to be influenced by the purely superficial resemblance of emotional utterances to linguistic forms, and by their chronological sequence in ontogenetic development; if we start off by evaluating the two types of utterance on the basis of the needs and purposes they satisfy, it will be seen that the two modes of expression are essentially different in nature and wholly divergent in function. Spontaneous expressive gestures and sounds are based on the tendency to give free rein to inner emotions; their purpose is the instinctive furtherance of vital aims. In fright, for example, inner tension is released directly by the mimic, pantomimic or acoustic expression of the emotion, and at the same time a mechanism of flight is set in motion for speedy escape from the dangerous situation. The act of speech, in contrast to this, is based on the need for communication. Its aim is personal and social contact, with the accruing advantages for the persons thereby brought into contact.

A further difference between mere emotional expression and language is in the respective unity or multiplicity of their experiential content. The mere expression of emotion does not add anything to the content to which it relates, but simply and directly

---

[1] K. Bühler expresses the same thought in saying that expressive gestures only become language when 'the natural eloquence of the human body is developed and transformed into a system of symbols on the model of an evolved language; as in the gesture-language of deaf-mutes'. *Sprachtheorie* (1934), p. 70.

displays it; language, on the other hand, splits the content of experience into the subjective experience and the 'object' to which or concerning which something is being communicated. Further, language basically *means* something; and as Husserl argues with special clarity, this 'meaning' is something quite different from the 'expression of a psychosomatic state', no matter what external form the expression may take.[1]

A further difference between these two modes of expression is in their relation to volition. The most obvious characteristic of the purely expressive gesture is its involuntary nature. Not only is there no intention to indicate the subjective experience of which it is the expression, still less to indicate outer circumstances; there is not even the slightest intention or tendency to produce any particular effect on others. Purely expressive sounds and gestures have an indicative or symptomatic function; they indicate inward conditions, but do not communicate them. Hence a gesture made with the purpose of frightening off an enemy is no more a purely expressive gesture than a greeting is an expression of pure affection. If the expressive gesture is associated with the tendency or intention to establish contact with others it ceases to be purely an expressive gesture and becomes either a sign or a linguistic symbol.[2]

Thus expressive gestures and sounds do not constitute a means of communication as such. Their only relation to the linguistic function is that to some extent they have found entry into living language after modification under the influence of speech sounds. Such cases are, however, exceptional. Very few words in human language can be derived from expressive sounds; and the numerous interjections used by children in their prelinguistic period do not normally survive as speech. It is therefore much more likely that it is not the expressive sounds that have played a constructive role in the origin of language, but rather the reverse: the linguistic function has transformed some expressive sounds

---

[1] E. Husserl, *Logische Untersuchungen*, I (1922).

[2] On the concepts of sign and symbol see p. 166; further discussion of the subject of expressive gestures is on pp. 152 ff.

into a means of communication.[1] But this could only be the
result of a change in their function and of a gradual phonetic
change. Hönigswald takes the same view when he says that 'the
proposition that the word could have originated from the animal
cry remains totally empty and vague as long as it is not shown
how that which lacks meaning acquires meaning'.[2] Why do
animal cries, so plentiful in nature, not also develop into words?
Indeed, why do we shrink from asserting that parrots talk, when
they do actually utter words that are ostensibly coherent and
intelligible to man?

In view of these circumstances and the salient fact that the
purely expressive reactions have nothing generically in common
with language, it follows that they cannot be accepted either as
the earliest form of language or as the antecedent form from
which speech symbols could be presumed to have arisen according, as it were, to biophysical laws. They arise, as stated, from a
different need and pursue a different object; hence they have
nothing to do with the tendency leading to language.

Though the difference between expressive reactions and actual
speech sounds and gestures is clear in theory, it is often difficult
in practice to decide whether or not an expressive gesture or a
spontaneously uttered sound has communicative intent. This
applies to a number of instinctive expressive gestures belonging in
animals and man to the inventory of innate sensory-motor reactions. A baby's smile, for instance, not only expresses its own
contentment but very soon serves as a means of putting its
environment into a friendly mood. To this extent, but only to
this extent, is it possible to accept such transitional forms between
expression and signal-making as an antecedent stage of language.
But one must be extremely cautious in drawing such conclusions,
and not lose sight of the fact that one is thereby attributing
to ontogeny a phylogenetic significance unwarranted without

---

[1] The language of Phi Tong Luang, which has few calls but many exclamations, must
be regarded in this sense. (H. A. Bernatzik, *Die Geister der gelben Blätter* (1938), cited by
Fr. Kainz.)

[2] R. Hönigswald, *Philosophie und Sprache* (1937) ,p. 18.

c

further proof. The fact that children in early stages of development produce forms transitional between spontaneous expressions of feeling and word forms is insufficient proof that the same relationship prevailed in linguistic prehistory. The infant as yet incapable of speech is already inclined to language by nature; he has latent powers that prepare him for the understanding and use of speech. For this reason we should not regard his utterances and gestures just before the onset of speech as a model or plan of the phylogenetic origin and development of language. The fact that gesture language employs some signs deriving from the inventory of original expressive gestures (as is the case, for example, when the meaning 'away' is expressed by a turning of the head or an energetic wave of the hand) is therefore no more proof of the relationship between the two functions than the fact that expressive sounds (*ah*, *oh*) are taken up in speech is proof that language originates from such affective utterances.

With that we come to the special interjection theory, which regards expressive sounds alone as having importance in producing language (the Epicureans, Rousseau, Max Müller, Wundt, L. Geiger, Noiré, Bechterew and others).

To the extent that the theory of expressive sounds represents interjections as the original form of language, it must, as Giambattista Vico pointed out in his *Scienza nuova*,[1] be rejected, for reasons already stated. Interjections were originally involuntary forms of expressing affective states, just as much as were expressive facial or limb movements; the external expression is a direct indication or symptom of physical and mental states without communicative intent. Apart from these general grounds, there is also specific proof of the untenability of the interjection theory. If, as some linguists assume, the original interjections had in fact played a constructive role in language formation, they should show a marked resemblance to verbal constructions, at least in their phonetic appearance. But this is not the case. The phonetic character of the original expressive sounds is entirely different from that of words. They are not articulated; i.e. they cannot be

---

[1] Giambattista Vico, *Principi di una scienza nuova* (1725).

analysed into elements combinable in phonetic complexes. Further, their plasticity is extremely limited; they are hardly influenced by language, often preserving their original structure unaltered even when adopted into language as interjections. Above all, their function does not change in the course of linguistic development; they continue to express affective states mostly having no suitable linguistic means of expression. Now, how can language be a mere development of a form of expression that has no linguistic equivalent and preserves its form and function nearly unchanged in spite of language?

These remarks patently relate only to primary interjections—i.e., to those solely expressing inner emotions[1]—and not to onomatopoetic interjections relating to external events, such as pop!, whiz!, bang! These are doubtlessly of later date, mainly because they consist of syllables or syllabic combinations (clip-clop, jingle-jangle, snip-snap) and sometimes even employ old linguistic materials originally without interjectional character (rats!, drat!).[2]

Thus sounds by themselves are not sufficient to produce and give form to language. As in the case of movements and gestures, sounds can be converted into speech only through the medium of an *inner linguistic sense*; that is, an irresistible impulse to communicate with others by means of phonetic symbols. Sounds become words only when phonetic complexes are brought into relation with subjective or objective circumstances—thoughts, deeds, objects, events—and acquire a communicative function. Only when this happens does language itself arise. Just as a movement becomes an element in a gesture language, so does a sound become an element of a spoken language on acquiring a linguistic function, such as being used in a substantive, adjectival or verbal sense. Hence it would be wrong to derive language from natural,

[1] It is scarcely necessary to observe that interjections are here being considered only from a genetic point of view, in terms of whether they played any part in the original creation of language. Naturally the semasiological point of view is not touched upon; namely, the secondary significance of interjections as a linguistic tool, and their incorporation into language.

[2] H. Paul, *Prinzipien der Sprachgeschichte* (1909), pp. 179 ff.

expressive sounds on the assumption that, say, the Neanderthaler occasionally 'expressed' his anger against his foes by means of a particular grunt, discovered that it was suitable for frightening them away, and then habitually used it to express anger and threats. Such a conception overlooks the great leap taken in conferring a substantive or verbal sense on the original grunt. It overlooks the fact that the expressive sound can become a word, a means of speech, only by being made to serve *a linguistic function of communication* or description, and finds a place in language through articulation and phonetic change. But once this has happened it loses the character of a pure expressive sound, its symptomatic function having been converted into a symbolic function. These ideas were already expressed by Aristotle, who insisted that the decisive step to human speech was taken only when the significant sound attained primacy over those of emotion and excitement. This precedence, as Cassirer has stated, also finds expression in the philological fact that many words appearing in the light of superficial observation or in a purely speculative etymology as mere interjections, prove upon more exact analysis to be devolutions from more complex linguistic constructions, with a definite conceptual content.[1]

The ambiguity of the concept of 'expression' may have contributed much to the prevailing confusion of ideas. By expression the psychologist tends to understand the manifestation of a subjective state. Logicians, like Husserl, use expression to mean the representation of an objective situation.[2] But even if sounds used to *represent* may also be employed to *manifest*, the former nevertheless presupposes a new principle, the linguistic function itself. An involuntary expression of a mental state cannot directly become a linguistic expression; we can only repeat that there must first be a change of function, by which the expressive sound is adopted into language with a change of form conforming to its phonetic laws.

The proof that expressive sounds and gestures as such cannot be

---

[1] Cassirer, *Philosophie der symbolischen Formen*, I (1923), p. 136.

[2] E. Husserl, *Logische Untersuchungen*, I (1922), p. 32.

regarded either as elements or as antecedents of language naturally does not imply that they are entirely without significance in
its formation, but only that at most they have a value analogous
to that of unshaped stones in a building, e.g. in the formation of
exclamations. They acquire a closer relationship to language, or
rather to linguistic prehistory, only upon acquiring a signal function, as in the case of true mating-calls or signalling of animals.

All efforts to trace language back to mere expressive sounds
must be regarded as abortive in the light of these considerations.
This applies to the views of Regnaud[1] and Taylor,[2] who think
that language arose through the gradual differentiation of animal
cries, and to those of Darwin[3] and Spencer,[4] who attempt to
derive music from natural sounds.[5] Regnaud at least tries to
demonstrate a rudimentary stage preceding articulated significant
speech; but in so doing he completely overlooks the fact that an
utterance lacking in all criteria distinctive of language cannot be
its original form.

My negative attitude toward the role of the expressive reactions
in the origin of language naturally does not imply that I am
sceptical of the expressive value of living language. Language or,
more properly, speech, doubtless owes its immediate concreteness
partly to the expressive values which in their great variety constitute the *physiognomic character* of language. It is difficult to judge
what role spontaneous expressive cries have played in this respect;
perhaps comparison of the expressive sounds used by primitive
peoples with their own languages can shed some light on this
problem. The fact to be emphasized in this context is that the
emotional power of linguistic expression does not in any case
reside exclusively in the production of sound, and consequently
even less in unarticulated expressive sounds, but in significant

1 P. Regnaud, *Origine et philosophie du langage* (1887) and *Origine et philosophie du
langage ou principes de linguistique indo-européene* (1889).

2 E. B. Taylor, 'Origin of Language' (*Fortnightly Review*, 1866).

3 C. Darwin, *The Descent of Man* (London, 1871).

4 H. Spencer, *Essays* (London, 1858) and 'The Origin of Music', *Mind*, XV.

5 G. Révész, 'Der Ursprung der Musik', *Intern. Zeitschrift für Ethnographie*, 40 (1941)
p. 65.

phonetic signs which incorporate an element of emotional sound. If extra-linguistic expressive sounds originally had any importance in speech, they entered into the total phonetic complex of words and sentences, and only in this sense can they be considered as constituent parts of the acoustic word pattern.

2. THE THEORY OF ANIMAL SOUNDS

As we have already shown that expressive gestures and sounds cannot be regarded as the antecedent stage, much less the original form of language, we need not criticize in detail the theory that animal cries are the antecedents of language. For, apart from a lone exception to be discussed later, animal cries are also expressive gestures of a biological nature, even if at times they must be regarded as having a directed nature.[1] The arguments we have adduced against regarding human expressive gestures and sounds as antecedent or early forms of language therefore apply *a fortiori* to any analogous interpretation of animal cries.[2]

But, even apart from these fundamental considerations, the theory of animal origins breaks down. The theory presumes that human beings or their semi-human forebears borrowed their phonetic material from the animals of their environment. The question at once arises as to the kind of animal from which they might have taken their phonetic material, and why they should have needed animal sounds at all. Human beings and their forebears surely had an abundant supply of expressive and imitative sounds at their command for use in creating language; they were certainly not inferior to any sort of animal in this respect. The possibility would merit consideration only if there had been some variety of animal living in proximity to man with a 'language' of its own; and human beings had adopted it as a means of communication before they possessed a language of their own and

[1] The exceptions are the expressive sounds used by domestic animals in addressing themselves to particular persons to attain definite ends. For further details see pp. 161 ff.

[2] Aristotle entertained the possibility of an animal origin for language, but decided against it. He admits that there is something in common between human and animal sounds, but animal sounds cannot enter into fixed combinations; no animal has the native ability to form a syllable.

while they were still attempting to create one. This assumption can be rejected not only because it is unreasonable but because it has not the slightest empirical foundation.[1] The study of animal psychology shows that there is in fact no group of animal utterances that can be called an 'animal language' in the proper sense of the word.

It would be proper to speak of an autochthonous animal language if there were evidence that animals employed sounds or gestures for the purpose of communication, with a definite meaning appertaining to each sound, gesture, or complex of sounds and gestures; if, that is, they possessed a well-ordered system of signs for communicative purposes. They would need, for example, not one but several kinds of warning cry: one for the approach of human beings, another for the approach of members of the family, and a different one for hostile animals. If such a case existed—which is surely to be denied; even the so-called vocabularies of bird-sounds and horse and monkey 'languages' compiled by Maday, Garner, Boutan, Kellogg, Yerkes and Learned testify against it—an autochthonous language of chimpanzees, gibbons, dogs, cats and others might be admitted in a limited sense; but even in these cases the 'language' is lacking in all the essential characteristics of human language. This applies, without exception, to all the animal languages. Neither in external form nor in internal structure do these animal utterances display any of the properties of human language to the slightest degree. Phonetically, the sounds of the higher animals, such as the dog, cat, and monkey commonly adduced as plausible examples, are, by our acoustic standards, formless and unmelodious noises, screeches, bleats—in short, sounds without phonematic character. They have no structured sound elements resembling the phonemes of language from which speech material could as it were be constructed; hence they cannot be classified in a phonetic system. It

[1] To this we might add that if animal cries had been important in the formation of language we should expect that words bearing a resemblance to particular animal sounds would be found in language, and especially in the more primitive ones. But nothing of this sort is known. Cf. my discussion of this point in my previously cited article, 'Die menschlichen Kommunikationsformen und die sogenannte Tiersprache'.

is for this reason that they cannot be noted down. The written transcription of animal sounds in our alphabet is scientifically useless; the 'consonants' are not our consonants, the 'vowels' are not our vowels. Furthermore, in animal cries, there is no unequivocal link between expression and what is expressed; the same sound can indicate differing needs, and different sounds can refer to the same need. Furthermore, it is noteworthy that individual elements are not capable of being joined so as to form combinations expressing anything more than what is expressed by the individual elements *per se*. It goes without saying that they lack all trace of division into parts of speech, let alone a grammatical structure. Finally, from the point of view of developmental psychology it is worthy of note that the 'animal languages' are not the product of a long and gradual evolution, as is human language. On the contrary: they are an inherited, immutable, fixed means of expression. They have no history; during the lifetime of an individual they undergo little or no development or change. With slight local or individual variation they are produced almost identically by animals of the same species in all parts of the world. Animals do not learn expressive sounds from their environment, as do men, but essentially inherit them readymade.[1] It follows from these facts that the so-called animal languages and human speech share no common basis; which is to say that animal cries, no matter how expressive they may be, cannot be related to human language. It requires no further discussion to show that we are not merely making a verbal distinction when we exclude animals from the concept of language *ex definitione*. It is a matter of fact, not of argument arising out of conflicting definitions.[2]

[1] Imitation plays a part only in certain species of birds.

[2] Here we may refer to the works of some older advocates of animal language, such as F. Müller (*Grundriss der Sprachwissenschaft*, 1876-87) and G. Jäger (*Über den Ursprung der menschlichen Sprachen*, 1867). Recently R. J. Humphrey ('The Origin of Language', *Acta Psychologica*, X, 1953) has examined this problem in detail. Jespersen (*Language*) and Grace de Laguna (*Speech, Its Function and Development*) are not entirely free of an animal-psychology approach. Cf. my argument against animal languages in *K. Ned. Akad. v. Wetenschappen*, Amsterdam, Vol. 43, 1940, and in 'Der Kampf um die sog. Tiersprache', *Psychol. Rundschau*, IV, 1953, and 'Is there an Animal Language?', *The Hibbert Journal*, 1954.

We have gone into this question rather deeply because the error is often made in genetic psychology of proceeding from the phonetic material and not from the need to communicate, thereby postulating a relationship where none exists. If this distinction is ignored we are liable to regard the entirely different cries of animals as a means of communication, and thus as being closely related to human language. It is this erroneous idea that gives rise to the so-called 'animal vocabularies', in which sense and meaning are ascribed to more or less differentiated animal cries without regard to their function. Thus Yerkes and Learned obtained thirty-two 'words' from two chimpanzees, of which sixteen were used by one, fourteen by the other, and two by both. The words were arranged into five groups according to their initial sound, depending on whether they began with guttural G or K, H-aspirate, nasal or labial sounds or vowels. The number of phonetic complexes that could be clearly distinguished was very small. If one can rely on the notes taken simply by ear, there were not more than six or eight sounds phonetically distinguishable to any degree; the first group (of the type gakh, kgak) comprising as much as 45 per cent. of the thirty-two 'words' listed. If one studies the list of these 'vocal expressions' in detail, it appears that the sound complexes all relate to a few emotional states, specifically to the conditions of hunger, excitement, restlessness, fear, bodily pain, pleasure and contentment. Directed utterances, arising out of the need for communication, do not seem to appear.[1]

[1] R. M. Yerkes and B. W. Learned, *Chimpanzee Intelligence and its Vocal Expressions* (1925). Yerkes does not regard the spontaneous utterances of the chimpanzee as language, not even as chimpanzee-language; yet he does feel justified in assuming that 'there certainly is a useful substitute (!) which might readily be developed or transformed into a true language, if the animal would be induced to imitate sounds persistently' (p. 66). From such remarks one gathers that the investigator is not convinced of the essential impossibility of animal languages. To be sure, Yerkes says in his fine book *Great Apes* (1929, p. 179): 'Everything seems to indicate that their vocalizations do not constitute true language in the sense in which Boutan uses the term. Their word-like sounds always lack ideational meaning.' But despite this he believes that the anthropoids would be capable of learning human speech if they could imitate speech sounds as well as the parrots. Yerkes thereby declares his opinion that the anthropoids have a disposition for language and are only prevented from conversing by their undeveloped speech technique. Nor could Delacroix (*Psychologie du Langage*, 1933) entirely free himself from this view.

The same conclusion emerges from analysis of the utterances of gibbons, investigated by Boutan.[1]

It is curious to find how stubbornly zoologists and sometimes even animal psychologists cling to the idea of 'animal language' despite theoretical objections and observed evidence to the contrary.[2] Here I would like to cite for its historical interest a passage in the *Discours de la méthode*, where Descartes with characteristic simplicity and logical clarity denies the possibility of animal language:

> Car on peut bien concevoir qu'une machine soit tellement faite qu'elle profère des paroles et même qu'elle en profère quelques unes à propos des actions corporelles qui causeront quelque changement en ses organes . . . mais non pas qu'elle les arrange diversement pour répondre au sens de tout ce qui se dira en sa présence aussi que les hommes les plus hébétés peuvent le faire . . . car au lieu que la raison est un instrument universel qui peut servir en toutes sortes de rencontres, ces organes (sc. des animaux-machines) ont besoin de quelque particulière disposition pour chaque action particulière. . . . Or, par ces deux moyens on peut aussi connaître la différence qui est entre les hommes et les bêtes: car c'est une chose bien remarquable qu'il n'y a point d'hommes si hébétés et si stupides, sans en excepter même les insensés, qu'ils ne soient capables d'arranger ensemble diverses paroles et d'en composer un discours par lequel ils fassent entendre leurs pensées et qu'au contraire il n'y a point d'autre animal tant parfait et tant heureusement né qu'il puisse être, qui fasse le semblable. . . .[3]

The complete absence of a linguistic function in animals is also shown by the fact that they cannot understand human language even to a limited extent, much less acquire it. Command words supposedly understood by animals are merely simple aural

[1] L. Boutan, 'Le pseudo-langage', *Actes de la Société Linnéenne de Bordeaux*, 1913. The same is true of the dictionaries of ape speech of R. L. Garner, L. L. C. Faidherbe and particularly of the well-known but scientifically valueless material of G. Schwidetzky.

[2] Buffon was the first of the modern students of natural science to accept language as the criterion of the human mind and to reject the possibility of animal language in principle. *Histoire Naturelle* (Paris, 1749-67).

[3] R. Descartes, *Discours de la méthode* (Leiden, 1637).

impressions which they associate with particular actions or prohibitions as a result of individual experience or training. The
animal is able to establish a meaningful connexion between the
sound and the object or activity only to a very limited degree.
The sound or gesture can at most be a signal which calls forth a
particular reaction. From a dog's point of view it is a matter of
indifference whether he is trained to leave the room at the word
'go', the sentence 'go out', a whistle, a letter displayed to him, or
the appearance of the colour red. For the animal the command
word 'go' is not really a word, the expression 'go out' is not a
sentence, nor the optical sign 'A' a letter; to him all these are
merely signals, and no different from the colour red in sign
value. All are equally significant sense perceptions, to which the
animal can be trained to respond.[1]

It had already been pointed out by Hobbes, Locke, Descartes,
and Leibniz that even if some animals learn to 'understand' our
verbally expressed wishes and commands by becoming accustomed to them, or even if they learn to imitate articulated sounds
by training, they do not actually grasp the meaning of the words.[2]
If, in spite of all this, attempts are still being made to obtain
words from apes, it only goes to show what little account the
experimenters have taken of the real nature of language, or even
of the origin and significance attaching to the imitation of
phonetic elements in the sphere of language.[3] They have never

---

[1] The great number of command words which Sarris adduces in his work on the
alleged word-comprehension of dogs can be very greatly reduced by detailed analysis
of the 'speech sounds' employed in them. It is not difficult to prove from the author's
own recorded observations that it is not word-comprehension that is involved with his
dogs, but simply ordinary drill. 'Sind wir berechtigt, vom Wortverständnis des Hundes
zu sprechen?', *Beihefte der Zeitschrift für angew. Psychol.*, 62 (1931).

[2] T. Hobbes, *Elementorum philosophiae, Sectio secunda: De homine* (London, 1658); J.
Locke, *An Essay Concerning Human Understanding*, III, Chap. I (London, 1690); R. Descartes, *Discours de la méthode* (1637), 58; G. W. v. Leibniz, *Nouveaux Essais sur l'entendement
humain* (1765), III, Chap. I.

[3] Upon succeeding, after six months of trying, in obtaining the word 'papa' from an
orang-outan, W. H. Furness ('Observations on the Mentality of the Chimpanzee and
Orang-Outans', *Proc. Amer. Phil. Soc.*, Philadelphia, 1916) said: 'I think this showed
conclusively, that there was a glimmering idea of the connexion of the word with the
object and with her desire.' He did not succeed with the word 'cup'. Nor did the Kelloggs
get any further with their chimpanzee than the 'vocalization' of the word 'papa' (*The
Ape and the Child*, 1933).

really grasped the fact that language cannot be learned by imitation alone. If animals allegedly on the 'threshold' of language were really in a position to step over the threshold, it would only be a matter of time before they began to converse with us. Though the animals possess vocal organs they do not have speech organs; for speech organs presuppose a linguistic function, or rather the innate capacity for speech.

These remarks point to an important fact of linguistic psychology; namely, that true language makes its first appearance only when the living being is no longer exclusively governed by instincts and emotions, but is motivated by conscious purposes and goals, and by insight into the means appropriate to their accomplishment. It is just this sort of purposefulness that is the necessary precondition of man, distinguishing human life from animal existence.

We meet a similar theory in the study of the origins of music, where the attempt has been made to trace back human song to that of birds. Human beings are said to have been impelled for some reason, presumably sexual, to imitate bird song; and thus is music supposed to have originated. The proponents of this theory fail to understand that bird song differs from human song in having a different function and a different structure, and is subject to different laws. Here too, as with so-called animal languages, it has not been clearly understood that the song of birds is not the product of a long development and gradual differentiation, as is human song, but an inherited and unchangeable means of expression. The song-bird essentially brings with him ready-made his whole art and repertoire; which is not to deny that some animals 'sing' better than others, and that practice, and especially the imitation of good singers, may improve results. That bird songs, such as the song of the nightingale, the call of the thrush, the robin and the finch occur in our music does not, of course, in any way affect the problem of origins.[1]

These arguments rule out the possibility that our presumed ancestors at any time in human prehistory adopted from animals

[1] G. Révész, 'Der Ursprung der Musik', *Intern. Archiv für Ethnographie*, 40 (1941).

of any sort either the initiative for linguistic communication or the material for it. The same may be said of music. In view of all this we are entitled to eliminate the animal-psychology hypothesis once and for all from the question of origins, or for that matter from comparative and genetic linguistic science as a whole. We can consequently declare that the misleading expression 'language', which has given rise to so many misunderstandings, is inappropriate for use in animal psychology.

We may now turn to the anthropological theories of origin. We begin with the imitation theory, which represents a transition between the biological and anthropological theories. Imitation is indeed not peculiar to human beings, but it does constitute one of the principal mechanisms of human development for individuals and for the species as a whole. Imitation governs the formation of Man's habits of life and all his training and education; but among animals its role is subordinate or non-existent. The survival and well-being of animals is largely independent of their imitative ability; even the imitative apes acquire, when isolated in captivity, all the skills requisite for their sustenance without making much imitative use of the experience of older generations.

(C) ANTHROPOLOGICAL THEORIES

I. THE IMITATION THEORY

The idea that spoken language is a collection of onomatopoetic sounds is open to the same objections as the expressive theory. It is based on the assumption that there is a causal connexion between the original words of language and the purely sensory impressions of the sounds of nature. Language was not, in this view, spontaneously produced and developed by primitive man from his own sound material; instead, he paid close attention to natural sounds, and acquired his initial vocabulary by imitation of these tonal stimuli. As a rule the proponents of this theory neglect to separate the sphere of sensory impressions from that of ideas, and fail to make a clear-cut distinction between unconscious development and conscious creation. They regard the origin of language as a matter of chance, and suppose man to have done no more than eavesdrop on the voice of nature, creating a means of communication through sheer mimetic ability.

Leibniz was perhaps the first to suggest that the solution to the question of why the most diverse languages have so many common roots is to be found in an *Ursprache*, a primeval language whose root-words would be of onomatopoetic origin. In his opinion the origin of words was subject to natural causes, traceable in the connexion between particular things and the sounds representing them, i.e., in the phonetic imitation of natural sounds.[1]

Steinthal, one of the best spokesmen of the Young Grammarians, considers articulated speech sounds as having originated in primitive man by a reflex coupling of a particular onomatopoetic sound with a particular sensory impression.[2] This assumption, for which the origin of speech poses fewer difficulties than that of silence, is challenged especially by Marty.[3]

According to Marty, Steinthal's assertion that an onomatopoetic sound can be found for every perception or observation is in conflict with experience. Marty takes the contrary view that all imitative sounds are the result of deliberate and conventional, not of instinctive and natural expression. He even denies that observation is capable of causing the instinctive production of onomatopoetic sounds.[4] Steinthal himself later acknowledged the

[1] G. W. v. Leibniz, *Nouveaux Essais*.

[2] H. Steinthal, *Abriss der Sprachwissenschaften*, I (1871), p. 389, and *Der Ursprung der Sprache* (1877). Steinthal here uses the word reflexive in place of instinctive; his doctrine is therefore called 'the reflex theory'.

[3] A. Marty, *Über den Ursprung der Sprache* (1875) and various articles in the *Vierteljahrschrift für wiss. Philosophie*, Vols. 8 to 16, reprinted in the first volume of his collected works (1916).

[4] In recent times Grammont and F. de Saussure have demonstrated the accidental character of onomatopoeia. The imitative sounds of children in their prelinguistic period testify against the deliberate nature of onomatopoetic word formation, in so far as they are not learned from listening to adults (as for example tick-tack, wow-wow, etc.) De Saussure, *Cours de linguistique générale* (1923).

deliberate character of most onomatopoetic speech sounds, without on that account abandoning onomatopoeia as the underlying principle of linguistic creation.

We do not wish to review in detail Marty's acute criticism of Steinthal's views, since Marty and his opponents are not really concerned with the problem of the actual *origin* of language, as they had erroneously thought, but rather with linguistic forms and development, which are outside our problem. The onomatopoetic theory has had an immeasurable attraction for students of the origin of language, especially on account of the large numbers of onomatopoetic words in all languages. Thus Renan saw onomatopoetic imitation as the road to the invention of linguistic elements (*De l'origine du langage*, Paris, 1859). The same is to be found in L. Geiger (*Der Ursprung der Sprache*, 1869). More recently Jespersen (*Language, Its Nature, Development and Origin*, 1922), A. Johanneson (*Origin of Language*, Reykjavik) and H. Kelso de Montigny (*How Did Language Originate*, Havana) regard onomatopoeia as one of the principal sources of language.

From our standpoint, the theoretical impossibility of founding a doctrine of linguistic origins on the onomatopoetic theory can be proved without difficulty.

Assuming that onomatopoetic sounds do represent the antecedent stage from which language developed, there would be two possibilities for discussion, depending on the meaning ascribed to the concept of instinctive imitation. There is no doubt an imitative instinct, as may perhaps be seen in the sound imitation of birds; but this instinct does not go beyond the production of patterns of sound resembling those on which they are modelled. Mere similarity to the phonetic model does not, however, confer a sign function (which alone would enable it to symbolize a situation) on the sound pattern that has been imitated. To concede an important influence in the formation of language to onomatopoeia is to use the concept of imitation in a different sense, going beyond mere reproduction to include the representation of something. An onomatopoetic expression representing an object or condition aims at more than merely reproducing the sound pattern; it uses the resemblance as a means of making the reference immediately comprehensible. Such extension of the concept of imitation is surely admissible in view of infant behaviour; although most onomatopoetic expressions used by infants are first taught to them by adults. Now there are only a small number of words of onomatopoetic origin in language, and even these are mostly of late origin.[1] The concept of onomatopoeia must therefore be extended still further, to include all spontaneously produced phonetic signs connected with and indicative of particular perceptions and feelings, and yet not having the character of words or symbolic function. In addition to natural sounds, other sounds make their appearance which owe their origin to the impulse to make communicative contact. A creature not yet capable of, but predisposed to, language, instinctively makes expressive sounds and gestures drawn from the reservoir of sounds previously employed that are phonetically more or less distinctive. In consequence of the urge to communicate, these sounds gradually develop into phonetic gestures immediately intelligible to members of the same species because of their similarity to the accompanying emotional overtones or by analogy with them because of their physiological character. These phonetic gestures gradually acquire greater uniformity in character through repetition and tradition until they finally attain a conventional form that conceals their outward relationship to the original spontaneous phonetic gestures.

If the word onomatopoeia is employed in this larger sense, it will have to be admitted that onomatopoetic sounds played an important role in the preparation of spoken language in the antecedent phase and even in the early phases of language proper. They appear to be rooted so powerfully and deeply in human

[1] But one should be careful not to underestimate the role of onomatopoeia. Languages no doubt exist that are very rich in onomatopoetic constructions. Thus according to Schuchardt the Basque language especially favours echoic word formation (*Schuchardt-Brevier*, 219 and 246). In any case this preference for onomatopoeia rests not with the language itself but with the speakers, who use onomatopoetic words in varying degree depending on sex, age, and social class.

nature that even when language had later completely attained its conceptual and symbolic character they continued to find employment as a supplementary part of language.

It is here that contact occurs between natural sounds and speech physiognomy, which involves the physiognomic content of words and sentences as well as sounds. Onomatopoetic words presumably date back to a transitional period during which the non-linguistic means of communication came to be adopted into language. The more symbolic speech formation came into the foreground, the more the imitative element was pushed into the background. There is thus an element of truth in the paradoxical statement that language begins where sound imitation ceases.[1]

With onomatopoeia the question is not whether the sound patterns are taken from nature, but whether they have meaning. If imitative sounds were employed by primitive man without a sign function, they remained outside the sphere of language and cannot be regarded as its original or antecedent form. But if they did possess a sign function, they were accordingly expressions of the linguistic function, which could no more be limited to the imitation of natural sounds than to expressive sounds. Both forms of utterance have been adopted into language and applied to the communication of subjective experiences (expressive sounds) and to the description of external perceptions (imitative sounds). But this certainly did not happen until language had already come into existence in an elementary form.

Finally we wish to call attention to a limitation of the imitation theory which makes it quite clear how inappropriate imitation is as a basic principle of language development. Imitative sounds can only relate to natural processes that produce sound, and consequently cannot represent silent phenomena, whether in the external world or in the mind. Furthermore, onomatopoeia is untenable as a theory of linguistic origins because it is only suitable for description or picturesque representation, but not for communication. Neither statements nor questions can be expressed by it. These considerations should be enough to show

[1] Josef Schmidt, *Language and Languages* (in Hungarian), Budapest, 1923.

the utter impossibility of a primeval language based on imitation.

Here it should be stated that the concepts of linguistic symbolism and linguistic physiognomy are misused in the imitation theory in relating them to sounds of the external world. Expressive language tries in the first instance to depict the speaker's subjective world, not simply by passive reproduction but by creative expression through an intellectual act. This has been impressively described by Herder and Humboldt and has been set out systematically recently by H. Werner.[1] The latter quite rightly makes a fundamental distinction between the phonetic structure and the physiognomic content of words, sentences and sounds. But he takes the very rash view that an objective symbol of their meaning is directly recognizable in words.[2]

2.   ONTOGENETIC THEORIES

(a) *The Babbling Theory*

Nor can the problem of the antecedents and early forms of spoken language be solved by reference to the beginnings of language in children at the babbling stage. If the original form of language be defined as phonetic expression already possessing essential elements of language, and therefore determined by the same tendencies as fully developed language, then babbling sounds cannot be regarded as its original form. Babbling, a reflexive and spontaneous activity preceding speech, has a primarily physiological character, the automatic continuation of movements once initiated; and a general psychological aim, the imitative repetition of a phonetic result once it has been obtained.

[1] H. Werner, *Grundfragen der Sprachphysiognomik* (1932).

[2] It cannot be doubted that certain words and even certain sounds possess expressive value; that thanks to their specific expressive power they are able to signify more than simple signs or neutral symbols for particular things, processes or situations. But exaggeration is to be avoided in this connexion; otherwise there is great risk of falling victim to self-deception, for the autochthonous physiognomic element cannot always be distinguished from accidental associations and other incidental matters in physiognomic analysis of the parts of speech. They may in fact be impossible to tell apart. In particular, one should be less generous in the use of analogies, so as to avoid being forced to conclusions that cannot be scientifically verified.

Besides the above-named authors, Jespersen, Cassirer, Bühler, and Hönigswald have also dealt with problems of expressive language.

Although it is true that learning to talk requires babbling as a preparatory activity; indeed, if, as Wundt[1] and van Ginneken[2] assume, the spontaneous babbling sounds form the hereditary basis of speech articulation, developing later into babbling words (papa, mama, dada, etc.) through a selective process (Delacroix),[3] it is nevertheless true that language is based on an essentially different function from babbling.[4]

The so-called 'babbling words' are not true words; they do not have definite meaning; they have only emotional significance, with no tendency toward contact, let alone communication. Undoubtedly a disposition toward speech is already present in the prelinguistic period; it is possible, even most probable, that at this stage the linguistic function is already preparing to become effective in an inward, as it were underground way, although its actual appearance only comes later. But once it is expressed it takes its form in correspondence with the *usages of language*. If a correlation is occasionally established between given babbling sounds and particular situations, it means simply that the babbling sound has become a sign, consequently losing the function of a babbling sound.

The new-born child is unable to speak because it is still incomplete in all respects, physically as well as intellectually. Our admittedly ´imaginary primeval man, however, was neither physically nor intellectually 'unfinished', and is therefore not comparable to infants. Such a comparison would indeed compel us to assume that the first human expressions resembling speech were babbling-sounds; but the assumption seems quite nonsensical. Primitive man was not an infant, and if he was unable to

[1] W. Wundt, *Die Sprache*, I (1911), pp. 284 ff.

[2] J. v. Ginneken, 'Die Erblichkeit der Lautgesetze', *Indogermanische Forschungen*, 45 (1927).

[3] H. Delacroix, *L'enfant et le langage* (1934), p. 63.

[4] In so far as words have arisen from babbling sounds they were formed by speaking adults utilizing the sounds produced by infants before they could talk. The earliest babbling sounds were used to refer to the parents. In this way all peoples have developed homophonous names for father, mother, grandfather, grandmother and nurse, such as papa, mama, muhme, papi, mami, mamina, apa, anya, nyanya, nono, nona, dada, baba, babo, dadé, tata, dad, daddy, pa(ter), ma(ter), pater *et al.*

speak it must have been for quite different reasons than is the case with the child.

If, on the other hand, our hypothetical speechless primeval man was already predisposed to language, it is difficult to understand why he should not have been capable of speech in the proper sense of the word. In this connexion, Wundt correctly observes that it is impossible to imagine a mental state mature enough to invent language and yet not doing so.[1] If, on the contrary, he lacked the capacity to lend his sounds a depictive sense, he could not yet have been human, since he lacked the very traits that distinguish human beings from other forms of life.

These arguments relate to the utterance of unarticulated sounds and the more or less articulated ones of children in the babbling stage considered as a supposed antecedent stage of language. A different question relates to the phylogenetic significance that should be ascribed to the first linguistic utterances of children, and whether and to what extent they could be employed in reconstructing the early forms of language.[2]

(b) The Child Speech Theory

In comparing the earliest stages of linguistic development of an individual human being with the beginnings of language in general, we must take account of the fact that with children the linguistic function is not first expressed by means of sound or gesture language. It is expressed in the *understanding* of language; or, more correctly, in the understanding of words—that is, in the comprehending of the relationship between words and the objects, circumstances and events denoted by them. Even if active speech only develops later, the child has reached the first stage of language as soon as it partly understands and lets its

[1] W. Wundt, *Logik*, I, pp. 16 and 47.

[2] We shall not consider the theories of origin that seek to establish the nature of the so-called original phonetic units, which are supposed to have constituted the phonetic material from which the first words were formed, by investigating the reflexive production of sounds (Whitney, Sievers, Murray, Sayce, Jespersen, K. Hĕrman, v. Ginneken, also Trombetti.) Perhaps something can be made of the phonetic form of the earliest words on the basis of the mechanism of speech; but this approach is irrelevant to our problem of the origin of language.

actions be influenced by the language of its environment.[1] Even with adults, the mystery of a foreign language is gone as soon as it can be understood. Once the understanding of speech exists, the way lies open to the activity of speech, and the capacity for the activity of thought is already assured.[2] But no chronological sequence of this kind can have existed in the early history of language, for the understanding of speech presupposes its earlier existence. With early man active and passive speech capacity must have emerged simultaneously, and both forms of speech activity must have stood in reciprocal relationship to each other during the period of emergence and development. It follows that the ontogenetic sequence of the speech functions cannot correspond with the phylogenetic development of language, for in the ontogenesis of child speech the distinction between the first phase of active speech and the first emergence of word comprehension—the meaningful reaction to certain words or word combinations—is quite clear. As is well known, the child may understand certain frequently repeated words for some time before it actually utters them and makes meaningful use of them. Before the beginning of active speech, which takes place only in about the fifth quarter-year, the child on hearing the word 'grandpa' will already follow the person concerned with its eyes, and even in the absence of that person will react in a way that adequately denotes comprehension of the word. Another fundamental difference reveals itself in the fact that a child does not form its language spontaneously, but derives it from adult speech material. As soon as a child is sufficiently developed to grasp the relation of meaning between a sound and what it denotes, it makes use of speech material derived from its environment. Hence no further proof is needed that the primitive speech of a child, deriving as it does from existing and mature forms of adult language, cannot represent the archaic form of language.

[1] Child psychologists, unable to dissociate themselves from the analogy with adult speech, commonly regard the initial phase as one of understanding sentences and word combinations, whereas the child in fact responds to phonetic complexes comprehended with the aid of emphasis, accentuation and mimic gestures.

[2] *Thinking and Speaking, Symposium.* Edited G. Révész. Amsterdam (1954).

Nevertheless, a certain evolutionary significance does attach to the *forms* of speech used in early childhood, as comparative philology has often pointed out. We agree with W. Stern,[1] F. Kainz[2] and others that in the development of child speech there is an interaction between external and internal factors in terms of immanent evolutionary tendencies determining the development of speech in general. If a major role is attributed to the spontaneity of the child, it is feasible to assume that the development of child speech, as Stern correctly emphasizes, is based on an immanent tendency of mental growth, and this is also likely to be the case in the linguistic development of mankind. In the sphere of semantics, vocabulary and especially syntax clear parallels exist between child language and the development of human language generally. But these similarities should not lead one to conclude too readily that there is a parallelism of linguistic development, and still less to see in child speech the components of earliest language. An idea of this kind can serve as a useful working hypothesis, but one must not be misled into conceiving the ontogenetic development of speech in the child as a schematic reproduction of the general evolution of languages, particularly as the phylogenetic value even of primitive languages is still a debatable question.

(c) *The Theory of the Priority of Song*

The idea of song as the first form of speech permeates the whole of Greek philosophy. But only with Charles Darwin did it attain influence in scientific thought. According to Darwin the origin of language is to be found in the musical exclamations of men before they had learned to talk. To support this idea from an evolutionary standpoint, he maintains that bird sounds constitute in many respects the closest analogy to language, since all members of the same species utter the same instinctive sounds to express (or describe!) their emotions. According to Darwin human imitation of such musical utterances in articulated sounds

[1] W. Stern, *Die Kindersprache* (1922), p. 262.

[2] F. Kainz, *Psychologie der Sprache*, II (1943), p. 69.

finally resulted in the production of words.[1] This doctrine of the priority of song recurs in Herbert Spencer's theory of music[2] and more recently in Jespersen's theory of the origin of language.[3]

It hardly seems necessary to subject this ingenious but untenable theory to criticism. It should be sufficient to point out that the two types of utterance differ fundamentally in purpose. The aim of song is to intensify and give free outlet to passionate feelings, and, in addition, rhythmically to order and facilitate physical movements and activities: language, on the contrary, aims at inter-personal contact and understanding. Each type of utterance consequently has its distinct materials and forms of expression and its own autonomous laws of development. The argument particularly stressed by Spencer, that numerous primitive peoples chant their speech,[4] has broken down. Even if it were true it would still be no basis for arguing that there was a prehistoric period in which human communication took the form of wordless song, nor that the two activities were ever inseparably linked.[5] It is easy to cite many primitive languages lacking in all musical quality; whereas there are highly developed languages, such as certain Semitic and Romance languages, with a marked musical lilt.

As will be explained in greater detail below, we take the opposite view and derive song from the most primitive form of linguistic utterance, the directed call.

(d) The Theory of Psychological Predisposition

The problem of linguistic origins has also been approached by inquiry as to what general human predisposition could have given rise to language, and as to the manner in which this predisposition

---

[1] C. Darwin, *Descent of Man and Selection in Relation to Sex* (1871).

[2] H. Spencer, *Principles of Sociology* (1876).

[3] O. Jespersen, *Progress in Language* (1894). He says, for example: 'If the development of language took the same course in prehistoric as in historic times—and there is no reason to doubt it—then we must imagine primitive language as consisting (chiefly at least) of very long words, containing many difficult sounds, and sung rather than spoken' (p. 345).

[4] H. Spencer, *Study of Sociology* (1873).

[5] So far as I know, wordless song occurs only very rarely among primitive peoples. It is the text that carries the melody and not vice versa.

might have effected its origin and development. Here again, expressive movements, gestures and interjections are taken to constitute the 'rudiments' of language; and this conception has already been shown to be untenable. A purely logical explanation is then given of how language developed from these rudiments. 'The instant a particular call, designed to attract, warn or frighten, takes on a form that not only describes a state of mind but also (!) the object or activity provoking the call, in that instant language as communication of thought may be said to be born.' So says Jodl in his *Psychology*.[1] Indeed yes; but the whole point is that Jodl's 'also' introduces a completely new element, namely the intervention of a spontaneous activity of the mind. What we are dealing with here is an *objectivization* of the state of mind, a use of the sound as a general symbol for certain groups or categories of things—in short, with a *word*. The real problem left unelucidated by these theories is, how does this instant arise at which the emotive call becomes a word? A similar objection applies to the attempt to derive indicative gestures from the action of grasping (Wundt, Cassirer) by arguing, firstly, from superficial similarity of the two actions, and, secondly, that among children the former function develops after the latter. The error lies in assuming that specific activities occurring in chronological succession must be intimately connected; whereas chronological succession, no matter how regular, need not necessarily imply internal development.[2] The mere occurrence of linguistic activity after that of grasping is no indication of any reciprocal relation. Though occurring in chronological succession, they are so different in nature that they cannot be interpreted as successive stages in the development of one and the same function. The extent to which such a theory goes beyond the facts is demonstrated by the consideration that any indicative gesture presupposes understanding of speech. Experiment has confirmed that a child points to an object or person only after having developed an active or at least passive speech function.

---

[1] F. Jodl, *Lehrbuch der Psychologie*, II (1903), p. 230.
[2] On the problem of continuity and discontinuity in development see pp. 171 ff.

It could also be argued that particular functions of consciousness are a prerequisite for linguistic development. Though not incorrect, the laying down of such conditions gets one no nearer to discovering how language originated. The conditions in question include functions such as the capacity for abstraction, for forming concepts, etc., which are inconceivable without speech. It would be only partially correct to regard thought as a basic prerequisite of language and to maintain that language as a meaningful system of signs is just a product of thought. That wordless thought exists is proved by the fact that we so often find it very difficult to formulate verbally a thought that is vivid in our minds. Certain mentally creative activities of non-verbal type, such as thinking out chess moves and composing music, point to the same conclusion. Such thought, however, implies capacity for speech and is based on a system of ideas or, at any rate, on a comprehension of things in terms of categories, and this again is impossible without speech. In any case it seems senseless to regard *wordless thought* as an antecedent *form of language*. The fact that words defining kinds of things can only be selected after thought has established the specific common traits of objects does not imply a priority of one of the functions over the other. On the one hand, thought inherently strives to find symbols with which to record its achievements; on the other, appropriately chosen symbols appreciably foster definiteness and clarity of thought. Hence there is a reciprocal relation between thought and speech invalidating any conception of an individual capable of thought but not of speech. Such a separation of thought and speech would result in a concept incompatible with experience and with significant interpretation of animal and infantile utterances.[1] In any case this theory merely avoids the difficulty by substituting for the problem of the origin of language another problem, that of the origin of thought.

What is true of language is also true of the disposition toward language and speech. This disposition is uniformly present in all human beings, and in human beings only. This explains why all

---

[1] G. Révész, 'Thinking and Speaking', *Acta Psychologica* (1954).

men, including the deaf, are fundamentally able to learn any existing language. Learning a language is closely connected with learning to speak; the same mental conditions are therefore requisite for each individual language.

(e) The Theory of the Priority of Gesture Language

The problem of the chronological sequence of the two forms of language, phonetic and gestural, occupies a special place in theories of origins. The problem is not the actual origin, but the *original form* of language. Some investigators, and especially Wundt,[1] whose views are strongly influenced by the concept of evolution, maintain that gesture language is the initial stage, from which phonetic language gradually developed. Though plausible at first sight, this theory lacks clarity.

The theory of the priority of gesture language asserts that inward conditions and external objects and processes were initially indicated by a system of motor signs, and that only later in human evolution was the indicative motor function overtaken by the phonetic sign function, involving a sort of transposition of natural and conventional gestures to phonetic symbols. The validity of this statement is based on two tacit assumptions; first, that man at first responded to internal and external stimuli exclusively or predominantly by motor reactions; and secondly, that he communicated his responses by motor signs forming a rich system of natural gestures.

It is easy to show that both these assumptions are erroneous.

Creatures with organs for sound production achieve emotional expression as much by the use of audible sounds as by bodily movements. One need only think of the whining and growling of dogs, the cry of the frightened blackbird, the cluck of hens, the feeding noises of apes, or the irate cry of the gander. To these we could add the many and varied hissing and growling noises and cries of warning, of fear, pleasure or pain, and the mating calls of many kinds of animals. In some species, such as

[1] W. Wundt, *Elemente der Völkerpsychologie* (1912), p. 59, and *Die Sprache*, II (1912), pp. 648 ff.

birds and apes, expression by means of sound is far more important than by means of movement. Thus it does not follow from the anatomical or physiological equipment or from the use of audible sounds that gesture language precedes the language of sound.

The fact that man is physiologically equipped for expression both by motor and acoustical means does not of course exclude the possibility that gesture language represents an earlier stage of speech activity than phonetic language. But if one examines the consequences to which this doctrine leads one can only wonder that so much recognition is accorded today to so purely speculative a theory (Spencer, Allport, Stout, Paul, van Ginneken and others).

One of its most obvious corollaries is that primitive men would have communicated with one another in the same way as do deaf mutes. To compare fully normal people and those with defects is unsound. The deaf mute uses a gesture language not because it is simpler, older and more concrete than phonetic language, but simply because his deafness makes him unable to hear his own speech sounds or those of others. But primitive man, not being deaf, must have employed vocal sounds as indications of his presence, or as directed calls, even before he began to use speech. A further fact invalidating such a comparison is that deaf persons tend to speak more loudly whenever they observe that they are not being understood. They feel their inferiority, as it were, because the most important means of communication, phonetic language, is not at their command.

To argue that infants striving for personal contact in their pre-linguistic period make use of gestures first, tells us nothing about the phylogeny of language; and, what is more, it does not agree with the experiences of child psychology. Linguistic ontogeny favours the assumption of the simultaneity of the two kinds of language. In newly born infants phonetic expressions of pleasure and displeasure appear in the first few days in the form of crying and whimpering, at the same time as movements of the extremities such as stretching of the arms and legs and turning of the head. Deliberate movement and the first babbling words appear fairly early, and roughly at about the same time.[1] The first gestures, those for pointing and indicating, do not occur until after the child has learned to understand at least a few words as such, *i.e.* until it has begun to understand speech. The fact that babies in their prelinguistic period have such limited command of unambiguous gestures suggests that their speech function has not yet become effective because of their mental immaturity. The fact should not be overlooked that the majority of gestures, apart from the purely indicative ones, are ambiguous and can be understood with certainty only when the reference is given by speech.

It has been suggested in support of the priority of gesture language that creatures incapable of speech express their desires gesturally. Thus Köhler reports that one of his chimpanzees expressed its wishes by gently touching its master or pulling his hand, at the same time looking at him and taking steps in the direction it intended to go. Sometimes the chimpanzee enacted what it wanted to do. 'Thus Rana stretched her hand out toward us when she wanted to be treated tenderly, but walked up to us clumsily with an eager glance, at the same time embracing herself as a gesture of friendship.'[2]

For the moment we shall not attempt to decide whether these communicative actions of the chimpanzee are to be regarded as speech gestures. As indications of the evolutionary priority of gesture language they are irrelevant, simply because the chimpanzee also has expressive sounds, and makes use of them to a greater extent than gestures. Hence there is no proof that among the anthropoid apes gestures preceded expressive sounds. The facts cited above can therefore be used neither for nor against the theory of the temporal precedence of gestures. Besides, we are not dealing here with a gesture language capable of being considered as a forerunner of spoken language, but only with individual gestures expressive of desires and tenderness arising only in human company (perhaps through imitation). Furthermore, one could ask with some justification, why the anthropoids, who

1 W. Stern, *Die Kindersprache* (1922), pp. 300 ff.

2 W. Köhler, *Intelligenzprüfungen an Anthropoiden* (1917).

have presumably been practising such 'gestures' for more than 100,000 years along with a variety of expressive sounds, could never take a single step toward spoken language? The objection that the phylogenetic development of language did not start with the recent anthropoids but only with the hominids, can be overcome by reference to the fact that even among the hypothetical ape-men—as among the anthropoids—phonetic reactions may well have far exceeded gestures in number and variety.

The attempt to find support for the gesture theory from study of the spontaneous language of deaf mutes has also failed. The agreement can be explained on the basis of the general form of all spontaneous expressive movements and gestures, their concretely representative and imitative character, which distinguishes all gesture systems including those accompanying phonetic language.

Van Ginneken attempts to prove the priority of gesture language in a unique way.[1] He asserts that gesture language appeared long before the birth of phonetic language, and that the latter did not arise out of the former directly but indirectly by way of hieroglyphic script. He attempts to show from the old Chinese, Sumerian and Egyptian pictorial scripts that pictographic signs depicting gesture and action as well as objects acquired phonetic values and thus gave rise to phonetic language.

Notre revue a donc donné le résultat assez remarquable, que tous les systèmes d'écriture, que nous connaissons dès leur commencement, suivent dans leurs trois prèmieres périodes entièrement le modèle d'un langage par gestes, lequel est donc antérieur aux hiéroglyphes. Et ce n'est évidemment qu'avec l'aide, et par le soutien des langues hiéroglyphiques qui possédaient déjà un lexique, une grammaire et une syntaxe, que dans les civilizations avancées moyennant les clics interjectionnelles les langues orales ont apparu et se sont développées assez lentement, en se créant des clics lexicaux. . . . Or, notre revue vient de montrer que les langues orales n'apparaissent dans l'histoire de l'humanité qu'environ l'an 3500 av. J. Chr. au plus tôt (pp. 123-4).

[1] J. van Ginneken, *La reconstruction typologique des langues archaïques de l'humanité* (1939). Although the theory of van Ginneken is untenable for psychological and biological reasons, the material which he has collected is extremely interesting.

The arguments by which van Ginneken and Chang Cheng Ming[1] seek to demonstrate the priority of gesture language through hieroglyphics and the ancient Chinese script are untenable. The fact that gestures and objects which can be perceived visually are represented in these primitive pictographic signs by no means excludes a contemporary everyday language with an oral rather than a kinesthetic character. The form of representation used in a script tells us nothing about the type of language used. One could just as well conclude from the fact that savage peoples use knots to represent number, that they have no numerals. A further difficulty is that according to van Ginneken man would have been mute for hundreds of thousands of years despite his continual development, and would not have begun speaking until a few thousand years ago. Van Ginneken must have overlooked this consequence of his theory; or he would surely have recognized the impossibility of the Egyptians having had an extraordinarily expressive written form of communication five thousand years ago and not the ability to speak.

Against the chronological priority of gestures, and in particular against the view that gestural symbols were somehow transposed into phonetic symbols, is the fact that there are neither phenomenological nor structural similarities linking the two modes of language. Nor could such similarities exist, because of their completely different nature. Each kind of language has its own sign material, its own organ, its own mode of appearance and its own structural laws. This is why descriptive and structural linguistics never goes back to gestures to explain morphological and phonological phenomena.

The supposed structural resemblances of sound and gesture language among the Sudanese and Hottentots—a circumstance stressed particularly by Wundt in his *Elemente der Völkerpsychologie* and used by him as evidence of the likelihood of a gesture language having been a kind of '*Ursprache*'—are irrelevant for the supposed primacy of gesture language. Even if such resemblances could actually be proven, they would only show that sound and

[1] Chang Cheng Ming, *L'écriture chinoise et le geste humain* (Paris, 1938).

gestural symbols assist one another. They would not in any way support the assumption that gesture language is more original or historically earlier than sound language. Such a view could only be justified to a degree if one could establish the probability of the common structural elements having originally arisen from gestures, and that these particular structures form the necessary basis for phonetic language. Such proof has not yet been furnished, and would be difficult to find.

There is no people on earth that preferably, not to say exclusively, uses gesture language for communication. It is true that gesture language seems to be a widespread speech form among primitive peoples, although only a few of them can rightly claim the name 'gesture language'. It is equally certain that all these peoples also possess a much more highly developed phonetic language, which they use for intercourse to a much greater extent. Among individuals of the same linguistic community both kinds of speech or language are used simultaneously, supporting and supplementing each other, as can be observed among some oriental peoples, such as the Arabs, to this day.[1] If, however, communication occurs occasionally only through gestures, this does not mean that these peoples have no vocal expressions for these things, but simply that they do not use the accompanying word, either because the gesture is adequate for communicating or because soundless communication appears to them for some reason as more suitable.[2]

The fact that in the extremely primitive, essentially monosyllabic Ewe language, existing gestural signs possess greater clarity and immediate comprehensibility than words and sentence structure, tells us little about the priority of gestural over phonetic language.[3] It is probably true that much can be expressed more directly and clearly by means of gesture than by words, as is the well-known fact that gestures naturally make possible a very close and direct relation between meaning and sign. One need only

[1] I. Goldzieher, 'Über Gebärden-und Zeichensprache bei den Arabern', *Z. f. Völkerpsych.*, p. 16.
[2] W. Wundt, *Die Sprache*, I, p. 153.
[3] D. Westermann, *Grammatik der Ewe-Sprache* (1907); *Die Sudan-Sprachen* (1911).

think of emotional gestures or of mimetic actions in theatrical representation of religious ritual. On the other hand there are innumerable instances where the events to be communicated can be represented much more directly by means of spoken language supported by intonation than by gesture language, which is often able to represent quite simple communications only with considerable circumlocution, and even then not always without ambiguity. It is for this reason that deaf mutes are forced to employ a conventional or finger language whose development indirectly presupposes spoken language.

It is worth noting in this connexion that the *development* of gesture language is dependent on sound language, and not the reverse. This is demonstrated by the poverty of the gesture language of deaf mutes. They are restricted to spontaneous gestures because their condition has denied them the chance of learning conventional gestures which have originated under the influence of sound language.

From the point of view of practical life—and after all, that is what matters here—the fictitious view of the primacy of gesture language is really absurd. When 'pre-linguistic' palaeolithic man sought a more differentiated mode of communication, he could not have been satisfied with one that permitted communication only with people in the immediate neighbourhood, or that necessarily excluded conversation with people at a distance or in the dark.

Against the priority of gesture language we may finally adduce the fact that in many (perhaps the majority) of languages the name of the organ of speech, or part of it, is used for language itself. In these cases there is also only one word for language and the organ of speech. A number of examples will illustrate:

Language and tongue as homonyms: Greek, γλῶσσα; Latin, *lingua*; French: *langue*; English: tongue (applied mostly to foreign languages and the Bible); German, *Zunge*; Dutch, *tongval* (dialect); Danish, *tunge*. In Finnish and Hungarian there is only one word for the two concepts: *kieli*, *nyelv* respectively. The same is true of Russian: *jazik*; Bulgarian, *jezik*; Serbian, *jezik*;

Albanian, *gjuhë*. Compare also the many expressions occurring in cruder forms of speech derived from the word 'mouth', such as: *avoir bon bec, n'avoir que du bec, flux de bouche, des mots de gueule,* to have plenty of jaw, to mouth, to lip, *grosse Schnauze, anschnauzen, afbekken, vuilbekken,* etc.

Homonyms for language, tongue and mouth occur even more frequently in primitive languages. Malayan: *moeloet* (mouth), but also: *bermoeloet* (speak); Samoa: *fofoga*=face, voice (of a chief), also mouth (chiefly word); Bantu language in the Congo region: *yànga*=language and mouth, *légŏ*=language, throat, and voice; Egyptian Sudan language: *dôk-dôk*=language and mouth; a Hamitic language from North Africa: *afàn*=mouth and language; or *affa*=language, but also mouth and tongue; likewise in the Somali language: *af* and Nubian: *lisān*; the Rama language in Central America: *kŭŭp*=language and tongue; the Ewe language, West Africa: *gbe*=voice, sound, tone as well as language and dialect.

On the other hand, there are languages in which language and the organ of speech are designated by entirely different words, as in Swedish, Sudanese, Buginese, Makassaar. Also in Sanskrit the word for language, *bhāsā*, is unrelated to the word designating parts of the organ of speech (*lidah*=tongue). The question that now arises is: what could have induced the gesture theorists to consider early man, in his efforts to establish closer contact with his fellowmen, as deliberately giving up the most expressive means of self-expression and communication, the sound of the human voice?

I suppose it is due to the observation that people who do not understand each other's language instinctively communicate through gestures, and that these natural gestures generally serve their purpose without previous knowledge or agreement. Palaeolithic man has been thought of in a similar way. In intending to communicate with one another they employed the means adopted by people who do not understand one another, natural gestures, which in the course of time developed into a full language. This analogy fails to consider, first of all, that our

E

hypothetical pre-human beings (like highly organized animals provided with vocal organs) certainly communicated by means of both sound and gesture even before this stage; secondly, that even completely deaf people accompany their gestures with inarticulate sounds, pointing to the biological inseparability of the two means of expression; thirdly, that humans endowed with speech employ gestures as a subsidiary language only in extraordinary circumstances, and even then only side by side with phonetic language; fourthly, that primitive peoples who use fully developed gesture language do not by far belong to the most primitive ones, especially as this means of communication demands great inventive talents. Finally we must repeat that gesture language, by virtue of its autochthonous nature and special characteristics, is not a step on the road to phonetic language.

If one visualizes early man in a concrete way it is impossible to imagine that men with normal hearing and vocal organs should have failed to use sound for the purpose of mutual communication and restricted themselves to gestural signs. When prehistoric man became aware that calls and pointing gestures were no longer adequate in intercourse with others of his kind he began instinctively to 'search' for more appropriate and more differentiated means of communication. The means at his disposal were sound and gesture; he therefore had to adapt these means of expression for his purposes. Thus sound and gesture came to be used simultaneously in the very earliest period of speech; from which arose the word and the linguistic gesture, the two basic elements of speech and gesture language. Both types of speech have developed from the beginning, supporting and supplementing each other, until finally sound language gained the upper hand and gradually pushed gestures into the background, though without completely eliminating them. Just as language could never be purely gestural, so it could never be purely phonetic. *Language, even in its most primitive form, was phonetic language shot through with gestures, mimic and pantomimic movements.*

This view of the role of the two kinds of language during the prehistory and early history of language agrees with that of

Cushing[1] who on the basis of a detailed study of the language habits of some primitive Indian tribes believes that the two kinds of language are autonomous in their development among primitive peoples. According to him neither type is more primitive. Both types of language are said to be an immediate expression of 'unitary thought'. This view induced Cushing to postulate the existence of 'manual concepts' alongside verbal concepts. Both are supposed to exercise considerable influence on each other, so that there is a particularly strong interaction between them. If we wished to reconstruct the development of language from this perspective, we would come closest to the truth if we considered the two kinds of language as direct expressions of unitary thought and the communicative impulse, springing from two sources: from phonetic images and from gestures.[2]

To summarize: the assumption of the chronological priority of gesture language is not borne out by the evidence of ethnology, child psychology or animal psychology. On biological grounds early man can be imagined only as a creature expressing his thoughts and wishes by both phonetic and gestural symbols. Against the assumption that phonetic speech originated out of gestural language is the fact that word and sentence constructions

---

[1] F. H. Cushing, 'Manual Concepts', *Amer. Anthropologist*, V, p. 291.

[2] It would be a rewarding task to analyse in detail the gestures of normal persons and those of deaf mutes with reference to the supposed 'manual concepts'. I do not doubt that there is some truth in Cushing's view, but it seems to me rather questionable whether we are dealing here with a specific kind of concept. The fact that linguistic gestures are executed without verbal concepts is not sufficient proof of the existence of specifically manual concepts. The same applies to utterances which cannot be executed without gestures and mime. To give an example, shaking hands, combined with a particular facial expression, can be interpreted as a sign of complete devotion, of unlimited mutual assistance. The feelings and decisions on which it is based and the obligations resulting from it can be expressed only with difficulty or not at all in words. In this case we are dealing with the direction of the whole personality, with an inner attitude which can be expressed most clearly by means of an action or symbolically through a special kind of handshake and mime. Is this action based on a manual concept? Is such a concept a psychological or a logical one? Do the same criteria apply to it as to other concepts? Is it therefore justifiable to classify concepts as verbal or manual?

These remarks are intended only to indicate the difficulties and the necessity of an analysis of the facts reported by Cushing. We do not regard it as impossible that Cushing's view could, after critical cleansing, provide a valuable theoretical approach toward the understanding of the natural and symbolic gesture language of deaf mutes.

have no similarity of form or structure with natural gesture language and that the development of gesture language is profoundly dependent on phonetic language, and not the reverse. In this connexion another fact of importance in cultural history may be adduced. The oldest form of writing, hieroglyphics, is related to phonetic speech and only exceptionally to gesture language. In general, the pictographic representation of an event involves the pictorical representation of a phonetic communication.[1]

In all probability human language incorporated within itself from its very inception all the characteristic constituents of fully developed speech—that is, on the one hand, the sounded word with meaningful content, together with its phonetic and rhythmic formal properties (articulation, intonation, rhythm and melody) and, on the other hand, the natural eloquence of the human body, gestures, motions of the hand and arm, facial expression and pantomime.

(f) Theories Based on Ethnology and the Pathology of Speech

For the sake of completeness I shall discuss two other approaches which are sometimes invoked in connexion with the problem of origins. The first of these employs ethnological material, and attempts to deduce the beginnings of language (including 'the' earliest language) from the language of primitive peoples.

Even if the possibility of reconstructing the earliest form of spoken language were conceded, this method would not apply to the prelinguistic period and its stages. Theoretically it is not impossible that languages of very primitive structure could cast some light on the sound and gesture material used by 'mankind' in the stage of early speech. In practice, however, this possibility is very slight, because of the great antiquity of the primitive languages. They are surely no younger than our own languages, and have a long history behind them.[2] Furthermore, all existing

---

[1] G. Révész, *Die menschliche Hand* (Basel, 1944).

[2] 'Le linguiste n'a jamais affaire qu'à des langues tres évoluées, qui ont derrière elles un passé considérable dont nous ne savons rien.' Further: 'On a renoncé à rien demander aux sauvages. Leurs langues ont une histoire.' Delacroix, *La langue et la pensée*, 128-9.

primitive languages, including those called 'root languages' by linguists, are true languages, and possess all the essential characteristics of mature languages. They are complete with a variety of classes of words, a rich vocabulary, grammatical categories, syntactical forms, phonetic laws, etc.[1] They are unsuitable as a starting point for the hypothetical reconstruction of a primordial language (or several such languages) if only for the reason that in most cases their complicated structure indicates that they are chronologically very remote from the primordial stages of linguistic activity. They are somewhat primitive compared with our languages, but are superior in their greater wealth in certain classes of concepts. This wealth of vocabulary and syntactical forms which has so often evoked the admiration of philologists is, however, known to be based on the primitive character of their thought and expression. Since the speech of primitive man is determined by concrete, vivid images and hence by immediately perceptible differences between objects, he is virtually compelled to create a special word or combination of words to define any concrete peculiarity. In this way primitive man arrives at dual and triple as well as singular and plural forms, verbs and auxiliary words dependent on the numbers of subjects and objects, and prefixes which not only indicate time and place but other concrete circumstances such as form, dimension, direction, movement or position.[2]

These considerations are of importance in any attempt to form a conception of the early forms of language. For we must assume that during the early history of language there prevailed generally a need for concrete modes of expression—a need favouring concrete terms as against general and abstract conceptions. A linguistic tendency to adapt to concrete situations must therefore have operated, thus giving much scope for the spontaneous invention of words.

Primitive languages are not to be regarded as reflexions of

---

[1] P. M. Plancquaert, S. J., *Les sociétés secrètes chez les Bajaka* (1930); R. Thurnwald, 'Psychologie des primitiven Menschen', *Handb. d. vgl. Psych.*, I (1922).

[2] H. Lévy-Bruhl, *Les fonctions mentales dans les sociétés inferieures* (Paris, 1922).

primordial ones because we cannot assume that the earliest languages were as complicated as those of existing primitive peoples. Earliest speech must have been exceedingly simple and confined entirely to essentials. Only in succeeding ages, as increasing needs made greater demands on language, did speech become circumstantial and hence complicated. During the ensuing stages of development (primarily for reasons of convenience) it became simplified, and this was particularly fostered by the increasing preponderance of conceptual thought over direct visual impresssion.

Another reason for treating ethnological material with caution is the fact that we know virtually nothing about the historical development of primitive languages. We must however, assume that in general they are no younger than our languages and here too, despite a vast accumulation of material, only a very small part of the total is known to us.

Although the results of research into primitive languages are of no great theoretical value for the early forms and still less for the antecedent stage of language, they nevertheless retain their importance for linguistic history, providing useful evidence for comparative philology.

Alongside these approaches from ethnology and child psychology, an attempt has been made to employ speech defects, and in particular the pathologically reduced capacity for speech in cases of motor aphasia, for reconstructing the 'primordial language'. But if we study the complicated reductive and regressive phenomena symptomatic of aphasia it becomes difficult to understand how they came to be regarded as paradigms of the emergence of human speech. Presumably it was because restitution in aphasia to some extent recapitulates the main stages in the development of child speech. Apart from the fact that there can be no logical justification for supporting one supposition by another, the process of destruction and restitution attending aphasia produces phenomena which cannot easily be related to the origins and prehistory of language. According to one scheme suggested by a speech pathologist the speechless stage is followed by one of agrammatical speech in words of one sentence, achieved by a stringing together of single words without grammatical construction and syntactical order, then by a paragrammatical use of sentence forms, until finally proper speech is recovered.

There can, however, be no question in the phylogenetic development of language of a paragrammatical stage, that is, of imperfectly or incorrectly used auxiliary verbs, conjugations, declensions, prepositions, comparatives, omission of interrogatives of time and cause, etc. There is no sense in the assumption that early man discovered conjugations and declensions but only later learned to use them correctly. The fact must also be taken into consideration that aphasic phenomena as a whole relate not only to concrete speech and to thinking intimately bound up with speech, but to the whole behaviour of the patient. The speech defect is merely a particularly striking symptom of the whole pattern of the illness.[1] It should be added that the speech of aphasic patients has primitive characteristics, but it is not primitive in the same sense as is the speech of children and savages. Moreover, phenomena of aphasia are so complicated and variable and are so intimately connected with the linguistic level of the patient before his illness that for this reason alone they cannot be considered as models of the preparatory stage of language.[2]

We do not wish to pass any definite judgment on the genetic significance of the processes of decomposition and restitution, since linguistic pathology has not yet succeeded in establishing generally valid laws of pathological occurrences. We do not, however, expect much advance in this direction from research on aphasia. The speech material of aphasia, fragmentary and unstable as it may be, definitely belongs to the sphere of language, and on that account cannot be used for the reconstruction of a

---

[1] H. Head, *Aphasia and Kindred Disorders of Speech* (1926); A. Gelb, 'Zur medizinischen Psychologie und philosophischen Anthropologie', *Acta Psychologica*, 3 (1937): K. Goldstein, ' "Bemerkungen zum Problem Sprechen und Denken" auf Grund hirnpathologischer Erfahrungen', *Acta Psychologica*, X (1954).

[2] In speaking of aphasia we have in mind those forms which display a gradual sensomotoric deterioration of speech activity. Cases involving the absence of reactive and spontaneous speech, difficulty in repetition or designation, are outside our problem.

condition anterior to language. These critical observations are naturally in no way intended to cast doubt upon the great services rendered by research on aphasia to the psychology of thought and language and to linguistic studies in general.

Thus all efforts to solve the problem of linguistic origins with the help of various apparent parallels are seen to be untenable. Animals do not possess a system of sounds and gestures at all comparable to the linguistic functions. Children are human; they are constitutionally equipped for speech and gifted with an inner linguistic sense; their phonetic utterances cannot represent an anterior preparatory stage, for even in the embryo they are already in possession of an inherited and highly developed speech apparatus, which is formed at an early stage and develops with astonishing rapidity. The languages of primitive peoples are true languages having perhaps hundreds of thousands of years of development behind them. Finally, the assumption that speech disturbances can provide an index to the first beginnings of language is based on empirical evidence that does not really provide any point of contact with linguistic prehistory.

(D) PHILOSOPHICAL AND THEOLOGICAL THEORIES

Finally, we wish to turn to the philosophical and theological doctrines, which are the best-known and most influential of all despite the fact that most of them exclude a genetic approach.

Philosophical doctrines relating to the formation of language can first be classified according to whether they regard the origin and development of human language as nativistic or empirical; and, secondly, according to whether they regard it as formed by design and conscious choice or through necessity and accidental circumstances.

Nativism, which regards the speech faculty as a form of expression that is directly given, prior to all experience, and not further derivable (W. von Humboldt, H. Steinthal, Max Müller, E. Renan, D. van Lennep, W. Wundt, and others) contrasts with *empiricism*, which ascribes decisive importance even in the beginnings of language to experience, volition and thought, and especially to the use of analogy (Condillac, Hobbes, Darwin, Taylor, L. Geiger, Carus, Michelet, Madvig, Marty, etc.).

Both groups of theories have deep-seated roots; they are expressions of epistemological conflicts that governed the development of philosophical ideas from Bacon and Descartes down to the end of the eighteenth century, and which claimed the theoretical interest of students of language even a century later.

Study of the most important nativistic theories of origin shows that their advocates concentrated their attention on the *beginnings* of language and did not study its later *development*. Had they also devoted their attention to speech development, as the nativist Wundt did, they would not have underestimated empirical factors. No nativist could deny that from the very beginning countless generations have consciously co-operated in the formation of language. This is also true of the speech development of the child. The idea that infants are already in possession of the main elements of language and are prevented from expressing themselves verbally only by the unprepared state of their speech organs is inconsistent with what child psychology has taught us. On the other hand, no reasonable empiricist would hesitate to grant that the human child could never acquire speech if it did not have the innate capacity for it. In the child's speech development, experience, the influence of the milieu, personal initiative and individual capacity undeniably play an important part, even though the child must inherit the capacity of speech activity as much as the disposition for running, playing, or thinking. It is thus clear that a theory taking account of both the origin and the development of language—phylogenetic or ontogenetic—would eliminate the antithesis between nativism and empiricism. The problem is rather one of the relative weight to be given to these factors in the early period of speech activity. Only theories that are moderately nativistic or empiricist are adequate. Either pure nativism or pure empiricism produces difficulties that cannot be argued away. We have already shown in our exposition of the theories of origin that purely empiricist doctrines, such as the theory of natural sounds or the imitation theory, lead to obscurities and confusions that cannot be eliminated except by a softening of the empiricist standpoint. The same is true of purely nativistic theories. I believe that my own theory of linguistic origins, the contact theory, is the only doctrine that reconciles these two fundamental ideas and is consequently free of the untenable theoretical and practical consequences of pure nativism or empiricism. On the basis of his inherited predisposition every human being must acquire his language by contact with his environment, and to a degree re-create it.

Connected with the problem of nativism and empiricism is that of whether the linguistic sense is innate or acquired. The answer depends on what is meant by the notion of a 'linguistic sense'. If it signifies simply the formal capacity for learning languages, it is doubtless innate;[1] but if we understand it to mean the inner structure of a particular language or language group, which controls the linguistic practice of a community and gives the spoken language its power of penetration, it could have arisen only through experience.[2]

I call the innate predisposition for speaking, i.e. the formal capacity for speech, for understanding the meaning of a vocabulary, and the active employment of words, the linguistic sense. The concrete working out of this functional readiness for the language of his environment which is more or less developed in each individual according to his particular disposition, I call the

[1] Whether a human being could, solely on the basis of his linguistic sense, without the help of a speech-using environment, invent a language structurally comparable to human language, is a matter on which opinions are divided. Despite the absence of attested cases, a number of linguistic psychologists incline toward a positive answer to the question. (W. Wundt, H. Paul, MacDougall, etc.) Cf. also the detailed discussion of F. Kainz in his *Sprachpsychologie*, II, 75 ff.

[2] To avoid all possibility of misunderstanding it should be noted that I do not identify the inner structure of language with its inner form. The concept of 'inner speech form' is formulated by Humboldt, Steinthal, Wundt, Cassirer and most incisively by Marty as the image-content of a linguistic expression, i.e. as the idea that surrounds and communicates the meaning of a verbal form. Reference may be made to the writings of O. Funke on this question, an important one for the philosophy of language, in his work, *Innere Sprachform* (1924) and *Studien zur Geschichte der Sprachphilosophie* (1927).

sense of linguistic form. The linguistic sense relates only to the general framework of language, but the sense of form to the specific details connected with a particular language. The linguistic sense is inherited, while ontogenesis determines the sense of form. To what extent the planned and orderly unfolding of ontogenesis also applies to linguistic form, and to what extent the first real linguistic utterances are themselves biologically determined, cannot be answered if we confine ourselves to what is empirically provable. The sense of form is to be understood as being very much like the sense of musical form, and the concrete forms of musical appreciation and expression connected with it. The sense of musical form of a European trained in music implies that he is confined in his perception, interpretation and production to the prevailing tone system of European music. Even in the most rudimentary examples of melodic improvisation among young children (five to eight years) the melodic elements of our Western music can be observed; such as the general laws of melodic lines, tonality, harmonic chords and cadences. The child growing up in a European environment of necessity sings in our diatonic scales, while a child in Siam similarly adopts the melodic forms of the heptatonic seven-note equally divided Siamese scales. Even adults find such exotic music completely incomprehensible at first, and considerable time is required to enable one to understand this singular musical language, let alone be able to express one's own musical ideas and moods in it.[1]

Language is quite analogous. We acquire a sense of linguistic form through the medium of our mother tongue and it is this form that governs the development of our individual speech. Even in the apparently freely invented 'private languages' of individuals or groups of children (W. Stern, Delacroix, MacDougall, Piaget), the secret languages of primitive peoples (Frazer, Lévy-Bruhl), or the special languages of somnambulists (Flournoy) the modes of word and sentence formation of the mother tongue are retained.

A characteristic example is a sentence used by a German boy

---

[1] G. Révész, *Introduction to the Psychology of Music*, London (1953), Oklahoma (1954).

who at the age of two to three talked only in private language. He once said, '*Ich haja kokodach, mach olol kap-näh,*' which means literally, '*Ich habe schönes Schokoladenhaus, das macht Rudolf kaputt; nein!*' How deeply the inner linguistic form takes root despite the exclusive use of a private language is shown by the fact that this boy, after clinging firmly to his self-invented vocabulary for two years, abruptly abandoned his private language one fine day, and without any sort of transition began speaking ordinary German.[1]

This can also be seen in the case of a spiritualist medium investigated by Flournoy.[2] The 'seeress of Geneva' made use of a special language during her trances, of which she knew nothing when she was awake. In fact, this language was exactly like French in syntax and grammar.

An example:

i modé, mété modé, iné,

o mère, tendre mère, mère bien-aimée.

palette is ché péliencheé ché chiré né ci ten ti vi.

calme tout ton souci, ton fils est près de toi.

je: cé	ton: ché
tu: dé	te: chée
il: hed	tes: chi
nous: nini	son: bi
vous: sini	sa: bé
ils: hed	ses: bée

The second problem involves the voluntaristic conception of linguistic development, as opposed to the deterministic or necessitarian view which regards it as unconscious and involuntary. Here again it is evident that these apparently opposite views can only be regarded in linguistic theory as interrelated and complementary.

The most extreme proponents of these points of view in recent times were Wundt and Marty. According to Wundt, language

---

[1] C. Stumpf, 'Eigenartige sprachliche Entwicklung eines Kindes', *Zeitschrift f. pädagog. Psychologie*, 3 (1901).

[2] Th. Flournoy, *Des Indes a la Planète Mars* (Paris, 1900), p. 202.

is, by its very nature, nothing but emotional expression; at all stages of its emergence and development it is in no way dependent on human intention. In his view, language is merely the particular form of expressive gesture that corresponds to a given stage in the growth of human consciousness. This necessarily entails the development both of expressive motions and gestures of language, and at each of these stages imagination, feeling and thought attain expression in the most exactly appropriate form.[1] Wundt categorically rejects the voluntaristic-teleological view of linguistic origins, which would admit the influence of communicative intent in language formation and in the selection of the means of expression. From his own point of view, he is correct. If thought were able to find its adequate expression at every stage of its development—as Wundt understands it—then intention would in fact have no role to play, and all of language could evolve involuntarily, unintentionally and without the slightest effort; words and forms need not be sought, they would appear of their own accord. But such a theory cannot explain either the strong synonymy or the varied idioms of language, nor can it elucidate the creative elements in human language. This extreme deterministic view is equally incompatible with the facts of man's desire to communicate and his mental efforts in attempting to establish communication and to find new words and forms of expression. It appears that the validity of the principle according to which language develops spontaneously partly on fortuitous grounds, partly on the basis of 'natural forces' working according to laws, was not entirely convincing to Wundt himself. Only in this way could one presumably explain why he admitted the existence of an 'exceptional voluntary creation' alongside his 'regular involuntary word creation'.

A similar but much more prudent position is taken by W. von Humboldt. Following his discussion of the phonetic laws he declares:

> One must beware of seeing anything genuinely intentional in this; in dealing with language the word 'intention' must generally be

[1] W. Wundt, *Die Sprache*, II, pp. 605 ff. and 636.

employed with reserve. To the extent that it signifies verbal agreement, or even simply the deliberate pursuit of a clearly conceived
goal, the concept of intention is (as we cannot too often be reminded)
foreign to language.

Despite this agreement, in principle, with Wundt, W. von
Humboldt conceives the process of language formation quite
differently, and his attack on the voluntaristic view seems to have
no other motive than that of cautioning linguists against exaggerated teleology. This is shown, on the one hand, by his deriving
of language from the 'depths of human experience' which precludes its being regarded as a deliberate product of peoples; and,
on the other hand, his characterization of language genetically as
an intellectual labour directed toward a definite aim. But if language is a form of expression dependent on the creative activity
of the human mind, if man by his very nature endeavours to
attain clarity and definiteness in his linguistic means of communication, then intention, intimately related as it is with voluntary
effort, cannot be eliminated. One need only try to imagine how
the multiplicity of verbal forms—cases and numbers, pronouns
and adverbs, the phonetic images in primitive languages, the
improvised indicative and descriptive gestures and symbolic signs
of deaf mutes—must have arisen, to estimate justly the role of
deliberate intention, initiative and invention in the formation and
use of language.

The origin and development of language have not the inexora-
bility of a biological function. Even if the mechanism of speech
and the disposition for it are biological in origin, living speech
requires the impulse of the will and mental activity, and these in
turn presuppose intention and conscious initiative. Starting with
this idea, the voluntaristic standpoint conceives of language formation as a conscious, deliberate process, not built up on a definite
predesignated plan but nevertheless governed by intention, free-
will and choice. Indeed, Marty, the most acute proponent of this
doctrine, is not a bit less extravagant in his exposition than his
opponent Wundt. Thus in one of his earlier works he propounds
the thesis that 'every individual step in language formation' is a

conscious one.[1] It is therefore not surprising that Wundt describes Marty's standpoint as purely an inventive theory. To this
Marty objects, declaring that he never conceived of language as
a form of communication that is planned and directed in the
entirety of its means and functions by reflexion or established
according to prior agreement. He wishes to admit invention in
language formation only in the sense that any other voluntaristic
teleological doctrine does so; that is, to regard language as an
instrument for the purpose of expressing mental life, formed by
intention and mental labour, without invoking planned reflexion
in its formation, or, in this sense, inventive sagacity. In his main
work Marty accordingly softens the crudeness of his earlier views
and finds the correct middle way between the opposing
doctrines.[2]

> It may be said of all words or forms [he states on p. 628] that at some
> time, one or more individuals first made the attempt to employ
> them with others for the purpose of communication, and in this
> sense to introduce them; certainly without a thought of the remote
> and distant future or of all time, nor of wider order, but probably
> only with the thought of his own small circle of fellow conversa-
> tionalists and the short period of the conversation in which he was
> engaged. This attempt, for the very reason that it was animated by
> the attempt at communication, was an action of the will in the
> true sense; indeed—since it mostly involves groping attempts and,
> according to the result, a dissatisfied dropping of it or approving
> retention of a means—an action involving a choice. And it was not
> only the first creator of the sign who exercised a fumbling selection;
> his comrades also did it—some more, some less—and only what was
> acceptable to the whole circle and definitely selected by it became a
> relatively lasting component of the common language and a subject
> of a fixed habit. But this selection of useful means of communica-
> tion was a completely planless one. Each individual who thus con-
> tributed to language formation thought only of the present need.
> No one of those who thus helped in its completion—some with more,

[1] A. Marty, *Über den Ursprung der Sprache* (1875).

[2] A. Marty, *Untersuchungen zur Grundlegung der allgemeinen Grammatik und Sprachphilosophie* (1908).

some with less skill and success—had any consciousness of the whole, or of the end result, or of the internal division of the work and the function of its different parts; and still less were any of them conscious of the method or methods by which the work was constructed. In this sense the formation of language was unconscious and unintended; and in the sense of the formula: not involuntary and choiceless, but unsystematic and planless, would I wish it to be understood when, for example, in the invention of equivalences and in the syntactical mode of sign formation, I speak of a tendency toward economy of signs or of a tendency toward convenience and brevity of expression.

In these final views of Marty the two apparently opposing principles of language formation, the voluntaristic and deterministic principles, are reconciled. Neither the one nor the other exclusively governs language formation. There are words that were produced as it were involuntarily through the communicative impulse, and words produced through intention and deliberation. In the first period of language the deterministic principle most probably exercised the strongest influence, in the later period of development the voluntaristic.

From this discussion it is not difficult to recognize that the whole attention of both the voluntarists (Marty, Herder, Bréal, Paul and others) and the determinists (von Humboldt, Steinthal, Wundt, Mauthner, and others) was focussed on language formation and not on its origins. A voluntaristic and teleological view of the question of linguistic origins is in the nature of the case untenable. It is inconceivable that earliest man should have arrived at his *first* linguistic utterances—be they concerned with form or vocabulary—intentionally. It is much more probable that after the first speech elements had grown involuntarily out of primitive phonetic communicative signs the need arose for man to express his wishes through specific phonetic forms, and to use the same phonetic signs repeatedly on similar occasions. With the successful introduction and development of linguistic representation, intention and choice became an increasingly decisive influence on language formation.

An extreme form of the voluntaristic theory is represented by the invention theory, which regards the teleological, spontaneous, creative impulse and the inventive mental gifts as the sole creative factors in the initial formation and subsequent growth of linguistic communication.

Its earliest form is met with in one of the writings devoted to the question of origins by the philosopher Tiedemann, well known for his study of the theory of knowledge. To him the problem of origins offers no difficulty; one need only suppose, he argues, that man was always a rational creature, and at all times could correctly judge how his need for mutual communication could be most appropriately satisfied. According to Tiedemann men first lived happily in an animal state. Gradually they became desirous of uniting and this aspiration gave rise to the need for a means of communication.

> Man probably first hit upon a language of gestures. This alone could not last long, and the inadequacy of this language must soon have been perceived. Human beings observed that the emotions called forth sounds. They also perceived that animals made use of them with good results. What was more natural than that they should seek to make use of this discovery and to employ these sounds as signs of their thoughts?[1]

All the individualistic theories of the nineteenth century basically resemble the over-simplified ideas of Tiedemann. L. Geiger also imagines language as an invention, as the personal creation of one or more linguistically gifted individuals,[2] and even Herder seems to subscribe to this view when he tries to show that man attained a language by exerting his powers in conscious effort.[3] To the extent that these views were intended only as a counterpoise to the voluntaristic ones they have a certain justification; as a theory of origins properly estimating the mental nature of early man they have failed.

A special, as it were refined, form of the invention theory is

[1] D. Tiedemann, *Versuch einer Erklärung des Ursprungs der Sprache* (1772).

[2] L. Geiger, *Der Ursprung der Sprache* (1869).

[3] J. G. Herder, *Über den Ursprung der Sprache* (1869).

represented by Fr. von Schlegel in his *Philosophy of Language*.[1]
He imagines language not as a product of gradual development,
but as something that sprang out of the full inner life and living
consciousness, so to speak all at one stroke, directly and all at
once. He naturally does not mean by this that language appeared
at once, richly expressive and grammatically differentiated, but
that even the very earliest human language appeared as language
from the beginning, incorporating the essential characteristics of
all language. Schlegel is of the opinion that the first formation
of the earliest languages was not possible until the essential idea
of language—in our terminology, the intention of mutual communication through the medium of fixed phonetic constructions
of a symbolic nature—had taken root in human consciousness.

> Just as a work of art could never arise out of individual lines and
> points of colour if a picture were not present from the beginning
> as an entity in the mind of the artist, so was language not assembled
> from atomistic fragments, but came into existence on the basis of
> the idea of the whole through the productive mental powers of
> man (pp. 80 ff.).

Here it would be a digression to pursue further the interesting
ideas of Schlegel, put forward with such profound philosophical
gravity, which in spirit and tone take their place beside those of
von Humboldt and Renan. We merely wish to observe that it
would not be difficult to reconcile our recent experiences and
more advanced conceptions of language with Schlegel's. It is
surprising that even so recognized a linguistic scholar as Jespersen
could not emancipate himself from the idea that the creative
linguistic activities of man were guided exclusively by conscious
intention, and conceived the original creation of language very
much as did Tiedemann 150 years before.[2]

Jespersen maintained that children in an uninhabited area, if not
exposed to immediate death through hunger and cold, have
the capacity to develop a language for mutual communication,
which could be so different from that of their parents that it could

---

[1] F. v. Schlegel, *Philosophie der Sprache* (1830).
[2] O. Jespersen, *Progress in Language* (1894).

actually form the starting point of a new linguistic stem. But if such Kasper Hauser cases are examined critically it appears that entirely neglected children attain at the most to individual 'phonetic images', which they use in combination with gestures to express their most important needs; at the most they make use of an incomprehensible 'language' arising out of garbled words of the language of their environment. It is remarkable that Jespersen himself investigated one such case, in which he recognized most of the words as belonging to the language of the environment. He must have known too that all the new words of children, the so-called original creations, consist of garbled words of the mother tongue and onomatopoetic transformations, and that in the first years of speech development the full free invention of words hardly ever occurs.[1] It is incomprehensible that in spite of this he adhered to the above opinion. In any event Jespersen does not say expressly that early man arrived at language in the same way as the neglected child; but from the example as construed one could hardly conclude anything else.

Aside from these theoretical systems there are linguistic theories that cannot be included under the general viewpoints indicated above. Among these we must in the first instance mention the views of two linguistic scholars of the first rank, whose works on the philosophy of language are distinguished by a wealth of fruitful ideas. These are Wilhelm von Humboldt[2]—who, as we have seen, cannot be regarded as simply a nativist—and Ernest Renan.[3] Both represent an *a priori* standpoint. In language there is said to be as it were a power transcending human wisdom and power which man obtains in principle from nature, without the intervention of his own conscious creative activity. They are accordingly of the opinion that right from the very beginning *all* the important functions of language were operative; that even

[1] W. Stern, *Psychologie der frühen Kindheit* (1930); H. Delacroix, *L'enfant en le langage* (1934); W. Preyer, *Die Seele des Kindes* (1904); J. Piaget, *The Language and Thought of The Child* (1924); etc.

[2] W. v. Humboldt, 'Über das verg. Sprachstudium', *Abh. d.k. preuss. Wiss. Berlin*, 1820; and especially '*Über die Verschiedenheit des menschlichen Sprachbaues*', 1835.

[3] E. Renan, *De l'origine du langage* (1859).

earliest man had command of a variety of linguistic forms. 'Language', declares von Humboldt, 'is thoroughly human even in its origins, and deliberately extends to all objects of incidental perception and objects of thought. Words well up voluntarily and there cannot have been in any desert a nomadic tribe without its songs, presupposing a considerable number of words and grammatical forms.' One could support this view to some extent with the language of peoples at a very low cultural level, whose language forms probably were defined from the earliest times onwards by the same formative tendencies. Wilhelm von Humboldt sees language as a whole as something directly given. It must, he believes, be understood as 'a mode of realization of the power of the mind', on the basis of a principle which governs language from the inside, by an inner linguistic sense. He believes that the inner linguistic sense is an inwardly present generative principle, so to speak the original image of language. There is no path from the Humboldtian dialectic to the genetic problem; therefore his metaphysically grounded linguistic philosophy automatically excludes consideration of origins. His interest is directed to the question of the diversity of languages, and for this problem that of origins has only peripheral significance.

The same view is represented by Humboldt's truest follower, H. Steinthal, who lends linguistic research a sharper psychological turn.[1] Steinthal correctly emphasizes that language is independent of logic (grammar), a view which has also recently been professed by Benedetto Croce.[2] But if Croce would solve the problem of origins simply by calling it a mental creation, he deprives the concept of origin of its true content—in agreement with his predecessors—connecting it not with the antecedent and early stages of language, but with the language-generative activity of man when he is already at the speaking stage. Neglect of the distinction between speech and language prevented him, as it did many

---

[1] H. Steinthal, *Der Ursprung der Sprache* (1851), *Grammatik, Logik und Psychologie* (1855).

[2] B. Croce, *Ästhetik als Wissenschaft vom Ausdruck und allgemeine Sprachwissenschaft* (1930).

others, from a genetic consideration of the problem of language. Renan's view of language may open access to a conception of the later development of language from already existing more primitive forms, but not to the true problem of origins. Renan's approach is expressed with great clarity in the following passage:

> Il serait absurde de regarder comme une découverte l'application que l'homme a fait de l'oeil à la vision, de l'oreille à l'audition: il ne l'est guère moins d'appeler invention l'emploi de la parole comme moyen expressif. L'homme a la faculté du signe ou de l'interprétation, comme il a celle de la vue et l'ouïe; la parole est le moyen qu'il emploi pour exercer la première, comme l'oeil et l'oreille sont les organes des deux autres. L'usage de l'articulation n'est donc pas plus le fruit de la réflexion que l'usage des différents organes du corps n'est le résultat de l'expérience. Il n'y a pas deux langages, l'un naturel, l'autre artificiel: mais la nature, en même temps qu'elle nous rélève le but, nous rélève les moyens qui doivent servir à l'atteindre.[1]

This view of language—to which we can add that Renan regarded language, in opposition to J. Grimm (1852), as 'from the first day of its existence' a means of communication and formulation that is expressive and complete in its basic structure —excludes all further discussion of linguistic prehistory. His discussion of onomotopoeia has nothing to do with the problem of origins; for him the imitation of natural sounds was, properly, not a prelinguistic phonetic expression but one of the sources of man's early word material. In accordance with his linguistic and historical outlook, Renan's entire interest was directed toward the development and transformation of language, which by and large he sought to explain in terms of general philosophical and linguistic considerations. It is therefore only natural that we can take as little account of him in our research as of Humboldt. In spite of this, their wide horizon, their rich thought and not least their incomparable capacity for linguistic presentation, together with their ardour for truth, guarantee a high educational importance for their works on linguistic philosophy.

[1] E. Renan, *De l'origine du langage* (1859), pp. 90 ff.

The philosophical and anthropological language theory of Gehlen avoids dealing with the problem of linguistic origins.[1] He attempts to specify the linguistic roots from which the nature and special character of language can be explained, whereby he emphasizes the motor aspect of speaking, following Palágyi's[2] and Noiré's work.[3] In his opinion, a deeper understanding of linguistic beginnings can only be obtained if speech accomplishments are considered within the framework of the eye-hand or optic-haptic system. Gehlen avoids the problem of origins, contenting himself with pointing to the unique nature and anthropological character of language and regarding it as an autochthonously developed form of communication.

Fritz Mauthner takes a similar view of language. In his opinion speech is as much an original biological activity as walking and breathing, and on that account it needs no explaining. Once the speech organs are present, he believes, language arises spontaneously. If we trace the development of language back to the distant past we never reach a point 'where we have to abandon the conception of concrete speech sounds, or where we have to inquire after the origins of the abstraction "speech" '.[4] It is entirely correct that if we were in a position to trace the history of languages back to their earliest forms we would never reach a stage where language ceases. But it all depends—as we explained at the very beginning—on what we understand by origin. If Mauthner is thinking of an original state in which man was without speech but already unknowingly possessed language-formative powers, such a state of affairs could obviously never be reached through the reconstruction of linguistic development. Thus far he is correct. But Mauthner does not discuss at all the possibility of extending a significant hypothesis beyond the language stage to give one an idea of the probable prehistory of linguistic communication. He contents himself with identifying

[1] A. Gehlen, *Der Mensch* (1940).

[2] M. Palágyi, *Naturphilosophische Vorlesungen* (1924).

[3] L. Noiré, *Der Ursprung der Sprache* (1877).

[4] F. Mauthner, *Kritik der Sprache*, I (1921), p. 14.

(in a manner that borders on sophistry) organ (speech equipment) with function (speaking), by which means he hopes to eliminate the difficulties, and hands over the problem of origins to the comparative physiologists and anatomists. Besides, it seems to me that Mauthner owes this idea to Goethe, who expressed it in a more worthy manner and in a way that is more deeply rooted in natural philosophy. He declares that—

> when man was created as man by God, language was implanted in him just as was an upright gait. Just as he had to observe that he could walk and grasp, he also had to learn that he could sing with his throat and modify these tones in various ways with his tongue, gums and lips. If man was of divine origin, language was too; if man was a natural being regarded in the sphere of nature, then language was likewise natural.[1, 2]

The theological theories of origin, which regard language, like human nature itself with all its innate gifts, as the work of God, assume what is perhaps an intermediate position between the inventive theory and the biologically oriented philosophical ones. We shall not enter into a detailed discussion of these theories according to which language is to be regarded as a present from God to man, or which attribute to Nature in the working of its law a kind of unconscious wisdom of itself, by which it creates something suitable that later comes to consciousness in man in his language. These doctrines reject any sort of psycho-genetic approach; consequently they exclude the origins of language as a problem of scientific research. This applies to the views of Jacob Grimm,[3] who as a follower of Süssmilch[4] regards language as a gift of God, which falls to man's share without any contribution by man himself, as well as to the theological theories such as those of Abelard, Duns Scotus, Pufendorf, Whitney, Jolly, Beattie, etc.

---

[1] Goethe, *Dichtung und Wahrheit*, Book X.

[2] The theories of origins are well and clearly set forth by A. Sommerfelt-Oslo in 'The Origin of Language', *Journal of World History*, I (1954).

[3] J. Grimm, *Über den Ursprung der Sprache* (1852).

[4] Süssmilch, *Beweis, dass die erste Sprache ihren Ursprung allein vom Schöpfer erhalten habe* (1767).

All the contradictions expressed in empiricism and nativism, voluntarism and determinism and in the metaphysical and theological doctrines of origins, can be harmoniously reconciled if the trouble is taken to go back to the methodological foundations of these views. It then appears with especial clarity that each of the various theories emphasizes only one of the factors or circumstances that were operative, continually or for a time, in the life of language. Particular factors or circumstances in language formation are highlighted at the expense of others. One-sided views are adduced in opposition to views no less one-sided. No consideration is given to fact that what is proved to be correct in the realm of experience is, from the point of view of the entire problem, an important detail, but not a decisive one.

Thus one-sided consideration of the nativistic-dispositional factor leads to *a priori* theories, and even provides an objective basis for the theological approach; the general and special laws established in linguistic development provide evidence for the deterministic theories; the conscious drive for adequate expression both in everyday and poetic language and the further possibility of a universal sign language favour the voluntaristic theories; while the multiplicity of chronological and regional forms of expression, the assimilation of languages, the borrowing of foreign speech material and the variety of tongues lend the accident theory an air of reality.

If language is conceived as something organic, one is led to the conception of a nuclear structure existing from the very beginning, from which languages developed in accordance with autonomous laws in the course of which were operative the most varied factors, such as intention, analogy, spontaneous invention or accident. From this point of view W. von Humboldt was right in saying that language could not have been invented if something of its type had not previously been present in the human mind (*Über das Sprachstudium*, p. 247).

Whether we claim that language is a human tool produced by intentional creative activity or that it spontaneously builds itself up from a nuclear structure on the basis of natural laws, each constituent part giving rise to the next one in logical natural order, is from the point of view of natural philosophy of no importance. From its first origins to the present day, language is the product of the human mind. It arose without deliberate intention as a function of the social community, and developed purposefully and intentionally, motivated in its formal development by the compulsive power of the general laws of the human mind, with the help of both conscious and unconscious creative human activity. The original stimulus was a common one; the means was the same; and the basic mode of development was predetermined by the logic of the natural order.

This philosophical conception is expressed with great plasticity in poetic form by Goethe, in a poem in which he endeavours to express the mystery of the individuality of the person and the living power of the individual:

> *Wie an dem Tag, der dich der Welt verliehen,*
> *Die Sonne stand zum Grusse der Planeten,*
> *Bist alsobald und fort und fort gediehen,*
> *Nach dem Gesetz, wonach du angetreten.*
> *So musst du sein, dir kannst du nicht entfliehen,*
> *So sagten schon Sibyllen, so Propheten;*
> *Und keine Zeit und keine Macht zerstückelt*
> *Geprägte Form, die lebend sich entwickelt.*

This synthetic view, mediating a reconciliation of opposing theories, in no way excludes preparatory and initial stages of language, or its evolution, the stages of which we shall attempt to set out in the following chapters free of the fetters of an extreme evolutionism.

(E) THE LIMITATIONS OF THESE THEORIES

The previous discussion has shown that the theories of the origin of language advanced in the past are either untenable or they evade the real problem. None of them is adequately grounded either theoretically or empirically. None is capable of bridging the gap between the prelinguistic period and that of mature language, or of explaining language as the culmination of a gradual development, linking up directly with the study of the evolution of languages in specific detail.

If we ask why these theories have been fruitless, we find that they suffer from certain inadequacies which have had a prejudicial effect on research and theory.

We have already, in Chapter II, referred to the ambiguous way the problem has been put, leaving it unclear whether we are concerned with the stage antecedent to language or with its early development; and to the failure to observe essential principles in the formulation of hypotheses. It must be added that all these theories have failed to unite under a common principle the two problems that are so closely related, the problem of origins and that of the earliest form of language. Consequently, they have failed to elucidate the inner forces that must have governed the entire process of development. In my view, a theory of origins only deserves serious consideration if it succeeds in developing a psychologically based and logically sound view of the psychic forces that are at the root of both linguistic activity and the genesis and growth of language. None of the groups of theories described above appears to be capable of doing this. The biological theories offer hypotheses regarding the source or reservoir from which man already in possession of speech drew his supply of words in the initial period of linguistic development. The imitative theories are concerned with the same problem, namely how man coined words out of onomatopoetic phonetic forms. The empiricistic and nativistic theories dealt with the question whether the origin of language rested on the experience of the hypostasized prelinguistic man, which led him to form symbolic speech, or whether the productive and formative power is to be sought in pre-existing talent, that brought language into existence and continued its development of its own power. The theological theories seek to trace the origin to the intervention of a higher being, leaving everything concerning the formation and development of language to the historical and comparative linguistic sciences. The voluntaristic and deterministic views do not really touch the problem of origins; their whole interest is directed toward language formation, the multiplication and differentiation of vocabulary and grammar. They inquire into the origin of words, and not into that of language.

There have been inadequacies in method as well as in content. First, there has been a failure to start off with a concept of language based on precise analysis. It should have been realized that clarity must first be attained on what is to be understood as constituting language. Only when a scientifically justifiable conception of language has been attained is it possible to approach the question of its probable antecedent and early stages. A clear definition, even if it is only a provisional one, is above all necessary to enable one to decide what is to be attributed to the expressive components of the antecedent stage and what is to be attributed to true linguistic utterance. It is the lack of care in the analysis and definition of language that has led to language being traced back to forms of communication that are themselves varieties of language (as, for example, gesture language or the language of primitive peoples) or to phenomena without direct relation to language at all, such as purely expressive gestures and phonetic imitation.

Definition of one's terms is invariably essential if one wishes to theorize on the prehistory of human activity. Thus in the problem of the origin of music one must know in advance what is to be understood as music. If the production of single-toned sounds is to be regarded as the first manifestation of music, then the monotonous drumming of primitive peoples will be regarded as music. But if we use the term music only when fixed intervals and their combinations appear, then monotonous drumming, the babbled melodies of infants and even bird songs must be excluded from the purview of music.[1] Not only is a preliminary definition not superfluous in these circumstances; it is quite essential. This

[1] See my paper on the origin of music in *Int. Archiv für Ethnographie*, Vol. 40 (1941) and my *Introduction to the Psychology of Music* (1953).

may also be seen in the problem of the origin of the arts. Here too the nature of the theories will depend on whether certain aesthetically pleasing forms and finds of human workmanship can be considered as 'expressions of art' even without any evidence of artistic aim, or whether only those executed with artistic intent may be so considered.[1]

Many theorists have blocked their own way to research on the question of origins by pushing into the foreground a secondary characteristic—namely, the medium of language: sounds and gestures. Their whole attention has been claimed by the medium, and none by the purpose and the motivating and formative forces of linguistic origins and development. Since the voiced sound is the most important means of expression in human speech, it is easy to understand that the origin of language should be sought in spontaneous phonetic utterances, since the latter show certain similarities to language sounds in their mode of appearance and their phonetic character. Thus arose the theory of expressive sounds and interjections and the theory of imitative onomatopoeia. In these the origin of language is confused with its development. It has escaped these theorists that expressive sounds and imitation may have been able to play a role in language formation, but not in its origin. These attain importance only after the appearance of linguistic activity as a new function, when man in intercourse with his fellows seeks new word forms. The same is true of expressive gestures. Their transformation into linguistic gestures starts only during the course of linguistic activity, and, to be sure, at an early date in the history of spoken language, since gestures are necessarily involved even in the most primitive speech situations. One need think only of command situations, the imperative, which is accompanied by expressive gestures even in highly advanced linguistic activity. Besides, one has not always been fully conscious of the fact that language originates only when sounds are associated with meaning—with

[1] I do not agree with the view that clear definitions are out of place at the beginning of empirical sciences, as O. Kraus insists in his 'Bemerkungen zur Gestaltpsychologie' (*Lotus*, 1921). Though this view may be justified in many problems of natural science, in psychology it causes mischief as a rule.

a suitable mode of thought for carrying the meaning, as Hermann Lotze has so clearly expressed it.[1]

Thus, no matter how important the material element may be in the later development of language, it can have played only a subordinate role in its origin. To be sure, language requires an organ, just as manual labour requires a hand. But as the hand by itself is impotent without a motivating mental force, as is shown by the instrumental incapacity of the hands of bears and anthropoid apes,[2] so are the vocal organs incapable of producing an adequate linguistic medium of their own power. This is shown in an obvious way by talking birds and by the babbling of idiots incapable of speech. It is therefore in no way surprising that theories oriented toward the material factor were unable to provide a fruitful point of departure for research.

Thus there can be no doubt that the essential element in language is not its overt medium, in which thoughts find an embodiment, but its *purpose*. From a teleological standpoint, language is a richly elaborated medium of communication. In order to arrive at an understanding of how the media of communication progressively adapted themselves to this purpose, and thus to reconstruct the prehistory of language, it is necessary to begin with those forms of contact or communication which already in the prelinguistic stage served the same purpose and were governed by the same principle as language. Linguists have failed to recognize the fundamental importance of this basic principle, which can form as it were the connecting link between language and its antecedents. They thought they were satisfying the idea of evolution by pointing to certain forms of expression which occur in man and which can also be assumed to have occurred in our hypothetical ancestors. They did not observe that such forms of expression as affective sounds and expressive gestures could never lead to language, simply for the reason that they serve different

[1] H. Lotze, *Mikrokosmos*, II (1869), p. 223.

[2] My paper, 'La fonction sociologique de la main humaine et de la main animale' *Journ. de Psychologie*, 1938. Also *Psychology and Art of the Blind* (1950).

purposes, have different functions and are subject to different formative principles.

It follows from these considerations that we must look for a principle which governs the origin, development and function of all types of expression employed for communicative purposes, inclusive of language; and from which those functions that constitute the most highly developed form of communication, human language, can be derived. To propose and to apply such a principle is the basic idea of the linguistic theory set forth here, on which is based a new doctrine of linguistic functions, which I call the functional theory, and a new doctrine of linguistic origins and prehistory, or stadial theory.

(F) THE CONTACT THEORY

The word 'contact' signifies the basic innate tendency of social animals to approach one another, establish rapport, co-operate and communicate. It is a universal principle of life for individuals belonging to social groups.

The contact theory seeks to explain the use of various forms of contact by living beings for communicative purposes, and to estimate their evolutionary significance. The contact principle enables us to identify the principal forms of communication, establish their mutual relationships and classify them systematically. It shows the forms of communication, beginning with mere contact sounds, progressively assuming forms more differentiated and wider in function, until in language they attain their morphologically as well as functionally highest stage. Unlike the genetic theories outlined above, this theory is not based on an exclusively linguistic orientation. It treats the individual forms of communication as autochthonous communicative media, which despite their independence are connected by the contact principle, and in respect of the gradual extension of their functions constitute an ascending series. Thus on the one hand, language fits into place in the total complex of communicative media; on the other hand, it carves out for itself an entirely special place among them. In treating language both as a product of development and as a communicative medium which is *sui generis*, it is neither incompatible with the views having theoretical objections to a genetic approach and regarding language as an absolutely unique and autochthonous structure, nor with those that see language as the last stage of a continuous evolution and consequently insist on a genetic approach as an essential basis.

The contact theory does not belong wholly to either the biological or to the anthropological theories, but equally to both of them. Its stadial theory (Chapter VIII) puts it in the biological sphere, and its functional doctrine (Chapter VI) in the anthropological. Thus the contact theory achieves a *balance* between these to some extent contradictory groups of theories.

The contact theory can be characterized as a theory of natural sounds, in the sense that it derives language from natural sounds by developing stages. From this point of view one might readily count it among the group of expressive, interjectional, animal-sound and babbling theories, which likewise start with natural sounds, and which we have rejected. The difference consists in the fact that while the other theories choose the most diverse natural sounds as the starting-point of linguistic evolution, without regard to the social aspect and to communicative intent, our contact theory confines itself to phonetic phenomena governed by the same tendency as language. As opposed to the purely anthropological theories, a natural sound theory has the advantage of proceeding in the spirit of the idea of evolution, and attempts to advance from a hypothetical primitive state of speechlessness to symbolic language. Among the natural-sound theories the contact theory has the advantage of being able to represent the origin of language as a gradual process of progressive differentiation, and provides a concrete idea of the prehistory and initial stages of language and an unforced transition to linguistic history. Its structure is so designed as to make linguistic evolution accessible to logical analysis (Chapter X).

IV

THE PROBLEM OF AN ORIGINAL LANGUAGE

Two other questions must be touched on briefly in connexion with the problem of the origin of language. The first is the question of an original language.

The conception of a linguistic genealogical tree has been abandoned in recent research. Even for Joh. Schmidt[1] the idea of an 'Ursprache' had dwindled into a mere phantom. Like 'the first man' and 'the first people', 'the first language' is a fantasy, an unfounded hypothesis based on an unjustifiable interpretation of the concept of evolution.

The earliest language, the *Lingua adamica* as it was called by Jacob Böhme, is supposedly the language employed by early man when he first 'began' to employ phonetic language for communicative purposes. There is no evidence at all, either historical or from comparative linguistics, for such a hypothesis. If one is loth to abandon the idea of a most primitive language, it would seem more sensible to speak of several original languages (polygenesis); such as the primitive forms of Indo-European, Semitic, Malayan, and other languages which are not derivable from one another. The assumption of a single original language (Ursprache) (monogenesis) presupposes an original state of paradise with a distinct geographical area forming man's original home.[2] This

---

[1] Cf. F. Mauthner, *Kritik der Sprache*, II (1912), p. 375. See also the Icelandic philologist A. Jóhannesson, *Um frumtungu indógermana og frumheimkynni* (1943), who argues on the basis of a vast material that the first language was an Indo-European one, and that the original home of the 'first' men was in the north-east of Europe.

[2] A. Trombetti was the most determined defender of the monogenetic view; whereas according to Schuchardt monogenesis and polygenesis are linked together from the beginning and determine the entire development of language. Oddone Assirelli of Bologna has endeavoured to reconcile the views of Trombetti with my theory in a paper which is worthy of attention. See 'Remarques et considérations sur le problême de la genèse et de l'unité d'origine du langage', *Acta Psychologica*, X (1954).

original home is, in the view of many palaeontologists and pre-
historians, Central Asia, from whence man is supposed to have
spread to all parts of the earth.[1]

There are palaeontological as well as geographical objections
to this view. It is known that human remains from early prehistoric times are to be found in all parts of the globe. In addition,
fossil remains of diluvial hominids, regarded as transitional forms
between diluvial anthropomorphs and recent man, have been
found in nearly all continents. To cling to the hypothesis of an
original home and an original language requires one to put the
time of this supposed prehistoric migration back in the early part
of the diluvial period, and above all one must establish a probability that the hominids taking part in such a migration had a
language, the assumed original language. But we know nothing
of such a language or languages, and there is no hope that historical or comparative linguistic science will ever be in a position
to throw light on them.

The attempt to draw conclusions regarding the original language of mankind from the evidence of primitive languages has
failed. The view that the languages of the Australian aborigines
provide a model for the language of antiquity is based on wrong
inferences and an uncritical interpretation of ethnological observations.[2] Theoretical considerations on the nature of probable
primitive phonemes point in a different direction. Van Ginneken
has, for example, attempted to develop a theory of the earliest
speech sounds and language on the basis of child psychology,
linguistics and physiology.[3] He envisages the very earliest form
of phonetic language as similar to the babbling of children. The
earliest oral language is supposed to have consisted originally of
'clicks' which were later transformed into consonants and words
and in the course of further development acquired the melodic
character of language through the introduction of vowels.
According to van Ginneken, the original clicking sounds

[1] T. Arldt, *Die Entwicklung der Kontinente und ihrer Lebewelt* (1907).

[2] H. Klaatsch, *Das Werden der Menschheit* (1936).

[3] J. v. Ginneken, *La reconstruction typologique des langues archaïques de l'humanité* (1939).

G

constituted the basic phonetic material of the earliest spoken languages. This theory, supported by rich linguistic material, probably has a bearing on the phonetic structure of the earliest words; but it has nothing to do with the original language.

Another possibility lies in the study of the factors and principles that were active in the origin of language and the development of its early forms. Among these are the role of the motor element in the development of spoken language, the gradual predomin-ance of the phonetic element over the motor element, and especi-ally the fixing of the basic functions which were dominant at the beginning of linguistic activity.[1] The last method involves not the reconstruction of an 'Ursprache' but the establishing of the psychological principles of language formation in general. In this way we have arrived at what we call the imperative language (Chapter VIII), which should correspond structurally to the hypothetical original language.

It seems to me that on the basis of comparative linguistic science little can be said regarding the nature of the earliest lan-guage beyond what Jespersen was able to say in 1894 following his critical discussion of the views on prehistory of A. Schleicher, H. Möller, Max Müller and V. Sayce. 'The evolution of lan-guage', he declared, 'shows a progressive tendency from insepar-able irregular conglomerations to freely and regularly combin-able short elements' (*Progress in Language*, p. 127).

[1] W. P. Pillsbury and C. L. Meader, *The Psychology of Language* (1928).

V

THE LANGUAGE OF
EARLY MAN

THE position is different with regard to the question whether language is to be ascribed to recent man only, or whether it is also justifiable to attribute it to his presumed ancestors, such as *Homo neanderthalensis* or to the earlier forms of *Homo sapiens* called Aurignacian man, Crô-Magnon man, etc.

Biologists have sought the solution of this problem through the methods of comparative anatomy. That none of these attempts would lead to a satisfactory conclusion was to be expected. Reference to the cubic capacity of the skull and accordingly to the supposed great weight of the brain of Neanderthal man was misleading (Keith, Bolk, Anthony). The relative size of the skull (i.e. the relation of skull size to the size of the whole body) may well be a sign of a higher average intelligence and may therefore be one of the conditions of linguistic activity. It does not, however, guarantee its presence; quite apart from the fact that we have only vague statements regarding the anatomical and morphological structure of the brain of these fossils. There are anthropologists who allow their conclusions to be strongly influenced by the bodily and skull structure of Neanderthal man. They attach considerable weight to the fact that the average cranial capacity of Neanderthal man is as great as our own. Although, on the one hand, these scientists warn us against drawing conclusions regarding level of intelligence, on the other hand they go so far as to ascribe a capacity for thought and language to Neanderthal man without sufficient reasons.

It is misleading to base conclusions regarding linguistic capacity

exclusively on comparative anatomy and to suppose that reference to the slight differences between the skull structure of earlier
human types and recent man suffices to attribute essentially the
same mental life to them both. This leads to fantastic theories in
which diluvial hominids appear as much more developed than
they were in reality, and to the inclusion of known pre-human
types in the classification of existing human types. This is shown
particularly clearly in Elliot Smith[1] and A. Keith,[2] who ascribe
speech capacity to *Pithecanthropus erectus* despite the criticisms of
Dubois.[3]

It is futile to ask whether man or language came into existence
first. The two are intimately interrelated; each presupposes the
other. In this sense W. von Humboldt is correct in believing that
language arose 'at a single blow'. This idea was obviously not
intended as a depiction of historical fact, but simply as a way of
representing the inseparability of the concepts of man and
language.[4]

In my opinion, the problem of the linguistic capacity of extinct
human types can only be attacked from one point of view, that
of culture. One must abandon the attempt to determine whether
or not diluvial man could speak, since the problem cannot be
solved directly. One may try to solve it indirectly by determining whether these supposed human types fulfilled conditions
which are necessarily linked with language. One of these conditions is in my opinion the preparation, gradual improvement and
handing on of tools and implements; and another is the making
of engravings on stone.[5] If it could be proved that man of the
later Palaeolithic did produce tools and modify them in accordance with his gradually changing needs, then he would be man

---

[1] E. Smith, *The Search for Man's Ancestors* (1931).

[2] A. Keith, *The Antiquity of Man* (1920).

[3] E. Dubois, 'De beteekenis der groote schedelcapaciteit van Pithecanthropus erectus',
Proc. Kon. Ned. Akademie van Wetenschappen, Amsterdam (1920).

[4] This statement of Humboldt need not be understood in the sense of Genesis, since
one arrives at the same conception in principle on the basis of the theory of mutation
(see pp. 171 ff.).

[5] This view is also taken by Bergson in his *L'évolution créatrice* (1910).

in the true sense, that is, *Homo sapiens* and, as such, a possessor of language. The making of standardized tools suitable for labour and adapted to specific purposes presupposes language. The power of constructive imagination and the gift of invention is linked with language, if only for the reason that conscious intention and the mental stimulus to execute it demand linguistic activity.[1] Man can only construct tools appropriate to a given end if he has the capacity to direct his activity toward it and is capable of surveying or visualizing the process of work to be carried out. Since conscious purpose and the invention of tools are based on mental processes that require linguistic fixation, we are justified in identifying *Homo faber* with *Homo loquens*. The designation *Homo sapiens* can therefore refer only to creatures that can speak and work. Thus the question becomes one of whether the fossil remains discovered do or do not belong together with the cultural remains discovered in the same deposits. If this is the case we are justified in assuming that these human types had basically the same mental life as historical man, and in consequence we may attribute a linguistic function to them. As this condition is met in the case of later Palaeolithic man, there is a high probability in favour of the assumption that he possessed a language essentially like our own. We can therefore place the beginnings of language more than 100,000 years ago, and according to one widely accepted theory of human origins at least as far back as half a million years.

[1] G. Révész, 'Thinking and Speaking', *Acta Psychologica*, X (1954).

VI

THE THEORY OF THE LINGUISTIC FUNCTIONS

(A) THE TELEOLOGICAL VIEW OF LANGUAGE

IT is not our intention here to recapitulate and criticize the various definitions of language offered in the literature of linguistics and psychology. That would be too great a digression from our problem and would lead to fruitless controversy. On the other hand, the progress of our study demands a definition of language to clarify the concept to the extent of distinctly stating what comes within its essential nature and scope.

Generally speaking, language can be defined both according to its nature and its purpose. Although we regard the distinction between definition according to nature and according to purpose as in general necessary, and admit that it leads to one-sidedness or even to confusion if one is replaced by the other,[1] it nevertheless seems to us that in relation to language this view requires further clarification.

If one undertakes a comparative study of opinions of the nature of various concepts, one soon discovers that definitions vary to an astonishing degree. Analysis shows that the diversity of opinions results mainly from differences in the point of view of the investigators. Depending on the point of departure, one trait or another of the object to be defined is stressed and decreed to be 'the' essence of it.

Let us take as an example the definition of man. A comparative anatomist will reject the problem as such, because from his point

---

[1] F. Kainz, *Psychologie der Sprache*, I (1943).

of view the human body does not differ fundamentally from the animal body, especially the anthropoids, so no essential difference between man and animals can be deduced. For the anatomist and the biologist man is only an animal that is more highly developed morphologically and functionally; for them, consequently, the problem of man's essential nature has no meaning. Their efforts are not directed toward establishing differences between man and the animals, but on the contrary to remove or bridge over the obvious differences by general laws of growth and variation. On the other hand, to the investigator concerned with man's intellectual and social behaviour this anthropological problem is of fundamental significance. A sociologist or historian will find the essential character of man in his link with and significance for the community; while an individualist who does not consider the relation of the individual to the community as the most important thing will look for characteristics or elements which characterize man as a personality. A metaphysician may find the essence of man in his sense of unity with the cosmos, a theist in the inner striving for personal contact with the divinity. A moralist who bases his system on personal liberty and moral responsibility will find an entirely different content in man's world of ideas, and hence in his nature, than will be found by an extreme economist for whom man represents an expendable part of an economic machine.

Each of these definitions includes a core of truth, as each brings out at least one aspect of the nature of the object to be defined. They do not, however, establish *the* essential nature of man. There does not seem to be any single characteristic from which all other characteristics could be deduced and from which man could be defined theoretically, nor does there seem to be any essential characteristic around which all others could be grouped to form a unity of a higher order. It is true that certain characteristics suffice to define man as a species and to differentiate him from other species of the same genus. They cannot, however, fix the total anthropological nature of man; such a definition remains fragmentary; it gets its meaning, indeed its persuasive power, only from the fact that the remaining constitutive elements are present as it were implicitly. Although in this case only one of a number of qualities is clearly illuminated, while the others remain in the shade, they do not disappear, indeed they make it possible to stress the most characteristic elements of the intuitively apprehended whole.

It is the same with language. Its definition will depend on the point of view from which its analysis is undertaken. Each definition stresses a particular trait of language or speech and neglects other elements which are equally basic, without excluding them. The elements selected as essential by a logician will not be the same as those chosen by the linguist, for whom the grammatical and syntactical structure of the language is fundamental. The phonologist will stress functions which the psychologist neglects and among the psychologists the phenomenologist will adopt a different point of view from that of the genetic psychologist whose attention is claimed mainly by the relations among the diverse forms of communication. The different points of view employed in the defining of the constituent traits of language may be seen clearly in the definitions of well-known investigators (p. 126).

Unless one is willing to leave the definition of language to chance or to the personal preference of the investigator it is necessary to discover a point of departure which will allow of a scientifically defensible definition and at the same time be capable of suggesting fresh paths of research. Here one meets at once the question of the *linguistic sense*.

Language is essentially, as Aristotle rightly recognized, an *organon*, a means, and its true import is therefore contained in its purpose. This purpose is the establishment of mental contact between men, the exchange of thought, the adequate imparting or reception of experiences, thoughts, wishes and desires.[1] As with all other means or *organa*, what is involved here is simply

---

[1] Cf. the discussion by Aristotle of the four formal principles in his Metaphysics where he identifies essential nature with purpose, since in his view the goal of every object and process lies in its own fully developed form.

the necessary relationship between ends and means. As a means, language is characterized by the fact that it serves definite and circumscribed purposes and that it can arrive at its goals through means which are distinctive to it alone.[1]

This definiteness of purpose emphasizes the instrumental character of language and involves its being directed toward more or less definite persons.[2] One talks to somebody, one expresses one's wishes to somebody; one talks to oneself. The person spoken to may have concrete existence or exist only in the imagination of the speaker (as, for instance, when a writer addresses himself to his readers) or it may be the speaker himself (as in monologue).[3]

Let us make clear what purposes are served by language and the means it is able to employ. One can distinguish between primary and secondary aims of language. The original purpose of language, to which it owes its existence and in part its development, is the establishment of mental contact, of inter-individual communication, by means of the exchange of thoughts and the transfer of will. Linguists do not consider this simply as the original and most fundamental purpose, but as the only one. This explains why language is so often defined exclusively by the

---

[1] The view that language, like music, decorative art and lyrical poetry arose from a mere need for the expression of the emotions of life and nature in some fashion is psychologically untenable. One could well imagine that early man began to sing and dance without a practical purpose; and that he adorned his tools with decoration for purely aesthetic and playful reasons; but it is impossible to imagine that he developed words and linguistic gestures without communicative intent or social purpose. Language of words developed out of original phonetic expressions that already served the purpose of mutual contact.

[2] The distinction between speaker and person spoken to coincides essentially with the distinction between 'speech significance' and 'hearing significance' of a speech act which has been stressed repeatedly by the Dutch semanticists and especially G. Mannoury.

[3] If one addresses animals, infants, objects or natural phenomena, this is based on personification: one speaks to them as if they could understand language. The tendency toward contact exists potentially in these cases too. I wish to take this opportunity to refer to the important psychogenetic work of my friend J. Piaget, and to point out that his stages of intellectual development (sensori-motor activity, egocentric representational thought, and rational and operational thought) have nothing to do with my functional theory. The two theories are concerned with quite different areas of mental development. See Piaget's works, *La Psychologie de l'Intelligence* (1947) and *Logic and Psychology* (1953); cf. Humphrey, *Directed Thinking* (1948) and *Thinking* (1951); Hearnshaw, 'Recent Studies in the Psychology of Thinking', *The Advancement of Science*, No. 42, September, 1954.

so-called communicative function as its general and most characteristic element.

Now it can be shown that apart from this primary purpose
language also has other purposes which are in no way inferior in
importance to the communicative function, and even to some
extent are presupposed by it. The secondary purposes of language
relate to the different fields of mental activity, and especially to
thought, self-consciousness and expression.

The role of language in the function of thought is well known.
Its role in mental operations, its function in the formulation of
latent thoughts in process of conception and development, and in
the interpretation of dreams, the share it has in ordered and
productive thinking, are all well known.[1] W. von Humboldt
declared in one of his works that language is not really a means
of representation of already recognized truths, but far more a
means for the discovery of truths previously unrecognized.[2] We
do not wish to interpret this dictum of von Humboldt as narrowly as does the school of linguistic philosophy influenced by
him, that is, either to see language as the 'formative organ of
reflexion' or to identify it with thinking; but only to regard it
as an expression of the fact that language has an active role in
facilitating and creating thought.

The relation between thought and speech has not yet been
fully clarified in the literature of linguistic philosophy, psychology and pathology. Discussion has led in the main to two
mutually contradictory views. According to the unitary view
thought and speech constitute a single indivisible function; while
according to the dualistic theory the two activities are essentially
independent of each other. Both these views are untenable,
because both lead to consequences which are in conflict with
experience. The former theory would require thought processes
to agree with the processes of speech in every respect; and this
cannot be reconciled with experience. There are many thought

[1] O. Selz, *Über die Gesetze des geordneten Denkverlaufes* (1913); *Zur Psychologie des
produktiven Denkens und des Irrtums* (1922).

[2] W. v. Humboldt, 'Über das vergleichende Sprachstudium', *Berichte d.k. preuss
Akad. d. Wissenschaften*, Berlin (1820), p. 255.

processes that actually resist verbal expression. Nor does the ontogenetic development of thought correspond with that of speech. An improvement in the capacity for thought is not always accompanied by an improvement in the capacity for speech, and *vice versa*. The dualistic theory similarly leads to contradictions; and above all to the unacceptable notion of 'thoughtless speech'. It is evident that this idea is incapable of clarifying the manifold relations between thought and speech. Furthermore, disturbances of speech very rarely affect speech alone or thought alone; usually both are affected simultaneously.

In spite of the great efforts devoted since the time of Plato to the study of this problem, no satisfactory conclusion has yet been reached. If we wish to appreciate the profound nature of the relation of thought to speech or to language, and to find a basis for a unified psychology of thought and language, we must inquire into the fundamental question whether the existence of one of these functions presupposes the existence of the other. This entails an answer to two other questions: is there speech without thought, and is there thought without speech?

The first question can be answered without difficulty. The use of speech without previous thought is unknown. Examination of one's own experiences will easily lead to the conclusion that every act of speech is prepared and accompanied by a thought process. Here we disregard phonetic utterances that have become automatic through habit, since these do not belong to speech in the true sense of the word. They are reactions determined by the momentary situation, and are to be compared with gestures appropriate to a given situation rather than with speech determined by thought. This view is supported not only by introspection but also by our knowledge of the evolution of mind and of the pathology of speech. If one adheres to a strict definition of language and thought, it is beyond doubt that the child does not employ speech before his first elementary thought functions have become effective. We must include among these, in my opinion, *conscious* decision and comparison; the recognition of categories and the classification of objects in them; and finally the acts of affirming and negating. It is true that in humans and anthropoids alike 'intelligent purposeful activity' can take place without the participation of thought, but such activity is not based on 'insight'. It is determined in accordance with the needs of an immediate situation. Further support is provided by phenomena of sensory aphasia, which indicate that disturbances in thought bring about serious speech defects. That the so-called 'speech' of complete idiots who are incapable of thought is not really speech in the true sense of the word is a well-known fact. It would therefore appear that speech activity is inseparably associated with thought; speaking without thinking does not exist.

The other question, whether thought invariably presupposes language, requires careful examination. In this question one of the greatest difficulties may lie in the fact that speechless thought is generally assumed to be possible; it is commonly supposed that there are thought processes that are carried out entirely without speech; that is to say, entirely without reference to thoughts previously formulated by means of language. Much misunderstanding has arisen precisely through the identification of 'speechless' with 'wordless'.

A thorough study of all the varieties of thought—ordinary thought, silent, unconscious, unformulated, intuitive thought, and thought activity in aphasia—does however lead to the conclusion that thought, including wordless thought, presupposes the linguistic function in every conceivable instance. Wordlessness does not justify the assumption that thoughts that have not been formulated verbally arise independently of language.

This view, which is of decisive importance for the psychology of thought and language, is based on the uninterrupted part played by non-conscious processes in mental activity. Our experiences, acquired knowledge, and forms of thought and speech are preserved mnemonically in such a way that they become available as soon as mental activity begins. In such cases they either appear in consciousness spontaneously as memory images or they influence our thoughts, values, and judgments without becoming conscious.

The great majority of these experiences and knowledge were already formulated linguistically before they sank into unconsciousness. Although removed from consciousness they did not disappear from the mind (which includes both conscious and unconscious). All thoughts, whether expressed in words or not, which are relevant to consciousness at a given moment, are very closely related to earlier thoughts and images previously given in verbal form. This must presumably be so because they exert a continual influence beyond the sphere of consciousness. Otherwise the continuity and development of thought would be inconceivable. Whether thoughts verbally formulated in consciousness retain their original verbal form we do not know and cannot discover, since we cannot experience unconscious processes as such. But the circumstance that thoughts often emerge verbally formulated, and further that even original ideas often make their appearance in full and faultless verbal form, permit us to assume that thoughts preserved in the unconscious which become activated there have in some way retained their linguistic structure. But it is not only the content of thought but those forms of speech and thought which we acquire partly passively and partly through experience and study, that must also be retained in an active unconscious. For otherwise it would be impossible to entertain the logically sound idea of thought unfolding wordlessly and following the sense of linguistic thought.

If we take these considerations into account and their necessary consequences, we see that only the view that verbal and non-verbal thought are invariably connected with the linguistic function can overcome all difficulties besetting the problem of the relation of language to thought. Since thought cannot exist without language, the statement that thought is necessarily and inseparably associated with language has a general validity. Thus both statements concerning the association and inseparability of the two mental functions become basic propositions of the psychology of language and thought.

The following brief summary may serve to clarify this relationship:

(1) Human thought presupposes speech. It follows that children in the prelinguistic state, to the extent that they are unable to understand the language of their environment, and the mentally ill who are completely lacking in the function of speech, are incapable of thought. Deafness does not exclude the function of speech, and in aphasia the speech capacity is apparently never completely broken off.

(2) Speech is introduced by thought. The content of speech and its representative and explanatory power is governed and controlled by thought.

(3) Through speech, thought is accompanied by the words and sentences required for the development of ideas. Thought is supplemented with new ideas produced through verbal thinking and the appreciation of relationships. It is structured by sentence formation and accentuation, and receives a verbal formulation in order to become fixed and communicable. Wordless thought is inseparably associated with the linguistic function as a result of knowledge which has previously received verbal formulation and continues to operate in the active unconscious.

(4) Thought and speech are inseparably associated with each other despite their disparity in function, intention and structure. The existence of the one presupposes the other. *Speech does not exist without thought, nor thought without speech.*

The new conception, at once dualistic and unitary, of the relationship of thought to speech (or to language) may accordingly be formulated in the following manner:

Thought and speech form an *inseparable duality* with manifold relations. Their functional and structural autonomy is expressed in their duality; the independence of their existence and content and the reciprocal influence of the two functions is expressed in their inseparability and their multiplicity of relationships. Thought and speech mutually complete each other; the right path in both guarantees uninterrupted intellectual progress.[1]

[1] On the problem of thought and speech see especially 'Thinking and Speaking. A Symposium', *Acta Psychologica*, X. (1954), edited by G. Révész with contributions from E. Buyssens, J. Cohen, W. C. Eliasberg, K. Goldstein, H. W. Gruhle, J. Jørgensen, F. Kainz, J. Piaget, G. Révész and B. L. v.d. Waerden.

After this somewhat detailed presentation of our views on the relations of thought and speech, we turn to the role of language in perception.

Here language appears as an active agent in forming, modifying and supplementing external perceptions, and helps in fixing them as memory. For illustration it should suffice to point out that the perceived image is influenced and enriched in content and form by linguistic formulation. A landscape seen without selectivity and grouping will appear quite differently if the viewer associates the perceived objects with others.[1]

The classification of perceived objects occurs as a rule through linguistic fixation, whereby the external world is given meaningful order. We would fail to receive a significant impression of a unified whole from a ruined building if we were simply passively affected by what is optically perceived. The general concept of ruins and the specific concept 'ruins of a Greek temple' have a supplemental and formative effect on the perception. Missing columns are re-erected in the imagination, broken architraves restored, destroyed parts of the building re-erected, so that in the end the architectural unity of a Greek temple stands before us as it were in its indestructible beauty and majesty. This visual conception cannot be awakened in a person who has no idea of a temple.

The importance of language for perception is seen nowhere so clearly as in the haptic impression of form. The structure of a somewhat complicated object unknown to the observer is grasped haptically only after the elements of the object's form have been conceptually fixed. It appears from this that the ultimate haptic image arises through linkage of abstract verbal with structural elements in a schematic image of the form.[2]

The formative function of language is also operative in internal

[1] Cf. my paper, 'Die Sprache', *Proc. Kon. Akademie van Wetenschappen*, Amsterdam, LXIII. (1940). Similar views are to be found in Herder, F. v. Schlegel, and W. v. Humboldt. 'To Herder and von Humboldt language is that intellectual activity by which the world is formed and named.'

[2] See my work, *Psychology and Art of the Blind* (1950).

perception. The visible and invisible objects of internal perception, such as thoughts, intentions, associations, abstractions, apperceptions, together with instinctive and emotional impulses, are in part produced by language, and in part raised to the level of consciousness by it, becoming part of the realm of ideas and thus becoming objects of reflexion.

It is beyond doubt that the recall or reproduction of things perceived or experienced is in most cases only possible when there has been earlier embodiment in words. It is mainly those impressions of a journey that are verbally fixed during perception that can be reproduced at a later date without significant changes.

Self-consciousness, a special field of employment of thought, also presupposes language. It is especially effective in tapping the secrets of our inner being and taking us into the world of the hidden and repressed. Without the verbal formulation of subjective experience and ethical standards, self-consciousness is incomplete, and self-knowledge and self-control equally so. To be conscious of one's own self, to examine one's own endeavours, motives, resolves and actions, necessarily presupposes language.

Finally, we would fall into an exaggerated intellectualism if we were to limit the role of language only to thought and communication. Besides its intellectual aspect, language also possesses an original expressive one. Emotions appear not only in the form of expressive sounds and gestures enriched by intonation, modulation and rhythm but also by means of symbolic phonetic signs with expressive value, i.e. words—a correlative conjunction of sounds and sense.

Linguistic constructions derive their physiognomic character not only from the melodies and rhythms of living language, but from the association of meaning with the sounds of language. The expressive capacity of language as a medium for the display of aesthetic experience and artistic effort appears in literature and in rhetoric and drama.

The purposes of language are less easy to separate in practice than in theory. It is not difficult to show the close relation between them and how they often intermingle. Thus verbally formulated thoughts, perceptions and expressions of emotions will furnish the materials for communication; linguistic expressive phenomena and conduct become objects of thought; self-consciousness appears as the product of thought and internal perception. But from the standpoint of the onset and directedness of linguistic activity these purposes prove to be so diverse that it is surely correct to distinguish between them as concepts.

Consideration of language from the point of view of purpose accordingly leads to the proposition that *language is a specially developed and unique means of communicating, thinking, conveying meaning, and facilitating self-consciousness and self-expression.* This definition applies to all speech situations, including dialogue, monologue, and unilateral speaking in a dual relationship.

The grouping together of these linguistic and related manifestations is justified by the fact that basically they all serve the same general purpose, that of permitting and furthering the development of human social activity and intellectual contact. Even if thought and the formation and expression of ideas are logically prior to communication, this does not contradict the assumption that they are not chronologically separated in the life of language, but existed in close mutual relation from the very beginning.

A second approach to defining the nature of language is to begin with the means by which it realizes its purposes. Language is so useful for such a variety of tasks and has the capacity for progressive and limitless development because it consists of phonetic and gestural symbols. Language is a complex of significant signs permitting the representation of objective and subjective circumstances in accordance with a fixed relationship of meaning to sign. Human language is distinguished from all other modes of communication by its symbolic form; it is precisely this that assured its potentiality for development and endowed it with its commanding importance in the evolution and intellectual history of man.

Thus, consideration of the means leads to a second proposition, that *language is essentially the representation of objective and subjective circumstances by means of phonetic signs and combinations of signs,*

H

supplemented by gestures, for communicating the experiences, opinions, aims and desires of the communicator. From this standpoint it is irrelevant what particular purpose language serves and under what conditions it is used, that is, whether communication, introspection, the fixation of thoughts, etc., is involved or whether the transposition of experiences into linguistic form takes place in dialogue or monologue.[1]

The symbolic function is singled out by many authors as *the* essence of language. This view is justified to some extent by the fact that language is brought into being by the very act of representing symbolically the content of one's consciousness. Language, like many other psychic functions, finds its embodiment in specific rendering as speech or writing, and these renderings are based on systems of symbolic signs of an acoustic, motor or optical nature. And it is these sign systems that provide the material studied by all linguistic science, grammar, syntax, semantics, phonology, and even logic. And since linguistic and grammatical research generally require little account to be taken of the purposes of language, it is conceivable that investigators who devote their attention to linguistic materials such as concepts, sentences, opinions and utterances see its symbolic form as the essence of language.[2] This standpoint is supported by the

---

[1] The pictorial languages of ancient civilizations such as the Egyptian, Chinese and Minoan and those of primitive peoples, as well as the pictorial character of dreams and visions, are connected in content with the expressions of phonetic language and mostly follow the structure of phonetic language. Their meaning can only be understood through translation into phonetic language. The picture sequences need to be read, and the images and visions to be interpreted.

[2] It would be an error to deduce from this the existence of 'pure language' as an end in itself maintaining itself independently of human needs and activities. We must accordingly reject the view of N. Ach, who regards 'language itself, i.e. language independent of particular functional purpose' as durable and lasting. To be sure, language can be isolated as an object of study without regard for its purposes, as is often done by linguists. But the results of such isolation have nothing to do with living language, which is what we wish to define in order to obtain a true conception of the significance of language. There is in reality no 'pure language', unlike mathematics, which does exist 'pure'. We have no more right to speak of 'pure language' existing for its own sake than we would have to speak of 'pure tongs' existing solely for its own sake and regardless of the function of tongs. 'To be tongs' means serving a particular purpose, and 'to be language' likewise implies a means of communication. Abstractions such as 'pure language' may entertain idle minds but they cannot advance research.

fundamental importance of symbolism in language. There is no objection to considering the symbolic function of language as its basic function; this view has sufficient basis in the dependent relation which the special functions have to the basic function. The existence and level of development of the special functions are dependent on the basic functions. One can even conceive the basic function as a kind of source function, furnishing the special functions with the sensory and conceptual material needed for their work. To call symbolic representation its basic function expresses the essential nature of language in the sense that it incorporates the basic characteristics of language, sound and sense; but it omits directedness, which is an integral component of the communicative intent.

However important the symbolic function may be in language, it cannot constitute its sole content, because symbolic representation is not characteristic of language alone. Many other activities and projections of thought such as cult practices, ceremonies, acts of greeting and above all the graphic arts likewise make use of symbolic signs. An unequivocal definition of language requires that both purpose and means be taken into account. This leads to the following formulation: Language is a medium of communication, thinking, idea formation, self-consciousness and expression, and represents in phonetic and gestural symbols the content of consciousness.

In this way language is defined unequivocally, but not exhaustively. To arrive at a definition taking into account all the categories of linguistic activity, it is necessary first to elucidate its functions, and to establish the basis of a functional system which is well grounded in logic, psychology and linguistic science.

The selection of the principal functions is not an arbitrary affair. If they are to fix the limits of language precisely and if their psychological content is to serve as a base for all linguistic activity, they must satisfy the following conditions. In the first place, like the principal functions of any biological or psychological organ, they must individually have a certain autonomy and a more or less independent field of activity. It follows from their independence that the failure or regression of one would not necessarily involve the failure or regression of another. As an example, we can cite the sense of sight. Two independent but closely related functions are possessed by the organs of vision, namely the sense of colour and the sense of space. Space and colour perception are constantly associated and seem to be inseparably related; but the sense of colour can disappear partially or completely under certain circumstances without interfering with space perception; the latter can likewise be greatly weakened without impairment of the sense of colour.

It is also characteristic of the principal functions that they serve various special purposes, at the same time forming a higher unity and being subordinated to a common principle. It may be an additional property of the principal functions that they lend themselves to study from an evolutionary point of view. In general we may assume that individual functions appear at different periods of development and are gradually integrated into a closed functional system under the guidance of a governing principle.

To my knowledge none of the recognized functional theories takes account of these requirements.[1] We shall refrain from examining these doctrines because their variety and diversity is so great that the points of difference do not readily form the object of fruitful discussion. The psychologically oriented theory of K. Bühler is an exception. Bühler's theory of language is characterized by the triad: *Kundgabe, Appell, Darstellung* (statement, appeal, representation). It might be assumed that by this triad Bühler wishes to express the individual functions constituting language. Detailed study of Bühler's doctrine, however, shows

---

[1] Such as: H. Maier, *Psychologie des emotionalen Denkens* (1908); K. Vossler, *Die Sprache als Schöpfung und Entwicklung* (1905); F. Mauthner, *Kritik der Sprache* (1921); K. Ogden and I. A. Richards, *The Meaning of Meaning* (1930); G. Stern, *Meaning of Change of Meaning* (1931); W. B. Pillsbury and C. L. Meader, *The Psychology of Language* (1928); H. Dempe, *Was ist Sprache?* (1930); and *Die Darstellungstheorie der Sprache.* Indogerm. Forschung, 53 (1935); O. Dittrich, *Die Probleme der Sprachpsychologie* (1904); H. Delacroix, *Le langage et la pensée* (1930); A. H. Gardiner, *The Theory of Speech and Language* (1932); G. A. Da Laguna, *Speech, its Functions and Development* (1927). Also: A. Marty, *Untersuchungen zur Grundlegung der allgemeinen Grammatik und Sprachphilosophie* (1908); E. Husserl, *Logische Untersuchungen*, I and II (1922), and *Meditations Cartésiennes* (1931); R. Hönigswald, *Philosophie und Sprache* (1937).

that he does not intend his three concepts (in a later version, expression, appeal, representation) to characterize the linguistic functions but only the general schematic concept of a 'concrete speech event'.

Bühler represents speech in terms of a three-fold relationship; A, the sender, addresses himself to B, the receiver, and makes something known to him by a particular sound.[1] In this way he arrives at three phases of linguistic utterance; the communicative act expressed verbally (Bühler calls it 'Kundgabe', later, 'Ausdruck'), then a request addressed to another person ('Auslösung', later 'Appell') and finally the representation ('Darstellung') of the subject-matter to be communicated. For the sake of clarity Bühler presents his doctrine of three fundamentals in the form of a triangle, in the centre of which is a point representing the mere acoustic phenomenon, the voiced sound; and to which the three factors mentioned are closely related.

The fact that in every speech act there is a speaker, an object addressed and subject-matter to be communicated is a generally accepted one. Plato in his *Kratylos* called language an *organon*, enabling one person to inform another of something: ὄνομα ἄρα διδασκαλικόν τί ἐστι ὄργανον καὶ διακριτικόν.[2] Bühler's analysis of the speech act is indebted to Ferdinand de Saussure, who was the first effectively to point out the fundamental distinction between the act of speech 'parole' and linguistic construction 'langue'.[3] It is Bühler's achievement to have recognized that *every* linguistic act embodies the three functions which he named. All three are present even in monologue and soundless speech, since in monologue the 'I' addresses itself to a second 'I' (though 'you' is often said instead of 'I'). That communicative intent and 'Appell' do not always go together in written language is explained by the fact that the conditions of speech do not always make themselves felt in writing.

---

[1] K. Bühler, *Sprachtheorie* (1934). Cf. also his work, *Die Axiomatik der Sprachwissenschaften (Kant-Studien,* 36, p. 19).

[2] Plato, *Kratylos* 388a, where he raises the question whether the names of things (*physei*) arise through natural suitability or (*thesei*) arbitrary selection and acceptance.

[3] F. de Saussure, *Cours de linguistique générale* (1916).

The correctness of Bühler's analysis of the fundamental relations of speech is also seen in the fact that the relative autonomy of their criteria can be seen phonetically. Even in an imperative sentence consisting of a single word, such as 'Come!', all three characteristics are present. The phonetic character of a volitional statement may reveal the membership of the speaker in a particular human group (sex, age, social position, occupation, geographical locality) and his personality as well. A command has not the same sound coming from a simple labourer as it has in the mouth of an educated person, and within a particular group clear and characteristic individual differences are phonetically perceptible. The address, too, which is indicative of the attitude and feelings of the speaker to the person, may show phonetic differences corresponding to differences of intention. The sentence 'You have done that well' can have various meanings, depending on its phonetic structure. By emphasising the 'you' or 'that' recognition or reproach may be expressed. Finally, the mere presentation of subject-matter has its own phonological requirements, the study of which is one of the most important tasks of phonology.[1]

We have no theoretical objections to raise against Bühler's conception of the fundamental relations of speech. But we cannot avoid mentioning certain gaps in his presentation relating first, to the sphere of validity of his *organon* model; and second to the apparatus of conception.

Bühler believes that he has provided a precise definition of language as a specific form of communication by means of the three speech factors named. But this cannot be reconciled with the results of our research on the phenomena of communication. For example, the spontaneous calls which will be discussed in detail later possess all three factors although they are not a linguistic means of communication. One must therefore admit a wider sphere of applicability than Bühler did, and extend it to certain extra-linguistic forms of communication; by which, to be sure, its importance for language is considerably reduced. What

---

[1] N. S. Trubetzkoy, *Grundzüge der Phonologie* (1939).

is specifically linguistic would then be expressed only by these relations of speech if the term 'description' were to be replaced by 'linguistic description'. This would also emphasize the symbolic nature of linguistic structure. None of the terms introduced by Bühler expresses clearly the specific criteria of language. *Kundgabe* exists without language, as in animal cries, calls directed to particular persons, and indicative gestures. Representation and expression are not limited to language alone, for all fields of art, especially dance and pantomime, have pronounced representational and expressive values. As for *Appell*, it can be expressed both by symbolic linguistic signs and by signals. Finally, *Auslösung* is really a phenomenon that results generally in response to a perceived stimulus appearing under the most varied circumstances in all living beings. This terminological gap can be remedied by substituting for Bühler's terms 'Kundgabe' and 'Appell' other terms which describe the linguistic facts with greater precision. The concept of 'Darstellung' is in any case not to be eliminated.[1]

We would not have examined Bühler's theory of language so critically were it not for the fact that it has created the impression among his followers that he was engaged, even primarily engaged, in establishing the basic functions of language, an impression to which his use of the terms 'Kundgabe' and 'Darstellung', which play such an important role in functional theories, contributed.

After this digression we can now turn our attention to the trifunctional theory. Although our theory is oriented primarily toward mutual understanding as the principal purpose of language, it extends, as we shall see, to all uses of language.

(B) THE TRIFUNCTIONAL THEORY

I believe that the following may be identified as the principal functions of linguistic communication. They appear in all speech situations and in all varieties of language; they are clearly distinct

---

[1] Bühler's theory is discussed critically in H. Duyker, *Extralinguale elemente in de spraak* (1946).

from one another in their autonomy of structure and purpose. They cast light upon new and hitherto unsuspected relationships, permit an evolutionary approach, and are in full agreement with the results of research in child psychology, general linguistic science and linguistic history. It needs no demonstrating to show that in his social relations man is governed chiefly by two purposes: to summon his fellows to action, and to indicate or communicate something to them. Without doubt these two social necessities have been the most powerful factors in the origin and development of language, since any communication of information, direct or indirect, is necessarily closely related to language.

To these two basic actions, summoning and informing, there should correspond in the most varied languages a number of activity words: and indeed in the Indo-European languages verbs occupy a central place. In the course of its differentiation language has to accommodate itself to the requirements of the communicative intent. It follows that the verb not only had to take over the task of 'governing' simple nouns and names, but also to attempt a closer definition of activity through the moods. Of all the moods, basic significance attaches to two in relation to the early history of language: *the imperative or command form, and the indicative.* To exclude any possibility of misunderstanding we wish to emphasize that we use the terms imperative and indicative (and also vocative and optative) in two quite distinct senses. We sometimes use them to refer to psychological categories: that is, human intentions and actions of commanding, calling, addressing, indicating, designating, independently of the manner in which these purposes are expressed, be they words, gestures, signals or other signs. At other times these terms are used to refer to linguistic categories. H. Paul in his *Prinzipien der Sprachgeschichte* (p. 263) pointed out the distinction between psychological and grammatical categories. He emphasized that each grammatical category is produced on the basis of a psychological one and that the establishment of a grammatical category does not affect the psychological one, which is independent of language and despite the origin of the latter continues exactly as before. The grammatical category becomes bound by a fixed tradition, but the psychological one on the contrary always remains free, living and effective.

The need for making this distinction can be seen in the fact that imperative and indicative intentions can appear without grammatical form, as in many primitive languages and in the gesture language of deaf mutes, which has no special signs for the moods; and also in natural gesture language, which even normal people employ to a considerable extent in support and extension of spoken language. The command or request is expressed in such cases by speech-related movements of the hand or by glances; indication is expressed through indicative, designative or other gestures of the hand. The separation of the psychological and the grammatical is also evident genetically; imperative and indicative conduct appear ontogenetically and probably also phylogenetically earlier than their corresponding grammatical forms. Furthermore, the imperative act can freely assume different grammatical forms (infinitive, indicative, and the syntactical form of a question), e.g. 'You will bring it to me', 'Are you not coming?' One should notice the way in which in German and Italian the substantive *Weg! Via!* assumes the significance of an adverb of place with imperative import. The same is true of the indicative. One can also point to languages that do not have moods, and are therefore compelled to represent these linguistic components in other ways. This applies, for example, to Chinese. Though it has no grammar in our sense, it can nevertheless provide all grammatical relationships syntactically, that is through word order or by special expressions. The Mbaya language lacks the imperative form: the imperative and optative are expressed by the substantive and a possessive pronoun. *L'emani* means 'He wishes', but is indicated by 'he' (*L*) and 'wish' (the noun, *emani*). In any case, one does not know what it was originally.[1]

---

[1] H. Duyker expresses these relationships so as to make language morphologically indifferent to the communicative intention.

Apart from these exceptions, the verb is the adequate linguistic means of expression of the above-mentioned two principal functions, and at the same time represents psychologically the most primitive act of speech and historically the oldest grammatical category. Its primitive character and prehistoric origins can easily be confirmed by psychological considerations and historical facts.

The first thing to claim man's attention at any time was unquestionably the event in all its manifestations; and in the first instance activities associated with movement from one place to another, such as running, coming, bringing, fetching, waiting, etc. Early man living in social groups was literally compelled to find suitable linguistic expressions for these vitally important activities. This effort led to the creation of action words (verbs), which probably constituted the basic element of language in its initial period of development.

The psychological pre-eminence of the action word is reflected in linguistic history in the lingual priority of the verb. The view that the verb is the oldest linguistic form has been accepted by numerous linguists. As early as 1770 J. G. Herder underlined the priority of the verb.[1] In his work on the origin of language he wrote as follows: 'Sounded verbs are the first elements of strength in the earliest languages. Thus oriental languages, for example, are rich in verbs as their basic roots' (p. 82). He even maintains that nouns are developed out of verbs and not verbs from nouns. In recent times is it Schuchardt who has especially defended the priority of the verb.[2] The experience of ethnologists agrees well with the historical view that in various primitive languages, and among others in the so-called agglomerating languages of the North American Indians, the process of activity, and along with it the verb, form the focus of linguistic communication. In these languages all other parts of the sentence are put into relation to the verb through modification of the original verbal word.

---

[1] J. G. Herder, *Abhandlung über den Ursprung der Sprache* (1770), I, 3.

[2] H. Schuchardt, 'Das Baskische und die Sprachwissenschaft', *Sitzungsberichte d. kaiserl. Akad. d. Wiss. Wien* (1925), pp. 202-4.

With equal frequency different verbs are used unaccompanied by other parts of speech to denote the same activity in diverse contexts. In the language of the Hurons there is a verb for seeing a man and another verb for seeing a stone. In both cases the verb is a 'sentence verb' which incorporates much more than our verbs do.[1]

The primitive character and great antiquity of the imperative and indicative grammatical forms are very closely connected with the genetic priority of the verb. This is reflected in linguistic history. The Indo-Germanic and Semitic language groups point back to an original state of verb formation in which the moods were limited to simple statements (the indicative) and to the most primitive subjective stressing of an action, the command (the imperative). M. Bréal recognizes these two modes of the verbs, the indicative and imperative, as the most primitive. He says, in part:

En toutes les langues où il existe une conjugaison, quelque pauvre et limitée qu'on la suppose, on trouvera une forme pour commander, une autre pour annoncer que la chose commandée est faite. . . . Ce deux formes, dont l'une peut marquer à tour de rôle un ordre, un avertissement, un souhait, une prière, et dont l'autre exprime un fait, un état, une action, un sentiment, sont les deux pôles autour desquels gravite le conjugaison. Tout le reste est venu s'ajouter par-dessus.[2]

If we disregard the linguistic differences between these two kinds of language activity, we can distinguish between them in two respects: firstly, in regard to the subject-matter to which they relate, and secondly, in regard to the chronological order of their origin.

In the sphere of function, the difference in their range of employment is evident. While the imperative can only express a demand for the carrying out of an act, the functional range of the indicative is significantly greater. The indicative function of

---

1 H. Werner, *Einführung in die Entwicklungspsychologie* (1933), p. 265.

2 M. Bréal, 'Les commencements du verbe', *Revue de Paris du 15 décembre* (1899).

language relates both to the communication of the subjective state of the speaker and to objective facts of the past, present or future; while the imperative function is directed exclusively to objective processes and relates primarily to the present, and only occasionally even to the future.[1]

The temporal priority of the imperative is supported on the one hand by psychological considerations and on the other by impressive arguments from child psychology and linguistic history, to which we will return in connexion with the problem of early language, on p. 186.

The remaining linguistic categories, like the optative, potential, and conditional, which partly possess their own functional forms and are partly expressed by the multiple functioning of the word categories, serve only to express the conditional reality of the situations they indicate: the optative the mere wish ('I would like to write'), the potential, the possibility of an event ('I can write'), the conditional supposing the possibility of the event ('If I write'). These moods are basically subordinate to the indicative and imperative. Since they imply the making of a distinction between reality and possibility, they most probably appear at a relatively high stage of linguistic evolution and can therefore be disregarded in considering the essential functions of language.

To the extent that linguistic philosophy and psychology have been based exclusively on human language, they have paid much less attention to the imperative than to the indicative. Husserl even falls into the error of interpreting the command as the mere communication of a wish, the expression of a command as the indication of one's mental state, a 'you shall' as an 'I wish'. Thus he confuses the imperative with the indicative or an optative derived from the indicative. This is quite understandable if the analysis of the linguistic function is based mainly on the way in which communication supposedly occurs; this can only be by indicating, referring and stating, and not by commanding. By

---

[1] Commands and prohibitions may relate to the indefinite future or to the duration of one's life or that of the social and religious order as well as to the present.

this over-emphasis on the indicative function the concept of language has been narrowed excessively. On the other hand a true language must be capable of adequately indicating and stating. The neglect of the imperative is understandable, besides, when one realizes that sentences which are neither true nor untrue, such as imperative, optative and interrogative sentences, do not belong to the field of traditional logic.

However important the imperative and indicative may be for communication, they are nevertheless one-sided in the sense that only the execution of the command or the reception of what is indicated is expected from the person addressed, and not a reply. The imperative and indicative speech situations do not necessarily imply reciprocal linguistic contact. A language cannot be regarded as complete unless the communicative intention is mutual, and is realized in the form of dialogue. But this speech situation cannot be brought about through imperative or indicative speech relations: the *question* must intervene. Thus we find in the question a third essential function of linguistic communication. From the point of view of concrete speech situations the question represents a special kind of linguistic communication, with a distinct purpose, its own acoustic-phonetic form and an important role in the exchange of thought. All this justifies its being included among the principal functions constituting language.[1]

The significance of the question in linguistic activity is also expressed in the fact that a child is regarded as having acquired mastery of speech when he can use interrogative as well as imperative, exclamatory and indicative sentences; when he is able to ask and to answer questions. It is characteristic that animal lovers, even in reporting the most remarkable speech activity among parrots, never claim that their pets have asked them questions. If they did, they would have to claim human consciousness for the parrots, but their admiration does not extend

---

[1] In Greek tragedy a player is opposed to the singing and dancing chorus, who answers questions put by the leader of the chorus (Koryphaios). The Greek word for player, *Hyokrites*, signifies respondent.

that far. John Locke's astonishment was justified when Maurice, Prince of Orange, told him of a Brazilian parrot that gave intelligent answers to his questions.[1]

In evolution, at least ontogenetically, the question seems to be a later linguistic form than the imperative and indicative. This is indicated by the fact that interrogative sentences appear relatively late in the speech development of children, considerably later than the imperative and indicative sentence forms. While the child can designate his most pressing needs in imperative form at nine to twelve months, and the objects in his environment by more or less articulated words at fourteen to fifteen months, the simplest one- or two-element interrogative sentences appear at the end of the second and beginning of the third year (W. Stern, Ch. Bühler, E. G. Scupin, Piaget).[2] For this it may also be argued that in every question there is to be found at least the beginnings of a distinction between truth and error, reality and appearance; and this distinction is at first beyond the powers of the immature child.[3] Whether the syntactical form of the interrogative also appears at a later date phylogenetically than the imperative and indicative forms must be left open. But it does not seem to us to be entirely out of the question that in certain primitive languages, and perhaps also in the historical grammar of advanced languages, indications of the later appearance of the interrogative form may

---

[1] The famous Prince told him that the parrot, on being brought into the room in which he and several other Hollanders were present, exclaimed, 'What sort of company of white men is here?' When it was asked, pointing to the Prince, what kind of man it thought he was, the parrot answered, 'Some general or other.' The Prince asked it: '*D'où venez-vous?*' It answered: '*De Marinnan.*' '*A qui estes-vous?*' '*A un Portugais.*' '*Que fais-tu là?*' '*Je garde les poules.*'

Locke did not wish to doubt the credibility of the Prince, and merely asked him what language the parrot had actually spoken. The Prince answered, 'Brazilian'. He then asked, 'Do you understand Brazilian?' The Prince answered in the negative, and added that the parrot spoke through a Brazilian interpreter. Locke was, of course, unconvinced of the honourable character of this man. Our philosopher might also have expressed his astonishment that the parrot could speak French as well as Brazilian. (*Treatise*, II, Chapter 27.)

[2] The interrogative appears especially late among deaf and dumb children. A rather long intellectual development is required before deaf-and-dumb children acquire a grasp of questions and participate in dialogue.

[3] It is obvious that this cannot be applied to questions as to the name of a person or object.

be found. This conclusion would not conflict with the assumption that the interrogative *function* was operative prior to the origin of the interrogative *linguistic form*. For it is impossible to conceive of a primitive human community that could have successfully dealt with hidden objects or persons or those out of sight without the use of questions. It can be argued in support of the view that questions are basically a higher linguistic accomplishment than the other two functions that many sufferers from mental illness and speech disorders are able to answer questions but not to ask them.[1]

While discussing the problem of the exchange of thoughts we must refer to an entirely distinctive form of expression which is intimately connected with language: namely *silence*. It is to be sure paradoxical to call silence a speechless form of speech activity, but it is so. The problem of silence has a place among the theoretical problems of speech. In Plato silence is used—as Hönigswald mentions in his work cited above (p. 13)—not as the οὐκόν but as the μὴ ὄν of speaking. Silence is based upon active speech; it is not oriented toward the reception of a command or communication, but represents a positive reaction to a question or other speech act, and is as it were a form of dialogue. Only a creature capable of speech can be silent. We only learn to be silent in the course of life after having learnt to speak.[2]

'To be silent at the right moment is wise and better than any amount of talk. It was partly for this reason that the men of early times introduced, as it seems, mysteries; by them we should accustom ourselves to be silent at the proper moment, and learn too to respect the Gods for the sake of human secrets entrusted to us.'[3] A silent attitude does not always have the same significance; it can be affirmative or negative, imperative or didactic, aggressive or comprehending. But for the most part it is

[1] A. Gelb, 'Zur medizinischen Psychologie und philosophischen Anthropologie', *Acta Psychologica*, 3, pp. 241 ff.

[2] H. Lotze, *Kleine Schriften*, I, p. 231.

[3] Plutarch, *Moralia*.

correctly indicated.¹ Often more can be expressed by silence than by speech; it allows the mental attitude of the person to be expressed much more clearly than words. The silent answer of Jesus to the question of Pilate lays bare the whole tragedy of mankind. (Cf. Tintoretto's 'Ecce Homo' in the Scuola di San Rocco in Venice.)

The basic functions discussed above are the main preconditions for the most primitive and most natural speech situation, the dialogue; but equally for the monologue, the methods, forms and usages of which are essentially indistinguishable from those of dialogue, independently of whether monologue occurs as an inner voice or is spoken aloud.²

The agreement between the two forms of utterance is to be seen most clearly when monologue takes place in a whisper or semi-speech. In this case the phonetic side of speech and everything connected with it, such as intonation, articulation, modulation, accent, rhythm, appears in the phenomenon of monologue exactly as it does in dialogue.

My three linguistic functions constitute a *functional system of language*. The three basic functions, in consequence of their equal weight, and their belonging to a single conceptual category, form a psychological and logical triad. They satisfy the conditions which must be required of any logical functional system, and especially one of language, and which have been neglected in earlier functional theories. The principal functions are, that is to

¹ Goethe once said that the conversation of cultivated people is instructive, but their silence is educational.

According to the *Upanishad*, Bhava was once asked to explain the Brahman, the principle of the world. Bhava became silent. After the inquirer had repeated his question a second time and a third time Bhava spoke: 'I am teaching it but you comprehend not. The Atman is silence'. (Atman means the Self and the nature of things). After F. Mauthner, *Kritik der Sprache*, I, p. 83.

Schiller indicated the literary value of silence in the following dictum: 'A master in any other field is recognized by what he says; a master of style is shown by what he wisely passes by in silence.'

² Monologue is not necessarily directed to the self; in most cases it is neutral, being merely a linguistic embodiment of thought. It is accordingly justifiable to distinguish between these two types of monologue (I-related and thought-related), ignoring the well-known spontaneous phonetic speech of children at play. Speaking with a neutral attitude is not called monologue but rather speaking aloud.

say, independent of one another, and neither cross nor overlap. Furthermore, they are—at least the indicative and interrogative—specific or necessary features of language or speech activity. The independence of the three principal functions also finds expression in the mutual relations of the subjects coming into contact with one another. The imperative indicates the dependence of the person addressed on the speaker, the interrogative indicates precisely the opposite, the dependence of the speaker on the person addressed, while the indicative puts both partners on an equal basis.

In the course of its early history the two basic functions, the imperative and indicative, in association with the interrogative, gave rise to fully-fledged language. A definite picture of this initial form of language is unattainable, but some indications could perhaps be provided by the languages of the most primitive peoples if they were studied from the standpoint of our trifunctional theory. Languages could very probably be found in which the three functions would be manifested in a much more primitive fashion than in developed language systems. It is by no means impossible that the archaic forms of our own languages established by historical and comparative linguistic science would be capable of affording points of departure for the reconstruction of these initial phases of language.

The earliest form of human languages must also have been a form of communication providing opportunity for the expression of the three I-functions, the imperative, indicative and interrogative, together with expressions of time and place. Since indicative information can be expressed in natural gestures only with extreme difficulty, and to a very limited extent, it is to be assumed that even in the antecedent stage of language sound played a decisive role. *The original form of language must therefore have been a phonetic language with imperative, indicative and interrogative forms of expression.* This is also shown by the fact that the three basic functions of language appear in children at the very beginning of their active speech. By the end of their second year children employ sentences consisting of several words in three forms,

I

namely imperative sentences (Papa, pottie! Go!), indicative sentences (It burns. There he is.) and interrogative sentences (What here? Where apple?)

In support of the trifunctional theory I would like to refer to two additional established facts of linguistic science. One of these is grammatical and the other phonological.

The grammatical point relates to the classification of kinds of sentences. From the history of Greek philosophy we know that Protagoras distinguished four kinds of sentences, the prayer, the question, the answer, and the command. These four types of sentence incorporate our basic functions; the prayer and answer including our indicative, the command, the imperative, and the question our interrogative linguistic function.[1] Aristotle distinguished a greater number; he justly ascribed fundamental importance to the declarative sentence (indicative) giving as a reason that this form alone is definitive in logic.[2] Among the Stoics, despite the multiplicity of sentence forms treated by them, the affirmative and wishing or command sentence (indicative and imperative) predominated. The Peripatetics advanced somewhat farther than Aristotle and the Stoics in respect to functional theory. They assigned first place to the declarative sentence (λόγος ἀποφαντικός) which corresponds grammatically to the indicative, just as their predecessors did, then follows the volitional sentence (εὐκτικός), on which the optative is based, and the sentence of command (προδτακτικός), which is the basis of the imperative. They also add the exclamatory and interrogative sentences.[3] In recent philosophy and formal logic the distinction is generally made between declarative and imperative sentences, to which the interrogative is added as a third class. This view is taken by leading linguists such as Delbrück, Paul, and Wundt.

It appears equally important to us that of the three basic functions each has its own phonological structure. The difference is great enough to enable us to recognize the true sense of a sentence

---

[1] Prantl, *Gesch. d. Logik im Abendlande*, I, p. 441.

[2] Aristotle, *de interp.* 4, 17a, 2 ff.; *poet.* 19, 1456b, pp. 8 ff.

[3] H. Maier, *Psychologie des emotionalen Denkens* (1908), p. 10.

solely by its phonetic character. In languages which do not have any special grammatical or syntactical form for questions it can be determined phonologically, and especially by the intonation, whether a sentence is interrogative or indicative. Analogously, the indicative form of the sentence can be given an indicative, imperative or interrogative import by varying the intonation.

Contributions have recently been made to the phonological problem by A. W. De Groot which have a close relationship to our functional theory.[1] He points out that three kinds of intonation can be distinguished in language, which he designates as call, assertion and interrogation. The agreement between his three kinds of intonation and our three language functions is apprent even at a glance. De Groot's terms assertion and interrogation correspond to our indicative and interrogative, which is to say that indicating (asserting, informing) and questioning are each associated with a distinct phonological structure, recognizable in speech through distinct patterns of intonation and in writing by distinct punctuation (full stop and interrogation mark). Only the third concept, 'Call', offers difficulty, because it has a wider application than the imperative. The intonation of a verbal call applies to commanding, requesting and volitional sentences as well as to exclamations. The last-mentioned is directed toward the expression of a momentary state of feeling (Glorious! Wonderful!) or a particular attitude (Fabulous! That's fine!) or sometimes an emotional assertion (He is coming!). These elliptical exclamatory sentences are indicative in intention (Glorious! means 'How glorious it is here!'; Fantastic! means 'I find this fantastic') but imperative in intonation.

In view of the correspondence between intention and intonation we prefer to use our own terms instead of the words call, assertion and interrogation. It should be added that the imperative

[1] A. W. de Groot, 'De Nederlandsche zinsintonatie in het licht der structureele taalkunde', *De Nieuwe Taalgids*, 38 (1941). De Groot's conclusions are limited to the Dutch language. It would be a separate problem to investigate the extent to which these kinds of intonation apply in other languages. To my knowledge they do apply in the Ural-Altaic languages.

intonation is also used for the linguistic expression of non-volitional experiences. The introduction of our terms would have the additional advantage of eliminating the heterogeneous character of the terms suggested by De Groot.

(C) THE DEFINITION OF LANGUAGE

Our functional analysis of linguistic activity has led to the conclusion that language is divisible into three basic functions, the imperative, indicative and interrogative. These three forms of expression encompass and exhaust all the forms of understanding among human beings. As far as we can discern in linguistic expression serving multilateral communication, there is no single linguistic act that cannot be assigned to one of these functions. When a human being enters into linguistic contact with his fellows he can order them to do something or invite or encourage them to some sort of activity (imperative, vocative, optative); indicate or communicate something to them (indicative); or ask them something (interrogative). To my mind there are no further possibilities within the sphere of the communicative function. Accordingly it now appears possible to offer a definition which will contain all the essential characteristics of language and none that are unessential.[1]

We would thus understand by the term language that form of communication by which, for the purpose of mutual understanding and with the aid of articulated and symbolic signs in a variety of significant combinations, commands and wishes are expressed, objective and subjective facts are indicated, and requests made for conveying information.[2]

In this definition language is unequivocally distinguished both in terms of its principal purpose and in terms of its aim and the

[1] Here we use the word 'language' to mean only the mature fully-fledged speech of adults; it excludes the speech of children, the mentally ill and the feeble-minded.

[2] The possible objection that indications or references may also be expressed by other signs does not affect the terms of our definition; for such signs only acquire meaning by being related to language and therefore by their verbal significance. Traffic signs and signals and the like are all conventionally established symbols for certain limited linguistic communications. They can only be understood when they are interpreted linguistically.

means of its attainment. The principal purpose of language is mutual understanding; its aim, the communication of facts, circumstances, intentions and wishes, and the inviting of others to action and communication; the means for the attainment of these aims are chiefly constructions of symbolic signs, taking the form of phonetic language, language-related gesture systems, and writing.

This definition of language is a synthesis of its outer form and inner content, connecting the sign function with the specifically intended linguistic activity. It applies to all kinds of language (phonetic, gestural, sign or written), each of which has its own structure and its own form of sensorily perceptible expression. Although it is based on the standpoint of the speaker, it takes account of the hearer. It embraces all activities or functions of language distinguished by other investigators from different points of view, such as the 'expression' of Husserl, the 'representation' of Külpe and Bühler as the communication of objective facts as opposed to the 'manifesting' of subjective states; and likewise the 'Appell' of MacDougall and the 'release' of Bühler as a coupling of the imperative with the resultant non-linguistic reaction. On the other hand it excludes all forms of expression that deviate from the criteria given in the definition, such as involuntary expressive gestures and imitative sounds.[1]

---

[1] In speech with its many rich nuances, one can easily find numbers of expressions not instantly classifiable under the three principal functions. Among these we can eliminate immediately all those that appear as the spontaneous expression of internal events. The others, such as signs of surprise, protestation, agreement, happiness, warning, sympathy, etc., can on closer examination without difficulty be grouped into one of the given functions, mostly the indicative, by which they lend the indicative an imperative, optative or interrogative touch.

A. H. Gardiner in his work, *The Theory of Speech and Language* (1932), p. 187, in connexion with the classification of sentences in an appendix to the 'Report of the Joint Committee on Grammatical Terminology' (1917) distinguished four sentence categories—namely statements, questions, desires, exclamations. The first three sentence forms are closely related to our three I-functions, the indicative, interrogative and imperative. His fourth, the exclamation, may perhaps be regarded as a specific form of sentence, but not as a special linguistic function. The exclamation may be directed at someone, but need not be (e.g. Woe is me!) Thus it need not belong among the forms of communication, much less among the essential functions of linguistic communication. It is an expressive gesture symbolized linguistically, and is therefore at the same level as interjections. The arguments of Gardiner are irrelevant to the evolutionary problem and to that of psychological development.

In the course of human development the functions originally directed toward inter-individual communication acquire an every-growing mental and spiritual significance. Through the medium of language we formulate and develop our ideas, express our feelings and moods, acquire guiding principles of conduct, make demands on the community, and discover our own selves. What were originally only media of communication are extended to become media of thinking, imagery, decision, self-control and expression. The I-you relationship, originally forming the basis of the exchange of thought and the projection of the will, is interiorized into one's own Ego. Alongside dialogue with others there appears dialogue with one's Ego. This form of linguistic expression is also carried on in indicative and imperative and sometimes (as in the questioning of one's own conscience) in interrogative form.

If we wish to define language as comprehensively as possible without loss of precision and logical integrity we must incorporate into the definition the secondary purposes of language other than communicative intent. The scope of the definition would thereby be extended, and would assume the following form:

Language is the medium by which commands and wishes are expressed, subjectively or objectively perceived facts are indicated, thoughts are formulated, and questions are asked to effect communication or self-control, for the purposes of mutual communication, ordered thinking, the meaningful appreciation of perceptions, introspection, and the expression of the inner life, through the agency of a number of articulated and symbolic signs appearing in a variety of significant combinations.[1]

---

[1] A selection of definitions of language are given here for comparison:
EBBINGHAUS: Language is a system of conventional signs that can be voluntarily produced at any time. CROCE: Language is articulated, limited sound organized for the purpose of expression. DITTRICH: Language is the totality of expressive abilities of individual human beings and animals capable of being understood by at least one other individual. EISLER: Language is any expression of experiences by a creature with a soul. B. ERDMANN: Language is not a kind of communication of ideas but a kind of thinking: stated or formulated thinking. Language is a tool, and in fact a tool or organ of thinking that is unique to us as human beings. FRÖBES: Language is an ordered sequence of

This definition represents the essential substance of language comprehensively. If we could imagine human beings completely unacquainted with language but capable of thought and imagination and somehow able to acquire knowledge of the definition, we could assume that on the basis of this definition they could reconstruct a language corresponding in essence to human language. In contrast, on the basis of a definition which puts the whole emphasis for instance on the symbolic character of language, these imaginary beings would arrive at a 'language' corresponding to mathematical symbols (in which, to be sure, many ideas and experiences can be expressed without the use of a single word or grammatical form of phonetic language).

It is theoretically possible to define language so as to include much more than is expressed *prima facie* by the word language. It could be made to embrace expressive sounds and gestures, imitative sounds, animal cries, in fact all forms of communication used by living creatures. From the biological point of view there is no objection to such an extension of the concept of language. It is only a question of whether there is any profit in so doing. In my opinion there is none; the neglect of the specific differentiae unavoidably leads to confusion, which is then only overcome by being compelled to distinguish between different kinds of

words by which a speaker expresses his thoughts with the intention of making them known to a hearer. J. HARRIS: Words are the symbols of ideas both general and particular; of the general, primarily, essentially and immediately; of the particular, only secondarily, accidentally and mediately. HEGEL: Language is the act of theoretical intelligence in its true sense, for it is its outward expression. JESPERSEN: Language is human activity which has the aim of communicating ideas and emotions. JODL: Verbal language is the ability of man to fashion, by means of combined tones and sounds based on a limited numbers of elements, the total stock of his preceptions and conceptions in this natural tone material in such a way that this psychological process is clear and comprehensible to others to its last detail. KAINZ: Language is a structure of signs, with the help of which the representation of ideas and facts may be effected, so that things that are not present, even things that are completely imperceptible to the senses, may be represented. DE LAGUNA: Speech is the great medium through which human co-operation is brought about. MARTY: Language is any intentional utterance of sounds as a sign of a psychic state. PILLSBURY-MEADER: Language is a means or instrument for the communication of thought, including ideas and emotions. DE SAUSSURE: Language is a system of signs expressive of ideas. SCHUCHARDT: The essence of language lies in communication. SAPIR: Language is a purely human and non-instinctive method of communicating ideas emotions and desires by means of a system of voluntarily produced symbols.

language, signifying a complete abandonment of the óriginal standpoint. But it would not occur to anyone, regardless of what standpoint he might adopt regarding the definition of language, to identify inarticulate human cries of pain, warning calls of elephants, the trilling of ants or the begging sounds of domestic dogs with human language and insist that these animals 'converse' with each other and sometimes with us.

The word language is a historical concept employed since ancient times to designate the entirely distinctive communicative utterances of *man*. This concept has a very positive if not too narrowly delimited content which is sanctioned as it were by linguistic custom and linguistic science. But in the second half of the last century—apparently under the influence of evolutionary doctrine—a tendency developed to designate phenomena having limited similarities with another group of phenomena by one and the same concept, instead of attempting by a broader generalization to find a new concept to designate both sets of phenomena. Huizinga, the historian, in one of his works, has described this tendency as an inflation of concepts and has shown how the idea of Renaissance, so characteristic a historical idea, was applied to intellectual currents of all ages and all peoples that showed particular parallels with the time of the Renaissance. People began to speak of the Renaissance of the thirteenth century, the Renaissance of the Carolingian period or of renaissance in general.

Completely analogous is the broadening of the concepts of language, music and tools. The tendency to generalize makes these concepts lose their clear and pregnant content. This tendency which is so contrary to linguistic usage leads among other things to attributing the production and utilization of tools to the anthropoids (Yerkes, Köhler), the art of song to birds, and language to all sorts of animals including insects (Garner, Buttel-Reepen, Wasmann). And animals are supposed to have acquired all this as a free gift of Nature, while we have to pay a heavy tuition fee for it.

In carrying over fruitful concepts to alien contexts one fails to notice that a concept firmly rooted in linguistic consciousness can easily lose its freshness and imaginative richness and soon become a stereotype, signifying too much and at the same time too little. Nor should it be overlooked that the broadening of the content of a concept easily leads to identifying with one another all the separate things brought together under it, and to deductions that give rise to misunderstandings and confusion. Nothing is more natural than deducing the identity of *phenomena* from the identity of their *designation*.[1] These considerations have led us to suggest using the word *communication* for language together with forms of utterance agreeing with it in limited respects; reserving the word *language* exclusively for the developed form of understanding of human beings with the faculty of speech.[2]

It would be a special task to study language from the point of view of the hearer. Little attention has been paid to this question, since it is outside the sphere of interest of the linguist. Material for it occurs in child psychology, animal psychology, and the literature on deaf mutes: but it is not enough to serve as a point of departure for a phenomenological and structural study of language.

The consequences resulting from our definition of language for the problem of the earliest language are as follows: Under our definition no form of communication can be deemed to be language in the true sense of the word unless it is endowed with imperative, indicative and interrogative functions. The earliest form of language must consequently include these basic functions so as to be capable of expressing the corresponding elementary communicative purposes. Since the indication or statement of facts is difficult or impossible without words, it is to be assumed that the earliest form of language was a form of understanding manifesting itself essentially in phonetic units consisting of words and combinations of words; which is much more probable than song, picture, or written language. These, and to a degree gesture

---

[1] G. Révész, 'Gibt es einen Hörraum?', *Acta Psychologica*, 3 (1937), p. 167.

[2] G. Révész, 'Die menschlichen Kommunikationsformen und die sog. Tiersprache', *Proc. K. Ned. Akademie van Wetenschappen*, 43 (1941).

language too, necessarily presuppose a language of words. The possibility is thus excluded of there ever having existed men who expressed their thoughts, wishes or intentions in any sort of sign, picture or written language in preference to phonetic language. All these symbolic forms of language are not languages in the sense of having the capacity for spontaneous development according to their own laws, but are based solely on a translation (sign and picture language) or fixation (written language) of a living phonetic language, and are moreover of much later origin than spoken language.

In reality the original form of phonetic language cannot be demonstrated, since, as already mentioned, the languages of present-day primitive peoples have far outgrown this stage. Certain clues may nevertheless be found in primitive languages and in the utterances of children; in the latter case the major linguistic categories are demonstrable before the end of the second year. But the value of these parallels as evidence depends on the evolutionary significance attributable to child speech and to the most primitive languages in general. If one is to be guided by these two types of language in the reconstruction of the earliest languages one must seek to establish or postulate a stage in the ontogenetic and phylogenetic development of language possessing the criteria of language of our definition in a primitive way.

After these theoretical comments, which will serve as the basis of our further discussion and exposition, we can turn to our real task. Remaining always on empirical ground, we wish to indicate those stages of communication that probably preceded the linguistic form, and which are found not only in speechless human beings but in present-day man. These antecedent forms open access to the early forms of language and beyond these to fully developed language.

If we proceed from the well-grounded assumption that phonetic and gesture language arise by means of functional adaptation from less developed forms of communication, and if we seek to reconstruct the stages of development leading to language from this standpoint on the basis of animal and linguistic psychology, there is only one practicable way open to us, that of proceeding from the most primitive forms of communication and of advancing in logical sequence to language. In this way we arrive at the antecedent stages of language, i.e. the forms of communication that cannot be reckoned as linguistic, but at least have in common with language the tendency to reciprocal communication which is the basic condition of all forms of communication, inclusive of language.

Theoretically the opposite method could be employed, arriving at the least specific kinds of communication in the classification from the highest or most differentiated form of the evolutionary sequence, fully developed language, by way of logical generalization. By this method ever more primitive forms of communication are obtained the further away the means of achieving them lie from the means by which human language is brought into use.

On methodological grounds we have decided in favour of the upward direction from the antecedent stages, conscious of the fact that in exploring the antecedent stages the guiding ideas, namely the essential functions of language, must be furnished by developed language.

With these definitions and leading ideas the path of our enquiry is indicated. First we shall consider the forms of expression that may be called the earliest manifestations of communication. Then we shall discuss the forms of communication that are already connected with human language by particular common characteristics. In this way we shall proceed gradually through the early forms to fully developed language.

VII

HUMAN AND ANIMAL
FORMS OF CONTACT

(A) INSTINCTS AND NEEDS

WHENEVER somatic or psychic equilibrium is disturbed, a need automatically comes into being to eliminate the disturbance. This instinctive need arises under the influence of driving forces, or stimuli, that guide the organism directly toward an objective. The need and the stimulus, teleological as they are in character, imply the adoption of particular means for the attainment of the objective and the satisfaction of the need. This process is most clearly observable in the sphere of pure instinct, where it operates without the intervention of consciousness or conscious volition.

A hungry animal is enabled by innate mechanisms to find suitable means of satisfying its need for food. The necessity of restoring equilibrium impels the animal to motor activities which lead to the desired result. In such a case there is a complete absence of conscious intention, motivation or decision. The entire instinctive process, from the emergence of the need to the execution of the activity, is determined by heredity; it can be regarded as a unified and automatic instinctive mechanism. All of it operates according to biological laws and consequently does not demand any rational decision. The inter-related phases of this process, the stimulus that sets the organism in motion and the instinctive regulation of the drive, which help the organism to seek (and most often to find) ways and means, can be recognized in all instinctive actions. This conception may be expressed in the following proposition: the need, the impetus toward satisfying it, and the finding of appropriate means for so doing, form an indivisible biological unit.

Actions determined solely by instincts also occur in human life. In general, to be sure, man recognizes his needs and the objects and modes of behaviour that will lead to their adequate satisfaction; and he evaluates them according to standards that can only be provided by intelligence. The application of intelligence, the balancing of motives and the estimation of consequences, lend to certain purely instinctive needs and the inseparable means of satisfying them an entirely different character and importance. In the course of human evolution and individual development the original instincts are sublimated, and are transformed into others, in part higher and under the control of consciousness, and in part mental, without thereby entirely losing their original instinctive nature.

The recognition of the instinctive basis of needs in general entitles us to contrast the intellectualized functions with their original instinctive forms, to put them into an evolutionary relationship and to reconstruct their temporal sequence.

A firm distinction must be made between objectives set on the basis of rational and voluntary decision and those toward which the individual is impelled involuntarily by biologically based drives. One must nevertheless guard against an error reaching back to Descartes which has been aggravated by psychoanalysis and which has triumphed in Behaviourism. This error is that animal reactions occur 'unconsciously', because their needs and instincts are not subject to what the psychoanalyst would call the 'censor' of the mind. In thus limiting the idea of consciousness to higher consciousness, where decisions are made on the basis of intellectual evaluations or where there are at least clear imaginative and emotional experiences, the unconscious is put into a twilight zone belonging neither to the sphere of purely physical phenomena nor yet to the phenomena of consciousness. In reality, consciousness is the broader concept, embracing both phenomena of consciousness in the narrow sense, that is the simple experiential 'givenness' of objects and processes, and the evaluation of objects and subjective and objective processes according to generally accepted standards. Among phenomena of consciousness in the narrow sense a distinction can be made, following Leibniz, between things that are distinctly and clearly experienced and those that are experienced indistinctly and unclearly. But unconscious phenomena are normally distinguishable only by the lesser degree of their clarity and distinctness from the other objects of consciousness, with which they otherwise agree in all other respects.[1] It is therefore unjustifiable to deny that a creature has consciousness simply because it has only a dark and confused consciousness, and in particular can only experience need and instinct as a 'dark pressure'.

This observation appears to be necessary because the extension of the contact theory to the animal world would not be permissible if the need for contact did not come to the consciousness of the animal at least as a 'dark pressure'.

(B) THE SOCIOLOGICAL BASIS OF COMMUNICATION

If we consider social organization as a whole it is evident that social contact offers great advantages to the individual creature. These advantages may be sexual or asexual. We know from animal sociology that associations arising on a sexual basis tend to appear as various forms of the family and as more or less closed groups, herds or swarms. Asexual communities are much more varied; they are formed to serve the security of the individual and the group, the acquisition of food and shelter, and even to promote physical and psychical development. The best known forms of asexual association among animals include groups that live, sleep or migrate together and which pursue such aims as

---

[1] Here we ignore unconscious processes without phenomenal content and of whose existence we become aware only in consequence of their indirect effects or their symbolic representation (as in a dream), to which depth psychology rightly attaches so much importance.

protection against climatic change or shortage of food and the finding of suitable breeding sites. It suffices to mention the dense colonies of wasps, the collective hibernation of bats and of otherwise unsociable vipers, the mass migrations of crabs, insects and fish at spawning time, and the roving bands of rats, wild horses, antelopes, reindeer and migratory birds. To the asexual associations also belong the food communities of beetles and birds of prey, the hunting packs of wolves, and the play groups of young animals.

The relations between the individuals within such communities can be reciprocal or unilateral. Reciprocity exists when the union is advantageous to both sides; it is unilateral when it is useful only to one of the partners. Unilateral relationships may even be harmful to one of the participants, as can be observed in parasitic societies where the guests eat the eggs of the hosts or drain their blood. In many cases it is difficult to decide whether the one-sidedness is complete or whether the combination does not in fact satisfy particular needs which partly counterbalance the disadvantages. The same is true of 'indifferent' combinations, in which the participants, who may or may not be of the same species, apparently derive no advantages from each other. In such cases investigation is required to determine whether advantages do not in fact accrue to both sides from the association. This is the case, to cite an example, with the mixed society of ostriches and wild horses. They graze together and accompany one another regularly, unconcerned with each other individually. But if one looks for the true basis of this 'friendship' it appears that the association of the two species increases their mutual safety. Ostriches have a particularly acute sense of sight, while wild horses make greater use of scent.

Animal societies display great variety in structure and type, based on the diversity of their biological organization and their circumstances and habits of life. It is interesting and of great evolutionary significance that there is only one variety of living being that displays nearly every form of social organization, and that is man. In man we find varying forms of the family, such as matriarchy and patriarchy; varying sexual arrangements, including monogamy, polygamy and promiscuity, and asexual associations for travelling, fighting, hunting, eating and dwelling.

All this indicates that in human societies the same or at least related collective powers and laws are at work as in animal societies. But this correspondence does not allow us to identify the complicated human societies with organized animal bands. The former are not only more complicated but point to ways of life owing their existence to human intelligence and the initiative of individuals. That in spite of all this the basic forms of human and animal societies show many resemblances and that these resemblances rest on biological laws going far beyond the sphere of human volition is a fact of basic importance.

If we now ask whether there is not a need that is common to all human and animal associations and societies—whatever social and individual purposes they may serve—we can point to the *need for contact* as the indispensable basis of their origin, development and differentiation and as that which governs them, whatever their size or degree of permanency.

When one studies the social relations of living beings one is struck by the unquenchable need among individuals of every species to enter into contact with one another. This urge for contact and the mutual and purposeful activity resulting from it are part of the biological plan of life. It is founded on the social nature of men and animals. Contact may accordingly be defined as a relation that is biologically based, necessary, and a condition of life for individuals of the same or sometimes of different species.

We must begin with this need for contact if we wish to attain a clear picture of the origin of human and animal forms of communication. On this foundation it is possible to reconstruct the evolution of the forms of communication, inclusive of language; a task which for lack of a suitable guiding principle has never previously been attempted.

(C) CONTACT AND ITS FORMS

If there is a danger of extending the concept of language to phenomena that do not possess its essential criteria, the danger is all the greater of identifying the concept of contact with forms of communication that are actually far in advance of it. A need to establish merely spatial contact with other living beings can be most easily defined by comparing it with related needs.

We employ the term contact in its narrower sense to mean the need for a simple approach, a coming into touch, without communicative intent. In its wider sense contact is the need for connexion of any kind in so far as it serves mutual interest, including the forms of communication distinguished by communicative intent.

The introduction of the concepts of *contact* and *communication* is a great gain from the psychological and evolutionary points of view, since their empirical scope embraces manifestations that were heretofore either not observed or were regarded as independent of one another. A further advantage of these concepts is that they include animal as well as human social activity giving the contact principle a general biological importance going far beyond human life.

The antecedent stages of contact include the most primitive forms of common life, the 'colonies' or communities of individuals produced by asexual multiplication and remaining in association, as in protozoa and in fungi, coelenterata and worms. Since the formation of the communities is simply due to germination from the common ancestor it cannot be regarded as the effect of an instinctive need. These animal communities can therefore be omitted from the ranks of social organizations whose origin is attributable to the need for contact. Only when the formation of communities is the sole means of enabling or facilitating the fulfilment of particular biological aims of its members can we say that the individual organisms come into contact for the fulfilment of those purposes. In the earliest stage

K

the need that welds together such contact formations is purely instinctive; and since it exclusively serves biological requirements it can be called a vital need for contact.

The forms of communities arising from this vital need for contact include groupings of animals for the sole purpose of affording greater safety to the individuals against the threat of danger. The need for common safety is very closely connected with the need for contact. For as soon as an individual is isolated from such a community it immediately feels insecure and uneasy; most stimuli appearing within its range of perception, such as noises, scents and movements, cause panicky reactions of terror and flight, ceasing only when the animal rejoins its group. Within the group the individual beasts bunch together more closely when danger appears, and they endeavour to offer resistance to the danger or to escape-from it by massing together. This is observable on innumerable occasions among chickens, flocks of sheep and groups of seagulls, pelicans, swallows, etc.

Many reactions appearing objectively as attempts to achieve safety, such as the crowding together of chicks under the wings of the brood hen, arise often enough from a need for contact that is satisfied merely by proximity. The fact that tame animals try to come into contact with people is evident to all who are acquainted with their habits and ways of life.

The merely biological need for contact also plays a part in all other instinctively based group formations having the immediate purpose of acquiring food, sexual activity, or play. Social groupings formed for the purposes of swarming, migration, feeding, sleep, hibernation, breeding and similar transitory or permanent associations are full of this need for contact.

The vital needs on which simple contact is based are directed by biologically determined instinctive mechanisms which are only to a limited extent modified by individual experience. In these cases the focusing of need and instinct on particular goals and the adoption of the means necessary to attain these goals is governed entirely by instinct, without the participation of consciousness or volition. The seeking out of other members of the species and their assembling in one place results from the instinctive direction of the individual animals and the group, without any deliberate intention.

In the main three basic drives are behind this association, namely, for food, sex and defence. These basic drives lead to the formation of animal societies, whose members belong to one or several species, as is the case with breeding and herding societies.

It is not difficult to find analogous cases in human society. The most convincing example of this kind of contact is given by the search for human fellowship in situations of danger. The individuals need not know or expect anything of one another, nor need they enter into mutual relationships; nevertheless their behaviour produces a sense of belonging together and of collective security. To this category belong those cases where a person associates with others to save himself from a sense of threatening isolation.

This 'herd instinct' is a pre-condition for the collective processes which can be observed during mass movements such as folk migration, unification of nomadic peoples, and colonization. Even the lone wolf who because of unhappy experiences is careful to avoid too close contact with man in the mass will at least attempt to establish contact with a domestic animal to keep himself from absolute loneliness.

But only in limited circumstances is this need for contact satisfied by merely spatial contact. The more the instinctive life of the person is overlaid by intentionally directed emotional experiences the more likely will the inclination for spatial contact deepen into a desire for emotional contact. Such emotional contact does not have the purpose of establishing intellectual communication. Its intention is neither to communicate nor to induce the partner to particular actions, but simply to find assurance of the emotional proximity of the other person:

> *Es ist so schön, zu zweit zu gehn und nichts zu sagen,*
> *Ganz einfach nur sich zu verstehn und nichts zu fragen.*

The contact goes deeper when the emotional relationship aims at the transfer of feeling. Emotional contact nearly always includes an intentional act, the act of understanding, of sympathy, of empathy with the other person; but at the same time the intention to transfer one's own state of mind and will aiming at the creation of an inter-individual connexion on an emotional basis. Emotional contact may occasionally arise even among strangers. They need not talk to each other, they need not even understand each other's language, and yet looks, gestures and expressive sounds may produce emotional contact between them. These individuals do not form a social unit or become carriers of intentions or purposes. What arises is rather a direct emotional relationship between persons or between person and group which can exercise a decisive effect on total behaviour. Relations within the group may vary noticeably but unspoken emotional contact remains their basis.

Since the emotional exchange must be mutual, emotional contact in the strict sense cannot be established with babies. The belief that there can be emotional contact with children who cannot yet talk, whom we touch or fondle, to whom we call out articulate or inarticulate sounds, is based mostly on an illusion. All that happens is that we attribute our own emotional reactions to the behaviour of the child. Very soon, before the child is a year old, spontaneous expressions and reactions pointing to the existence of emotional contact make their appearance. This is most clearly evident when the child plays with grown-ups. If the baby is able to distinguish between play and serious behaviour and interpret any given action (pushing, pressing, hitting, threatening gestures, etc.) according to the situation and the mimic expression of the adult, then there is no doubt that emotional contact has been established between the child and his surroundings. The objective data remain the same in both cases; nevertheless the child can, as a result of his close observation of delicate expressive gestures and sounds of the adults, correctly interpret the situation. If the situation suddenly changes, as for instance in the transition from playful to serious behaviour, he can even change his own behaviour accordingly.

These considerations call attention to the problem of whether it is in general justifiable to deny the existence of emotional contact among animals. Animal lovers and ornithologists who have the opportunity of observing animals over many years and of studying their reactions under different conditions adopt a positive attitude on this question. There is no doubt that great caution and reserve are necessary in the interpretation of animal behaviour, so as not to see in certain modes of expression signs of emotional impulses as if in answer to our approaches, without a thorough examination of the situation.

On the other hand, it must not be overlooked that with certain highly organized animals that live in family groups, one easily gets the impression that in their behaviour toward their fellows and offspring there is an emotional resonance or echo. In particular this impression is felt when watching young animals such as dogs, cats or apes playing together. The whole drama cannot be explained simply on the basis of a need for contact, because the manifold and often surprising reactions of the animals are often perfectly attuned to one another, behaviour which is inexplicable in terms of any mechanistic or reflex theory. It must be added that playful activity is not necessarily one of the essential needs of the animal (play is not so universal in the animal kingdom that one could take it as a biological necessity, as do the biological theories of play). Still less can we emancipate ourselves from this impression of emotional contact when we watch humans play with domesticated animals. How the domestic dog can distinguish between playful and serious behaviour; how it one moment answers a blow with a counterblow and in the next moment, noticing that the play is finished, reacts to the same blow with flight, is difficult to explain if one simply denies the existence of emotional contact among animals.[1] There are however facts which do not favour such an assumption.

[1] During my prolonged experiments with anthropoid apes I could not, however, convince myself that a play situation between young chimpanzees, orang-outans and gorillas and humans is possible. Every student of animal life knows how carefully one must treat young anthropoids and watch their movements in order to avoid painful surprise. Their sudden attacks on the warder rather point to the fact that they do not understand our movements and mimic expressions, which can be supported by the fact that play with adult anthropoids is practically impossible.

Emotional contact involves a *transference* of feeling, and not a sort of emotional contagion. If it were only the latter we could not deny the existence of emotional contact in domesticated animals, and in particular in dogs. When an adequate response is expected there is an intentional transference of feelings and when a response is lacking the establishment of contact is attempted in a different way, but it can hardly be assumed that animals participate in this contact. The same probably also applies to very small babies and to the majority of the insane. These are all occasionally able to react to our emotional expressions, but this does not require emotional response. The increase of emotional activity in the animal and the infant does not appear to create the conditions which would be adequate for the origin of emotional contact.

Sympathy and antipathy are based on the presence or absence of emotional contact, which is able to establish immediate relations between people without basing itself on previous experience. In such cases we have the impression as if an emanation from our partner were overwhelming us with irresistible force and were returning back from us to him. We do not question or reason, we only listen to the voice of the heart which arouses sympathetic vibrations. Through a kind of emotional exchange the personality of the partner is immediately comprehended. Genuine love and genuine friendship are based on this emotional communion. It forms the basis of that first impression which our intuition forms of a person. This explains why it is so difficult for us to free ourselves from the effects of a first impression, to correct the emotional echo by means of rational arguments.

On the other hand, emotional contact need not be based on sympathy, although in every case we are dealing with empathy into another ego. Even when we are facing an enemy we value emotional contact, in order thereby to understand the behaviour and intentions of the opponent and take the necessary countermeasures.

Collective emotional contact is not tied to a given numerical size of the group. It is true that mostly it appears within a numerically limited closed social structure but in certain circumstances it can also appear in a moving crowd. This can be observed at popular festivals, carnivals and similar social occasions when the reserved attitude of the individual is broken down by the heightened emotional state of the group. Within the framework of the heterogeneous group an atmosphere develops which owes its origin to emotional contact.

Vital and emotional contact can be established only by means which are perceptible to the senses. The biological urge for physical contact can obviously only be satisfied by the performance of bodily movements yielding direct contact between the individuals. Such movements are executed by us, for example in an emergency, when we instinctively draw into close physical contact with others; an expressive action which presumably is exceeded in intensity only by the sexual act. Although it may be true that in the movements of sexual activity the biological urge for contact predominates, yet it cannot be overlooked that they always spring from an urge for emotional contact as well as from a purely sexual drive, and this applies in a greater degree to movements which, as in the friendly handshake, there is no sexual element. But the emotional urge aims at indirect as well as direct contact; and the means which it uses for this purpose are actions such as of the hand or the hat, yodelling, etc. These are finally sublimated in the formal greeting, which can dispense with any kind of physical contact. Indeed, one need only compare the handshake of two lovers with the handshake exchanged with a mere acquaintance in order to recognize that this process of sublimation can be taken further and that a movement originally aiming at the establishment of direct contact can be formalized into a mere symbol, indicating no more than the respect of one person for the other, thereby divorcing the gesture from its original purpose.

This comparison likewise makes it clear that the 'contact reaction' (as we can now call it without risk of misunderstanding) assumes a characteristic intermediate position between expressive and communicative signs. It has in common with the purely expressive gesture the expression of subjective experience, i.e. the need for contact of the person who performs it. It is differentiated from it by being an act that is not carried out involuntarily, but with the intention of establishing contact with others. (As soon, for example, as the baby uses his smile, not only as the expression of a comfortable mood as at first, but to establish contact with his surroundings, then the mere expressive gesture has become a contact gesture.) If the contact reaction has in common with the communicative sign the intention, it differs from it by the fact that its intention is merely that of establishing emotional contact with other living beings, and not understanding. When the contact reaction assumes an interrogative or indicative function, as it does especially in forms of salutation, which are mainly based on contact reactions, then it has undergone an essential change in its significance.

Just as man all too often undertakes to identify the nature of objects and processes by reference to their purpose, so has sociology believed that the nature of communities could be established solely by classification of the practical purposes which consciously or unconsciously determine their behaviour at their formation. Examples of such aims going beyond the actual formation of a community and requiring an organized collaboration of its members for their realization, have already been met with above when we sought to differentiate the contact urge from other social needs. As opposed to these, the contact urge aims at the establishment of a community as an end in itself, and thus does not require for its satisfaction the *co-operation* of members of the community, but merely their *co-existence*. Since such a community has no immediate practical effects it has been completely neglected by sociologists. While the dictum *operari sequitur esse* is universally valid, communities capable of realizing their purpose or aim only through the collaboration of their members can arise only after the individuals have been unified in a community by the simple need of being together. If on the other hand reciprocal understanding is the basis of all co-operation, mere contact cannot be an early stage of communication: it does not induce the individuals to communicate with one another, but simply to come into mutual contact. The need for contact is therefore completely satisfied as soon as an emotional exchange takes place.

Contact reactions therefore also have a significance different from that of signs, which serve the communicative impulse. Unlike signs, contact reactions do not point beyond themselves, but simply provide expression for the contact urge. They are thus only a precondition of linguistic communication.

To ask, therefore, whether psychical contact can be regarded as an antecedent stage of language is to put the question wrongly. It is quite a different matter if one asks whether language would have been possible at all without psychical contact. The answer to this must be in the negative; for it is altogether impossible to suppose a need for linguistic contact without a previous emotional relationship; impossible to suppose that the need for linguistic contact could have arisen without the earlier existence of inter-individual relationships on an emotional basis. Man without sympathetic empathy, without comprehension of the experiences of others, is just as contradictory a concept as man without speech. It is difficult to imagine a conversation without emotional contact. If the inner connexions between man and man are lacking, an exchange of ideas based on mutual comprehension is impossible. One may even say that the purely non-linguistic emotional contact which arises between people who speak different languages is not altogether outside the sphere of the linguistic function. Both partners carry on a 'monologue', silently, speechlessly, each in his own language, and this silent speech, transferred through empathy and understanding, is experienced and divined by both. During this soundless and wordless contact the linguistic stage is in preparation, and in many cases it may even be activated. The inward dispositions of the person, the concepts that are forming, radiate emotional force in a way that is perceptible to the senses, putting one of the contact-seekers under the influence of the other, the more active one.

We therefore conclude that the speech act is only possible when personal rapport or emotional contact exists between persons capable of speech. When people having a common language are unable to understand one another, the cause is not the inadequacy of the language medium, but the absence of that emotional link or spiritual bond which when it exists enables the speakers by groping and probing to guess and grasp each other's meaning.

The human contact reactions and expressions which we have discussed here represent an important part of *semasiology*. They embrace an area of human behaviour to which no attention has hitherto been paid. This is explained by the fact that human contact has always been studied exclusively from the linguistic point of view, resulting in unintentional neglect of expressions and effects based on the urge for proximity and not on the communicative urge. But in considering language as a special form of contact we have had 'to take notice of non-linguistic emotional contact and from this it was natural to recognize its significance for *semasiology*.

The communicative urge is in the last analysis a striving for *intellectual contact*. Just as emotional contact stimulates an emotional echo, so intellectual contact gives rise to a link of an intellectual nature. Here it is not simply a matter of personal relationships, as with emotional contact, but of a relationship that is essentially super-personal, of individual minds whose content is handed down collectively. It is true that we address ourselves to an individual intending to establish intellectual contact with him; but this invariably occurs in respect to a sphere developed overwhelmingly in independence of the individual and therefore far transcending the single person. We address an individual mind that has been formed in the intellectual community of a more or less uniform group (linguistic or ethnic community, nation, community of ideas or moral standards, philosophy of life, etc.) received and adopted by the individual. In this way the supra-individual attainments of the human communality become the basis of intellectual contact among men and thereby define the collective mind.[1] Among the manifestations of the collective

---

[1] The concept of the objective mind which Hegel introduced into philosophy but obscured by vague speculations (*Phänomenologie des Geistes*, 1817) was most successfully dealt with by Nicolai Hartmann, who made it usable in the philosophical sciences. (*Das Problem des geistigen Seins*, 1933). Noteworthy contributions to this problem were made by K. Mannheim in his *Ideologie und Utopie* (1930).

mind are, in the first place, language, and with it the immanent spirit of spoken language; and also custom, law, morals, religion, education, art, science, and technology—manifestations that all find expression in varying degrees in the intellectual sphere of the persons establishing contact with one another. The immediate clarity and comprehensibility of living language owes its existence to the collective mind which is handed on by individuals and groups and is continually developed by them. It is the intellectual heritage of past generations which every individual, thanks to his innate intellectual potentiality and activity, takes over, and transmits when he learns his language, and this is a spiritual heritage which forms the basic pre-condition of collective intellectual work and therefore of mutual understanding.

Emotional contact serves the transfer of emotion, and intellectual contact, the transmission and exchange of thought. The goal of intellectual contact is understanding in relation to all intellectual, social and moral life, bound up with reciprocal communication and influence. Intellectual contact is the basis of the apprehension and comprehension of ideas, opinions and intentions of others. Everything that we have inherited from our forebears, justice, religion, morality, scientific and technical knowledge, intellectual orientation and principles of conduct, and equally everything that we learn from our contemporaries; in short, everything of transitory importance or of lasting and inestimable human value, has been won through the medium of intellectual contact.

Intellectual contact presupposes language. That many speech situations take place without intellectual contact (commands, everyday questions and statements) does not contradict this proposition. For it is not a question of demonstrating the existence of intellectual contact in every concrete case, but of the general existence and functioning of intellectual contact in relation to speech. One thing is certain: a human being who has never entered into intellectual contact with others cannot understand language, the intellectual means of communication and influence. This probably also applies phylogenetically: language could come into being only after the pre-conditions for emotional and intellectual contact were present among the members of primitive society.

The properties of contact reactions here discussed will appear more clearly as we turn next to the task of tracing the development of phonetic communicative signs from their antecedent stage through their early forms to the fully developed state.

VIII

THE DEVELOPMENT OF
PHONETIC FORMS
OF COMMUNICATION

In tracing the development of phonetic forms of communication in the following pages, the concept of development as it is used here is to be understood in a *logical* rather than a *historical* sense. We can therefore leave open the question whether the individual links in the evolutionary chain did actually take place in the sequence indicated, although, as we shall see, there is a good deal to be said in favour of this assumption. What matters is that each link in the assumed evolutionary chain is differentiated by an essential characteristic from the previous one, so that the means of communication are perfected progressively and by distinct stages. What matters here is not how the development actually took place, for we have no historical evidence, but how it could have taken place. It is still an open question *how one should conceive the changes which led to the development of language.* It should be noted that in accordance with the view, put forward above (on p. 50) concerning the precedence of the phonetic as opposed to the gestural elements, the origin and development of language will be described exclusively in terms of phonetic speech. The restriction to phonetic language is all the more justifiable because man can attain a fully developed language only by means of the transformation and development of speech sounds, while gestures —with some few exceptions—can only be considered as auxiliary elements which accompany and support language.

(A) EXPRESSION AND COMMUNICATION

Our discussion of the theories of expression (p. 20 ff.) renders it unnecessary to support with further argument the view that purely expressive sounds have no communicative significance. They are not produced to influence fellow members of the species, but exclusively as an outlet for emotional excitement and tension. Consequently the sounds merely represent a reflex process providing a definite emotional content characteristic of all expressive phenomena. The expressive sound is produced not only without communicative intent, but without any intention or tendency to interpersonal or collective contact. If the same sounds or gestures are later on produced with a conscious purpose as in the case of interjections, they are thereby transformed into a means of communication, or at least of intended contact. If expressive sounds do occasionally evoke an appropriate response in individuals belonging to the same or different species, it happens in spite of their involuntary and reflex character. Superficially this situation resembles communication; but the sound is produced without communicative intent and does not have for the hearer a symbolic significance learned by experience. Thus the instinctive cries of a frightened animal put the herd to flight, and the shrill screams and excited movements of startled birds incite the others to fly away or to greater watchfulness; migrating birds cry when they are frightened, as do cranes when their fellows pass them by in flight. Troops of monkeys fill the air with chaotic howling, without any demonstrable communicative aim. It is true that there are numerous animal cries which have at least the function of holding the herd together (contact sounds), but just as frequently we come across cases where such an interpretation cannot apply. The absence in purely expressive sounds of any intent of contact or communication is demonstrated by the fact that animals produce sounds without the expectation of any reaction on the part of others. Indeed, animals are frequently induced to perform superfluous and inappropriate, or occasionally even dangerous actions by sounds, regardless of whether these sounds come from their fellows or enemies or from inanimate nature. One must not forget that the prelingual child also produces a number of sounds (crying, snorting, yawning, coughing, sighing) which express nothing but his emotional state. Interjections themselves were originally mere expressive sounds, and acquired their communicative function only upon being adopted into language.

We particularly emphasize this interpretation of expressive sounds because it is precisely these sounds that zoologists and animal lovers wish to adduce as convincing examples of directed signals. Whenever 'animal languages' are discussed, these sounds are brought up as examples of communicative intent. A communicative significance is ascribed to each sound uttered by the animal because, from a human point of view, it is thought unlikely that living beings would produce sounds without the intention of making contact. The following example is very instructive. It was observed among subterranean bumble-bees that a bee stations itself at the entrance to the nest in the early morning, before the swarm starts its daily labour, and produces a loud noise with its wings. The explanation came readily to hand that the bee does duty as a sort of night watchman, and awakens its fellows from their sleep to signal the beginning of work. Later on it became clear that this behaviour of the so-called 'trumpeters' was in no sense signalling, but is induced solely by the instinctive need to supply fresh air to the nest.[1] It follows that expressive sounds are not functionally related to utterances serving a communicative purpose. Nor can they be linked, as is occasionally suggested, by their use of a common medium—that is, sound. Calls are necessarily associated with sound, for the simple reason that by nature their medium cannot be anything else; the phonetic relationship is therefore based on a biological necessity. This does not, however, mean that expressive sounds played no part at all in the origin of the original communicative sounds. The fact that communicative call sounds are, in essence, like

[1] Brehms, *Tierleben*, II (1915), p. 604. Cf. G. Kafka, *Tierpsychologie* (1914), p. 203.

expressive sounds, emotionally based reactions to subjective experiences, allows us to regard purely expressive sounds as a material precondition of contact sounds and the communicative cries.

(B) CONTACT SOUNDS

The interpretation of animal sounds has been rendered difficult by the fact that in approaching them with a classification borrowed from human psychology, one seemed to be faced with the alternatives of considering them as the involuntary expression of a state of inner excitement or of attributing a communicative intent to them. The fact that there are no reliable external criteria by which one could choose between these alternatives explains the great diversity of explanations which have been offered by various investigators. In general the tendency has been to ascribe comparatively far-reaching communicative intention to animals. That many of these interpretations cannot withstand sober criticism is due mainly to the neglect of the possibility that animal sounds, though they may be intentional, are nevertheless not produced for the purpose of understanding but simply for contact. Once one has become aware that human beings may raise their voices not only to give expression to their emotions or to communicate with their fellows but sometimes only for the purpose of establishing contact with their fellows by vocal utterances or physical gestures, many animal sounds seem to acquire a quite different significance.

It is because of the primitive nature of the biological need for contact that it has remained unknown to laboratory psychology for so long a time. Its character is so primitive that it is quite impossible to provide an altogether adequate linguistic formulation of the contact urge. Seen from the outside, the contact reaction appears to say, 'Here I am. I am getting in touch with you.' But when we express the attitude on which it is based in these words, we are adding to it two functions which transcend the realm of pure contact: a kind of communication, and a spatial reference, which—as we shall see later—ought only to be attributed to true media of communication.

Naturally it is impossible to decide on the basis of external evidence whether an animal utterance is to be interpreted as an expressive sound or a contact sound. But it is difficult to imagine that the comparatively rich register of sounds at the disposal of animals capable of voice production should be designed exclusively for the expression of their emotional state and not for the establishment of contact with their fellows. This applies in particular to the social noise as the expression of a communal feeling which we observe in crows and sparrows. It applies equally to bird songs, the humming of bees, the chirping of chicks, the purring of cats; in short, to many phonetic utterances of a variety of animals that live in groups. Thus the howling of wolves on the hunt may possess a contact function, which is yet absent from the growling of the bear, the chirping of the cricket, and the neighing and whinny of horses. The imitative sounds of tame mocking-birds and parrots are not entirely without contact-intent. The same may be said of the phonetic reactions of dogs on the appearance of strange people or animals, but it does not apply to the phonetic reactions of dogs to the barking of their fellow dogs, or to the crowing of a cockerel in answer to the crowing sounds of a neighbouring cockerel. For these latter cases are examples of reflex reactions, mere expressive sounds like those of children who begin to scream as soon as they hear their playmates screaming.

It is especially unlikely that an animal would express its sexual drives by means of sounds, gestures and postures without the purpose of establishing contact with its sexual partner. Although the playing and love-calls of the male are an effect of the sexual urge, they serve at the same time to establish that sexual contact toward which the sexual urge is directed, and they are therefore suited to evoking in the female, by means of 'emotional infection', a similar state of sexual excitement. Such love-calls, although they are no longer mere expressive sounds, are not yet contact sounds, because they do not have the signal function. Only when the male learns in the course of development that at the sound of the love-call the desired female appears, or makes herself evident in some way, can the love-call acquire the function of a signal. It thereby becomes a mating-call directed to the female, which no longer merely expresses the sexual distress of the male and its need for sexual contact, but at the same time addresses a more or less outspoken request to the female and in this way establishes a kind of 'communication' between them (p. 158).

A more sceptical approach seems to be required with the so-called warning cries, which might very well be directly attributed to a biologically based 'Urtendenz'.[1] Without a thorough examination of individual cases one cannot assume that warning cries are produced for the purpose of intercommunication: i.e. uttered by one individual as an alarm signal and understood as such by another individual. The warning cry seems rather to produce a shared emotional situation which has certain of the characteristics of biological contact, and to that extent appears to have a wider significance than the pure expressive sign. The phenomenon of panic among groups of people is to be evaluated in the same way. The emission of cries of fright or even the silent performance of a corresponding gesture is not meant as a warning signal; but its effect is the same because it produces direct biological contact among those present by a sort of emotional infection.

The communal life of highly organized insect societies is also probably based in essence on contact reactions. The need to establish biological contact is certainly recognizable in the trilling of ants. But even the 'round-dance' of the bees returning home with a heavy load of honey clearly displays the character of a contact reaction;[2] and although the state of satisfaction may provide a stimulus for the 'round-dance' of the scouts, it might yet at the same time be governed by the need for a specific form of contact, and the emotional infection which is produced by this contact with the bees in the hive might in turn induce them to fly out.

[1] G. Kafka, 'Verstehende Psychologie und Psychologie des Verstehens', *Zeitschr. f. Psychol.*, 65 (1928).

[2] K. von Frisch, *Bees, Their Vision, Chemical Senses, and Language* (1950).

The question whether the trilling of the ants with their antennae, the dance of the bees, or the leaving of a track of scent by animals really represents more than a contact sign is difficult to decide, since we are unable to form a proper picture of the mutual relations of the individuals and of their social needs, and therefore of the purpose of their utterances.[1] We are dealing here with animals so far removed from us in their behaviour and mode of life that we possess no reliable basis for an unambiguous interpretation of their activities.

In any case I am convinced on evolutionary grounds that a 'signal system' such as is postulated by ant and bee investigators is exceedingly doubtful. It is hard to believe that so primitively organized a creature as the ant can stimulate its nesting mates by 'feeler language' to feeding, change of nest, attack or flight, or bump its head against the breast of its mate to lend special emphasis to the message—and even continue to do so forcefully if the warning is not heeded (Escherich, Alverdes). This is certainly an attractive interpretation, but it is questionable whether it can be reconciled with their behaviour as a whole and with their almost complete incapacity for development, adaptation and learning. The widely prevalent view that organized communities are necessarily provided with means of communication is rather based on the inclination to look for means of communication in all animals, no matter how primitive they may be, and to find traces of individual motivation behind any collective activity. In research this attitude leads to misunderstanding of the nature of animal societies and of association in general as well. The existence of animal societies is based on the *collective instincts* of the individual members which are sufficient for the maintenance of the communities. Individual acts, spontaneous intervention, or special modes of communication are superfluous. That among lower animals mere contact can lead to a result that simulates communication is at once evident if one thinks of the

[1] Concerning this, see the controversy between the two well-known students of ant life, Wasmann (*Studien über das Seelenleben der Ameisen*, 1900) and Escherich (*Die Ameise*, 1917).

process transposed into human relationships. If after a long walk we see a group of men emerge from a valley looking completely refreshed, the mere encounter can lead us to discover a refreshing pool in the valley. We have been told nothing by the group nor have we been induced to any action; our conduct is the result of the simple contact reaction to which we have limited ourselves.

The transition from expressive sound to contact reaction may be followed with particular clarity in the human child. In the first period of the child's development he cries only when he feels unwell or uncomfortable. The child does not 'communicate' his condition to his surroundings and does not ask any one to come to his aid; at first he does not distinguish himself from his environment. Only when he begins in some way to feel separate from his surroundings does he acquire the need of entering into connexion with it. Naturally this connexion is not at first communicative but exclusively in the form of contact.

There are as yet no systematic observations on the phonetic contact reactions of adult human beings. In any case it is certain that phonetic utterances serving the purpose of mutual communication are logically, and most probably also genetically, preceded by phonetic utterances based solely on the need for vital contact. These utterances go beyond mere expressive sounds, in that they are produced deliberately and not involuntarily; but to the extent that they convey only the need for contact they are less advanced than phonetic utterances produced for the purpose of understanding. They can therefore be regarded as the antecedent stage of communication in general, but not of language.

(C) THE FORMS OF COMMUNICATION AND THE TRISTADIAL THEORY

Whilst the simple contact reaction aims only at the establishment of rapport by means of sound or gesture, there are situations in which man or animal seeks the assistance or co-operation of his fellows, and tries to communicate this by suitable means. In these cases a true communication arises between the two parties for the purpose of mutual influence. The contact sound is transformed into a directed call, and thereby acquires the function of a signal.

In principle all perceptible sensory stimuli, such as auditory, visual, tactile and olfactory ones, can serve as means of communication. Experience shows us that human beings as well as animals make principal use of stimuli which are acoustically perceptible; optical stimuli are used less often and tactile stimuli still less frequently. It has not yet been proved with certainty that olfactory signals exist in the animal kingdom, but this possibility cannot altogether be excluded if one takes into consideration the effect of the secretions of females when they are in heat and the track of scent left behind by certain mammals. Only phonetic and motor signals are of interest to us here since only these can have played a part in the genesis of language.

The difference between contact sounds and communicative calls is unmistakable. The communicative call is based on the need to communicate something to a visible or invisible partner. Call sounds are differentiated according to the impulse to be communicated. This differentiation manifests itself in special acoustic or motor characteristics which are not found in contact sounds. Furthermore, the call is especially characterized by a sense of expectation. The animal expects something, is attuned to something which is to come, to a result. The animal remains in a state of tension until the reaction follows or until its attention is diverted. If one can speak at all of anticipation of the future among animals it seems to lie in this very sense of expectation. Finally, communicative calls possess an imperative character, which is expressed in aggressive sounds constantly repeated and in excited gestures. The directedness, the imperative intent, and the sense of expectation give the call its specific signal character and thereby its pragmatic significance.

How far down in the animal kingdom communicative sounds may be found is a question which can be answered only by an animal psychology that has grasped the difference between purely expressive, contact and communicative forms, and has studied animal reactions from this point of view. Enough emerges from what has been said to suggest that a large part of the phonetic utterances which until now were considered as means of communication really belong to the expressive sounds or contact reactions. This much is however certain: that animals not only use phonetic utterances to express their emotional state and to establish contact but are able to 'communicate' with their fellows and even with man. From the outside it would naturally be difficult to decide whether a sound is really more than the expression of an affective state or of the mere need for contact; the total situation does however provide indications which in concrete cases usually make it possible to arrive at a decision. Among the communicative calls two kinds may be distinguished. They are the *wordless cry* and the *directed call*, which are next to the most highly developed form of communication, the word.

I. THE CRY

The cry is an instinctive unarticulated phonetic utterance directed to a more or less definite group, and has the tendency to give effect to a desire.[1] It is still unconcentrated and vague; but it is already *directed*. It does not aim at contact with definite individuals; it is merely an endeavour to induce the environment or more generally speaking the external world, to co-operate by performing some appropriate action. To be even more cautious we must say that a sound-producing animal takes refuge in the cry when it expects the satisfaction of its needs from the outside. It gets ready for a change in the situation by which it 'hopes for' the removal of the present tension, the disappearance of the momentary state of dissatisfaction. The communicative tendency is expressed in the fact that the animal as it were senses the proximity of a creature that can free it from its state of need.

Animal psychology provides us with numerous examples of this primitive form of communication, in solitary animals as well as in animal societies. Here one can point firstly to mating calls; and then to the cries of young nestlings when in danger and the cries of the mother animal calling her young.

[1] German, *Zuruf*; French, *cri*; Italian, *chiamata*; Dutch, *uitroep*.

Sexual mating calls are probably general among mammals and birds, and are said to be widespread even among certain insect species. Thus it is reported that the male grasshopper and cricket attract the female by means of chirping sounds, and the latter are said to react phonetically to these mating calls. To the category of cries also belong certain sounds of domestic animals when, impelled by hunger, fear or cold, they expectantly post themselves outside the door and express their needs by means of specific and definite sounds. To this category also belong motor signals such as the pairing postures and the graceful 'dances' and other wooing movements of birds. The family tie furthers the use of cries, since the welfare of the needy members of the family engages the entire interest of the parents. Even in the family group true mating calls are not clearly individualized, although they refer exclusively to members of the family.

The interpretation of animal cries requires extreme caution. It is not always easy to decide whether an animal's phonetic reaction originally possesses a communicative tendency, whether it is meant to convey something to another member of the same species. Animal psychologists have mostly failed to examine concrete examples in a way that would make clear whether certain emotional phonetic utterances really represent a signal aimed at turning a fellow away from danger and inducing a flight reaction or whether they are merely expressive sounds. In my view the animal has no intention of notifying his fellows that danger is approaching: the sound merely represents an expression of its own frightened state, which instinctively produces terror in the others and consequently leads to a flight reaction. If one has once had the opportunity of observing the whole drama of a herd set in motion by a cry of fright one would find it extremely improbable that the sound-uttering animal has the intention of warning its fellows. Its impetuous, inconsiderate behaviour during the flight does not point to a partnership or mutual relationship.

It is well known that the simplest form of phonetic communication, the wordless cry, is not monopolized by animals, and that

babies also make use of it at the start of their linguistic development. They communicate their needs through phonetic signs taken
either from the material of their babbling sounds or from their
spontaneous emotional reactions, and thereby attempt to direct
the attention of their immediate familiar surroundings toward
themselves, without addressing particular persons. They attempt
to establish communication with their surroundings, but it is not
yet a personal communication. The best-known cry sounds are
the unarticulated affective sounds produced by the baby when it
is unexpectedly left alone. Through cries and other more
differentiated expressive sounds (nä, ä, öö, nu, mmme) and gestures the child tries to induce his environment to stay near him,
or to pay attention to or at least watch him. Although in these
cases the cry sounds are produced without communicative intent
their communicative character is beyond doubt.

Phonetic utterances occasionally observed among adults which
are not directed to definite persons also belong to the wordless
form of communication which has been described, to the extent
that they resemble the unarticulated and spontaneous cries of
children and animals. Such utterances occur among civilized
peoples only under special circumstances; but we meet them
very frequently among primitives. As is well known the latter
when emotionally aroused often make spontaneous cries which
are clearly distinguishable from their conventionalized cries.
Among them it would be possible to trace out the whole range
of cries from the inarticulate cry to the call-like word. The
normal cries of people capable of speech necessarily follow speech
sounds. They are mostly articulated and phonematically differentiated, and are therefore of no concern for our genetic problem.
We may mention as examples cries from a distance and cries for
help, signal cries in mountains and at sea, and the great variety
of cries at work.

It should be mentioned here that cries with a warning and imperative purpose may also be made purely by motor mechanisms,
that is, by hand and arm movements.

2. THE CALL

Superficially one may see little or no difference between the wordless cry and the call;[1] especially as the instinctive aim and the means of communication are identical in both cases They both represent instinctive phonetic and motor utterances; both seem to induce fellow members of the species to actions serving a particular purpose. But if one observes the modes of behaviour of the individuals more closely, particularly those of animals and children before they have acquired speech and have only these two forms of communication at their disposal, the difference between the two appears clearly: even if there are cases where it is difficult to decide to which of the two wordless forms of communication they belong.

One may attribute this specific mode of behaviour to a special function, the calling function, based on the ability *to direct significant signs to particular persons by means of a wordless indication of the desired aim.* The most obvious difference between cry and call is thus the individual reference of the latter. The call is unequivocally addressed to definite individuals; while the cry, in spite of its directed character, is merely directed at the environment from which satisfaction of one's needs is expected.[2]

The call, because of its character of 'address', requires the immediate accessibility, the sensible presence of the partner. It is therefore uttered only when the recipient of the communication is within sight or sound of the communication. The dog turns toward the person from whom it expects something; the baby likewise addresses a call to the mother when she is in the immediate vicinity; the initially diffuse movement is transformed into a direct address. In contrast, a mating or warning cry can be sounded when the desired creature is outside the field of perception of the communicator.

[1] German, *Anruf*; French, *appel*; Italian, *invocazione*; Dutch, *roep*.

[2] It is useful to make a distinction between directing and addressing. We use addressing to mean a demand or communication directed to a definite individual. According to this terminology the cry is directed, while the call is addressed.

A further difference lies in the pronounced imperative character of the call. This imperative element appears unmistakably and with special emphasis in a distinctive kind of sound complex in association with characteristic motor reactions, and in the obstinacy with which animals and babies demand the satisfaction of their desires. The imperative character of the call is so pronounced that one might be inclined to describe these phonetic utterances with the word language. But this term must be avoided, so as not to give rise to false interpretations. For if one refers to the phonetic signals of animals as 'language' then one is easily tempted to overlook the fundamental difference between animal calls and the early form of language and to draw from it the most untenable consequences.

Cry and call are further differentiated from each other in respect to their origin. The call is bound up with individual experience, while the cry, like other primitive contact processes, is exclusively governed by instinct. In the cry the animal is led to phonetic utterance by means of an inherited and purposefully functioning instinctive mechanism, which impels it in a particular direction, in which it senses the desired aim. With the call it is entirely different. Animals and babies must learn from their own experience which individuals to address. Dogs and cats lie calmly in their accustomed places, and do not budge until that weak person appears who they know from experience can be made to satisfy their wishes.

The place reference may be considered a further essential difference between cry and call. By a glance or gesture the animal indicates the place, the object and the person it is addressing. It is not satisfied simply with uttering a call, but supplies place references for the sake of more clearly defining its desires. It follows, therefore, that the call includes, along with the imperative invitation to an action, a locative indication of aim; the cry contains only the first of these characteristics in rudimentary form, and lacks the second altogether.

The whole process of the wordless call can be demonstrated most easily in the behaviour of domestic animals towards man.

One observes frequently that domestic animals spontaneously express their desires to certain persons of their environment by perceptible indications of desired aims. It is well known that cats and dogs indicate their desire to leave the room by placing themselves in front of the door and turning their heads toward a familiar person, and usually producing a characteristic sound. It also frequently happens that dogs approach us directly and as it were force us to follow them by sounds and movements and even by using their paws. It is not easy to shake them off; they repeat their summons obstinately until we yield.[1] The same may be observed in cats. When driven by hunger and thirst, they begin to mew, they stroke our legs with their heads, they look up at us with erect tail, they virtually drag us along with them to the empty drinking bowl in the clear expectation that it will be filled. I have also frequently observed anthropoids such as young gorillas and chimpanzees extending their arms in the direction of an approaching warder, inviting him to stroke them.

Even if the animal thus indicates, in the simplest possible fashion, the two factors from whose interaction it expects the desired result, yet it only turns toward its goal, but never *points* toward it; not even when it possesses hands, as in the case of monkeys. This is only what is to be expected since pointing (as has already been explained) is a form of the speech function, which animals simply lack.[2]

Calling sounds have been observed only among dogs, cats and apes, but they doubtless also occur among other domesticated animals. I do not know whether calls are also used by animals living outside human society. In any case we have been unable to identify them with certainty in our observations in the zoo and in natural surroundings. On the other hand, reliable observers of animals have assured us that they have on occasion noticed call sounds among other mammals and birds. But since the various

[1] One of my Javanese students who kept a monkey in his house in Celebes told me that it behaved very much like our intelligent domestic dogs in similar circumstances.

[2] If a monkey is trained to refrain from grasping as soon as its hand comes close to the object of its choice, this inhibited movement can easily create the impression of pointing. Cf. N. Kohts, *Untersuchung über die Erkenntnisfähigkeit des Schimpansen*, (Moscow, 1923).

contact sounds are mingled together in these animals it was not possible to provide pure examples of calls. Threatening calls and mating calls are said to lead to directed calls; if a strange male or a desired female appears as a result of threatening or mating calls, the phonetic character of the cry is modified and is addressed directly to the individuals who have thus appeared. To the extent that such a change takes place, we are justified in considering these utterances as the most primitive form of the call.

Beyond the imperative and locative function of the wordless summoning action, one could—with, however, considerable reserve—speak of a vocative component of the call. When a dog looks at the person he is addressing, at the same time uttering a specific sound, and then directs his steps towards the door, these actions represent the imperative and locative components of the summoning act. If at the same time the animal produces a special sound which is undeniably addressed to the person concerned, and also, for instance, puts its paws on the person's arm, then this pronounced address behaviour could be interpreted as vocative.

Careful as one has to be in the interpretation of these utterances, one will have to admit that we are dealing with some kind of spontaneous communication, by means of which the animal tries to direct the attention of those present towards itself by some means which is comprehensible to us.

In babies we meet analogous situations when, for instance, they stretch out their arms toward their mother in order to be picked up, or, when by means of crying or gestures they indicate that they wish to be picked up or taken out of their cradle. The place reference is clearly expressed when they stretch out their arms in the direction of the desired object. This arm movement represents an intermediate form between grasping and pointing.

It is to be noticed that human beings capable of speech usually communicate their desires to domestic animals and speechless infants by similar means. If a person wishes to forbid or censure an action he makes use of expressive call sounds and gestures which have a striking similarity to the summoning actions of children and animals. In this sense the human act of non-verbal summons could represent an early form of the uninflected imperative and vocative, and also the archetype of adverbs of place.

Animal psychology does not provide a clear answer to the question of which of the two non-verbal forms of communication is the earlier. But the primitive and undifferentiated character of the cry, on the one hand, and, on the other, the fact that the call is restricted to the higher animals, prove that the cry represents the first manifestation of that functional change which leads in a direct line to the call. In addition, experience with human babies points to its genetic priority. At first the baby is incapable of associating with the help of his nurse the cry by which he expresses his displeasure. But it does not take long before the original expressive sound acquires the function of the cry, and then gradually changes into the directed call. On the other hand one could point to the fact that nestling birds, whose living conditions most closely resemble those of the human baby, behave differently; their desire for food is immediately associated with the expectation of the feeding parents. As soon as the peeping sound by means of which the nestling originally merely expressed its hunger has become a cry for food, the cry always appears to be directed to more or less definite individuals. But this cry is still not a call, which is unambiguously directed towards particular individuals; and it also lacks the other characteristics of the call mentioned above. One could also add that in cases of serious mental deficiency cries at best occur; in less severe cases, however, clearly recognizable calls are identifiable. From these observations one cannot, it is true, prove the temporal priority of the call but one can at least prove its more primitive nature.

It goes without saying that the richly differentiated call sounds of human speech cannot be used to determine the chronological sequence of non-verbal communicative forms, especially in view of the fact that man has all the varieties of communication at his command to use as the need arises. Thus cries of distress (as by mountain climbers or mariners in difficulties) necessarily imply awareness of the circumstances and hope of rescue, or anticipation of a desired situation. Such cries are therefore in no way more primitive than calls; for the most part they presuppose much more experience and deliberation and much more precise knowledge of the situation than calls which are uttered only in the perceptible presence of another.

The cry and the call are not simply hypothetical phases of linguistic origins; they are also communicative forms that endure. For this reason the more primitive forms of communication cannot be entirely superseded by more developed ones. If they merely represented prehistoric stages of language it would be hard to understand why they remained in use after language had assumed a more developed form.

After this discussion it is unnecessary to explain in detail the fundamental difference between non-linguistic calls and phonetic words or verbal gestures. These two means of communication have merely a correspondence phonetically, though not in phonetic form or in respect to the differentiated intentional content of the phonetic image. The difference stands out clearly in the *symbolic character* of the linguistic construction, as compared with the *signal character* of the call. The difference can be made plain by comparing the two concepts, symbol and signal.

A linguistic symbol creates a formal connexion between a sign (sound, gesture, written character) and some object of any sort. The linguistic symbol owes its representational character to transmission and adoption, to its being a convention. Naturally this does not mean that man can arbitrarily introduce phonetic constructions of any kind into language; but he does emancipate himself from natural sounds to an ever-increasing extent. He forms words out of the phonetic material at his disposal, but under the steady influence of the tendencies of his language, under the guidance of an inner linguistic sense. These words are much richer in content and much clearer than signal calls as signs of requests or information, quite apart from their ability to represent details, which signal calls cannot do because of their limited expressive capacity.

The signal, in contrast, is a non-verbal sign of a request or desire. It is mostly a direct and necessary result of a concrete situation, to which it is completely adapted. Its relationship to the reflex and spontaneously released expressive sounds and gestures lies in its directness and in its emotional and imperative character. It is directed toward an aim that is to be effected at once, and therefore no answer is expected. Because of this one-sidedness and this pronounced imperative character no signal system, no matter how complicated it may be, can produce inner contact between two persons in the sense of an exchange of thoughts. The sender and the receiver of the signal remain emotionally and intellectually apart, and it is only the concrete situation that links them for a brief interval. The situation-bound character of the signal accounts for the fact that people still use very similar signal calls under comparable conditions. It also explains why primitive signal calls are for the most part understood directly. The signal calls are derived in part from the very earliest period of human life and are rooted in the socio-biological organization of higher living beings. The later signals employed for definite purposes are either based on natural sounds (e.g. yodelling, work calls) or are formed from combinations of expressive sounds (e.g. distant cries). These later calls, associated with transmission and convention, no longer have an exclusively imperative function but are also indicative and communicative, as for example phonetic signals used in speech; they are therefore excluded from our purview.[1]

It is only the natural signals originating from cries that are of significance for evolutionary psychology, and it is only these that can be brought into relation with linguistic prehistory. Their primitive character is shown by these facts. Firstly, among present-day primitive peoples they still occur as signals in their original form; e.g. among the very primitive Kubus of Sumatra, who still use this form of communication to a considerable

[1] Pierre Janet has made very important contributions to the question of symbol and signal in his book *L'intelligence avant le langage* (1936). The discussion by Piaget 'La pensée symbolique et la pensée de l'enfant', *Archives de Psychologie* (1923), is also worthy of note.

extent. Secondly, certain spontaneous calls that arise out of an immediate situation still betray their archaic basis. Lastly, they occur in children at the beginning of their pre-speech period. It may accordingly be assumed that our hypothetical ancestors at a very distant period in the past, before they had attained the symbolic form of language, made their requirements known through (imperative) calls. It is therefore not a gratuitous assumption that the signal has played an extremely important role in the prehistory of language.

The linguistic development of the child provides us with some understanding of the transition from calls to words. At the beginning of the second year we often observe the gradual transition from sounds, babbling constructions, calls and onomatopoetic creations to more or less clear verbal expression (statements without a subject, calls). The speech activity of primitive peoples also provides suggestions regarding this change. Thus aborigines often seem to react to sense impressions or emotional states with spontaneously produced sounds which are at first phonetically unarticulated. If these spontaneous cries are often repeated on similar occasions by their original creator they are taken over by the speech community, modified to conform with their inner linguistic sense, and embodied into their language. The genetic connexion between call and word can easily be recognized in these phonetic images, which Westermann calls 'as yet undomesticated' words. It is to be emphasized that these prelinguistic calling sounds possess neither phonological structure nor the morphological and grammatical form of linguistic constructions.[1]

It follows that a special place must be granted to the imperative call in the system of communicative forms. The illustrations show that addressed communications having the character of a signal appear at a relatively early stage of living beings and necessarily produce partnerships. Poor as this form of communication may seem from a human standpoint, it nevertheless has in common with human language the tendency toward interindividual relationships, and an imperative and the beginnings

[1] D. Westermann, in *Festschrift für Meinhof* (1927).

of a vocative function; and it forms an expressive medium which has been and still is of very great service in human intercourse.

These correspondences with language entitle us to judge the imperative calls as the antecedent stage of language. This opinion is, of course, as we have already pointed out, valid only to the extent that language is seen as having an evolutionary background and viewed as the product of a development leading from the cry through the call to the word. If one grants this precondition, the view presented here is justified and, in my opinion, logically incontestable.

The general evolutionary significance of the imperative call is also shown in unexpected fashion outside the sphere of language. It has played a significant role not only in the origin of language but in that of music.[1]

It is a likely assumption that early man could produce different calling sounds for different purposes. A particular calling sound might serve solely to produce vital contact, another as a sign of one's presence, a third as a warning signal, etc. If distance hindered verbal communication he produced shouts, consisting partly of more or less articulated elements, partly of short call-like syllables and words, such as may still be observed among primitive peoples, mountain folk, and seamen. Closer inspection shows that these calling sounds possess a definite musical content. This is based, on the one hand, on the fact that every call consists of at least two different vocal sounds with a definite interval between them; on the other, on the sliding tonal movement at the end and often at the beginning of the sound complex, which contributes to the musical character of the call. The latter phenomenon is a natural consequence of vocalization. If one wants to produce a loud and far-carrying tone, one strengthens it more and more and then lowers it at the end, the tone gradually fading away. That this sliding movement is common in the songs of primitive peoples, although these have already lost their original calling function, points to a close relation between calls

---

[1] Cf. my Introduction to *The Psychology of Music* (London, 1954).

and song. It appears to be a case of survival from an earlier phase.[1]

Our conclusion that the cry and the call have played a decisive role in the origins of music is based not only on the similarity between the musical structure of the call and that of primitive music, but also on the traces which one finds in the small melodic phrases of the calls of mountain folk and in the songs of labourers.[2] The call as such also possesses a wider significance for the origin of music. For there is a kind of sound production which may be described as solely an expression of heightened emotion, and for its part contributes to the understanding of these vital emotions. The emission of sounds and especially of far-carrying calls indubitably awakens feelings of pleasure, as everyone knows from his own experience. How often in the mountains do we spontaneously call out loudly, with no other purpose than that of hearing our own voice ring out naturally and reach across wide spaces. One has the impression that inner forces are discharged and certain psychosomatic inhibitions relieved by doing this (yodellers in the Alps).

Now it seems to be beyond doubt that the same vital feelings of pleasure which we experience in calls are also associated from the beginning with song. We like to play with our voices. This need appears to be biologically based. Infants carry on babbling monologues for hours without any special purpose. The same is true of the 'singing' of birds. When we are in good humour we sing at our work, without always being conscious of it. Our pleasurable emotions cause us to sing, and the singing in turn enhances our pleasure. The activity of singing, the modulations of tone and volume, the tempo and rhythm, heighten the emotions and regulate the rhythm of life. They are elements common to the call and to song and serve to awaken the desire for activity and pleasure. This psychobiological relation means that the call passes over into song directly, probably without any distinct

---

[1] Cf. C. Stumpf, *Die Anfänge der Musik* (1911); E. v. Hornbostel, 'Über die Musik der Kubu', *Abh. z. verg. Musikwiss.*, I (1922); C. Meyers, 'Music', in C. G. and B. Z. Seligmann, *The Vedda* (1911).

[2] K. Bücher, *Arbeit und Rythmus* (1925).

intermediate stage. Since the call with its traditionally fixed tone sequences possesses the character and form of a musical motif, one can see it without difficulty as the antecedent stage of song. The wordless cry and call have the essential characteristics of music (intervals, transposibility, elements of larger tone combinations) without being music themselves. Thus the call bridges the gap between the stage without music and the earliest phase of musical evolution.[1]

The theoretical advantage which this theory presents is that it explains the connexion between the call and music without the interposition of any new hypothesis. It forms an entirely natural genetic link between two forms of expression quite different in nature, thus permitting the derivation of music from the call. Since the call acquired a verbal character even in the earliest period of linguistic activity, song and therefore music owe their origin in the last analysis to language. Thus the call, appearing in the prelinguistic stage of human development as an especially important form of communication, became the common root and starting-point for language and, as we now see, music.[2]

We may now turn to the question of the transformation of the wordless call into the word.

The theory of progressive variation in organic events would

---

[1] G. Révész, 'Der Ursprung der Musik', *Intern. Archiv. für Ethnographie*, 50 (1941), pp. 65 ff. Cf. also the discussion of P. Schmidt in *Mitteilungen der anthropologischen Gesellschaft Wein.*, p. 33.

[2] This conception is in polar opposition to the theory, which has been repeatedly revived since ancient times, that the first language of mankind was song. 'The language of love is sweet song in the nest of the nightingale, and a roar in the lion's cave', said Herder at one point in his discussion of linguistic psychology. Jespersen also subscribed to this romantic view, regarding the beginnings of language as something in between the lyrical tones of a kitten on a roof and the melodious song of the nightingale (cf. W. Wundt, *Sprachgeschichte und Sprachpsychologie*, 1901). A more serious form of this theory is that of Herbert Spencer, who endeavours to derive the origins of music from the accents and intonations of human speech. These theories, which are mentioned even by Rousseau, run into difficulties in basing themselves on speech, which admittedly does not use fixed intervals and which merely passes gradually from one tone to the next. All such hypotheses proceed by and large from the so-called melodies of speech, which cannot, however, ever lead to song. We believe that music goes back to an antecedent of language, the call, which, though it is not music, possesses its essential elements, the fixed intervals.

render it probable that the call also underwent countless transitional stages before becoming the word, and that these stages must form a continuous evolutionary sequence. The question to be raised here is whether on the basis of the knowledge at our disposal and the theoretical considerations arising from it we are justified in regarding the evolution from call to word as *gradual* or whether it is more likely to have progressed intermittently by *jumps*.

To answer this question, which is so interesting from the point of view of psychological development, one must start with the fact that there is no material available as proof; firstly because the transitional forms, assuming that they once existed, do so no longer, and secondly because neither child psychology nor ethnology is able to provide any point of departure for reconstructing the probable transitional forms. In my opinion the sole practicable way of answering this question is to frame an evolutionary hypothesis, which must be at once logical and factual. But such a hypothesis can only be arrived at if we first make clear in what sense we wish the concept of development here to be understood.

Development is a change, which is distinguished from other kinds of change, such as qualitative change (e.g. the change from red to yellow), extensive change (e.g. motion or spatial expansion) and intensive change (e.g. increase in the intensity of light) by the process of growth. Growth is a change from a less differentiated to a more differentiated state. In such a case the successive intermediate stages appear to the mind as the realization of an immanent 'total plan' embodied in the growth process, and accomplished through evolutionary change.

From a purely evolutionary standpoint we cannot attribute to development either an axiological or a teleological significance. So the idea of development is in principle equally applicable to gradual progression or gradual regression, regardless of whether the change is beneficial. In general the concept of development is used in the former sense, i.e. as continuous progress by imperceptible stages. One accordingly speaks of development when an organism (or an organ) is able through morphological or functional growth to extend its sphere of action and progressively to adapt its capabilities to the increasing requirements of life.

Thus it seems logically and factually justifiable to consider the concept of development in both a narrower and a wider sense. In the narrower sense development is to be understood as a change to a more differentiated, mature and capable stage: while in the wider sense it relates simply to change, independently of whether it is an advance or simply a qualitative change, or even a regression. Both the teleologically oriented definition and the value-free one are sensible and scientifically valid. There is no theoretical objection to employing either of them provided that one makes clear which one is being used. We wish here to employ the concept of development in its narrower sense, because it corresponds to the current conception of the life of language.

Biological growth is fostered and directed mainly by vital forces from within the organism itself; environmental influences are to be considered as secondary. The inner forces as it were point out the direction of change. If the growth of the organism or organ proceeds undisturbed, the change is consummated in the same way in all individuals or all organs of the same kind. The human embryo always develops into a man, the larva into an insect, the eye into an apparatus for perceiving space and light.

As we know, the process of growth in the organic system has been viewed as one that is as a rule continuous. It was assumed that changes of form and function during growth proceed in imperceptible steps, an assumption which implies that each successive stage is derivable by internal evidence from a preceding one (Darwin, Spencer). The continuous process of growth is supposed to apply to the entire plant and animal world. Against this view, which was for a long time very widely accepted, it may be stated that the continuity of change in perceptibly small intervals of time cannot be seen or demonstrated either microscopically or macroscopically. One must plainly recognize that the employment of the continuity principle does not rest upon a generalization of observed and incontestable facts, but upon the *assumption* that the discontinuous momentary stages which we observe are connected by countless transitional stages. The impression of flowing continuity is as it were put together, as Bergson has so clearly depicted it, from cinematic images, dissolving into one another with great speed.[1] These images, discontinuous in themselves, unite into an apparently continuous ordered total process, in which the main role of synthesis falls to our constructive sensory and intellectual activity.

But the apparently unbroken sequences perceived chiefly in the macroscopic world, and our firmly rooted faith in continuous change in the world of events, cannot be allowed to prejudice our view of the nature of reality. It has in fact been shown that the idea of continuity deduced from mere observation is no longer compatible with the framework of recent research in physics. The physicists have succeeded in demonstrating experimentally that phenomena produced by molecular motion do not display the continuity of macroscopic phenomena, but the discontinuity characteristic of isolated molecular collisions.[2] It is not difficult to conceive of organic development, especially ontogenetic, as discontinuous, by analogy with the discontinuous movements of atoms. Although there is no experimental proof of discontinuity in organic processes, its high probability can hardly be doubted; the more so because the question does not depend solely on observation, which may easily be mistaken or, methodologically speaking, incapable of verification with the required precision, but also on theoretical considerations whose weight often extends far beyond what is susceptible to direct observation. And these appear to testify against the assumption of continuity.

If discontinuity of growth within the single biological unit, that is to say, in ontogenetic development, may be regarded as possible, or even as highly probable, then it should possess even greater probability in phylogenetic development, where indeed

[1] H. Bergson, *L'évolution créatrice* (1910).

[2] H. Reichenbach, *Atom und Kosmos* (1930).

the hypothesis of discontinuity has already found experimental confirmation.[1] It was the very fact that sudden and precipitate variation is not at all uncommon in phylogenetic development that enabled Hugo de Vries to propound, in opposition to Darwinism, his principle of sudden hereditary change—a view that is constantly gaining new ground in the biological sciences. The biologists have many reasons for believing that plants and animals, including man, have developed from the forms of earlier geological periods by more or less clear mutational steps. From the point of view of scientific philosophy there is no fundamental conflict between Darwin's doctrine of continuous progressive variation and that of sudden variation introduced by de Vries; for Darwin also admitted sudden variation (single variations) alongside gradual ones in numerous instances. They differ in that according to Darwin the discontinuity is insignificant because of the accumulation of innumerable small changes; that is to say, of intermediate stages following very closely upon one another; while according to the mutation theory sudden change is to be seen quite clearly in natural events and has a general significance. If, on the one hand, all zoological and botanical evolution is not to be divided up into a sequence of successive steps, and if, on the other hand, sudden changes are of general occurrence in the mental development of individual human beings and especially of infants,[2] there can be no objection to extending this doctrine of the sudden appearance of new forms and functions by analogy to the mental evolution of man. The principle of continuous growth has less probability when applied as a general principle relating to all circumstances of human culture than it does in the biological field; because, apart from the unconscious collective inner forces that guide his mental development, man's own creative activity, manifesting itself in the changing course of time, and the traditions of past generations also exert their influence on

---

[1] H. de Vries, *Die Mutationstheorie* (1903) and *Species and Varieties* (1905).

[2] W. Stern, *Psychologie der Frühen Kindheit*, and C. Stumpf, *Der Entwicklungsgedanke in der gegenwärtigen Philosophie* (1900). The latter would see continuous advance as relating only to the physical sphere, while the discontinuous would be limited to the psychic world.

the trend of development. And our experiences in these fields are irreconcilable with the idea of continuous development. Phases of stability alternate with phases of jolting change. The process of Becoming, the tension of continually changing circumstances, is frequently interrupted by periods of peaceful Being. The changes do not disturb what exists, but simply deepen and enrich preceding gains.

It should be noted that the idea of creative development in nature, and consequently also in the world of the mind—an idea that assumes special importance in the philosophy of Bergson —accords only with the principle of discontinuity. In so far as an evolutionary process is continuous, the creative act has no opportunity to intervene in the process of growth; the unalterability of the evolutionary process, its development 'according to plan', precludes any creative act or deed. In contrast, discontinuous, sudden evolutionary change presupposes the introduction of new forces that were inoperative during the preceding stage, in order to produce sudden variation, modification or change of direction. These sudden and novel forces serve as the basis of what is called creative evolution. Creative acts cannot be wholly derived from what has gone before, or the attribute 'creative' would be utterly without meaning. New productive forces must be set to work, taking effect not planlessly or accidentally but in accordance with particular rules or tendencies.

Let us illustrate this with an example from the history of art.

The structural forms of the baroque were not a necessary outgrowth of the Renaissance. The rise of the baroque cannot be attributed to the same forces that created the art of the Renaissance and determined its development. The introduction of new impulses and stylistic principles was required to transform the one into the other. The idea of continuity of development here proves to be an illusion. For the direction of stylistic change[1] was determined by the first decisive step toward freedom and the enhancement of movement, made on the personal initiative of

[1] H. Wölfflin, *Renaissance und Barock* (1925).

Michelangelo, and with that the gradual retreat of the ancient tradition.

When we consider the development of language from this point of view we see that discontinuity in evolution, the sudden rise of variations which must be attributed in part to the creative powers of individuals, can be shown to exist in the infant and in the acquisition of new languages as well as in linguistic history. That the ontogenetic and phylogenetic development of language is governed by general laws, such as those of phonetic shifts, divergence, functional change, the differentiation of grammatical categories and the like, does not prejudice the fact that the development displays a clearly discontinuous and intermittent character. This is all the more understandable because in the ontogenesis and phylogenesis of language we dare not underestimate the role played by the initiative and invention of individuals and of social and cultural groups.

If we compare animal cries and the unarticulated phonetic utterances of idiots incapable of speech but using words and verbal complexes to serve the same purpose, and if we suppose that words have developed gradually out of these animal cries, we would be unable to form the faintest idea of the intermediate stages. We could not succeed in forming any picture of the changes the animal sounds must undergo in order to arrive at the articulated, rhythmic and melodic, differentiated forms capable of development and continuous modification such as are the properties of phonetic words.[1]

The difficulties are considerably fewer if human cries and calls are taken as the starting-point, the more so because in man's ontogenetic development his distinctively human character is

[1] At this point we wish to call attention to the difference between the communicative cries of children and animals, not only in form but in terms of the psychology of perception, instinct and volition. This is only what is to be expected if we realize that the infant has a predisposition to speech and that the linguistic function is in preparation within him during his pre-speech period. It follows that the assumed ancestors of man also employed other and much more differentiated communicative sounds during their prelinguistic stage than animals capable of sound production. It follows also that these creatures must have had at their disposal, to the fullest extent, call sounds, the possession of which by non-domesticated animals is very debatable.

present from the beginning in decisive traits fundamentally different from those of animals. By comparative study of the conventional and especially the spontaneous call sounds of primitive peoples and by taking into account, with due caution, the cries of infants during their pre-speech period, it becomes possible to reconstruct the hypothetical transitional stage with fair probability. Through such an investigation the phenomenal similarity between call and word would be brought out clearly. It would show that to a considerable extent the addressed calls correspond in respect to important phonetic properties with the most primitive words and roots. Many would see in these external similarities an indication of a continuous development of the word from non-linguistic forms. In fact, we do know of efforts in the literature of linguistics to put particular emphasis on unarticulated sounds in attempts to reconstruct the so-called 'Urwörter'. Ingenious as these may be they are unable to demonstrate the transitions from sound into word, from the emotional into the symbolical, from the merely imperative function into the linguistic function. If in examining this problem one not only considers the phonetic nature of the two types of communicative utterance but also their internal structure, the symbolic character and mental content of language, and not least the degree of mental development required for speech, it becomes clear that one cannot do without the assumption of a kind of spontaneous creative activity, and therefore of sudden advances in development, not only in the learning of language but in its origin as well.

Language could not have arisen from primitive non-linguistic calls by inner necessity, otherwise it would be impossible to understand why the animal world has never grown beyond non-verbal means of contact. Calls cannot have produced language by themselves; here too new impulses and particularly new creative forces must have taken effect to bring into being the first expressions of articulate language. We must accordingly assume that even at the cradle of language creative human activity exercised a powerful influence, that already during man's formative period the tendency made itself felt to designate needs, wishes, thoughts, etc., with varied but constant sounds in the interests of easier communication, and to address the individual to whom the request was directed with a particular calling sound. This spontaneous activity, like any other productive act, was associated with particular preconditions, in this case with the presence of suitable phonetic materials. The phonetic material we found in the addressed calls, which by virtue of their imperative and locative character were especially suited to facilitate the formation of the first phonetic words.

What is most probable is that initially cries, calls and primitive words overlapped, the cries and calls being predominant at first and gradually giving way to words, but without suppressing the non-linguistic calls. These must have survived, since the call's special function of contact over distances—one of the primitive community's means of contact overlooked by linguists—could obviously not be replaced by articulated language. Now, with the first step taken, the general course of linguistic development was prescribed; the spirit of language, the inner sense of form began to exert its creative effects and to govern language formation according to general and special laws. The later development of language also proceeded by leaps and bounds; external and internal causes, above all the influence of other languages and the emergence of new needs, entered into its development and unfolded new possibilities.

In this sense the call may be regarded on the one hand as the culmination of the development of non-linguistic communication, and on the other as the point of departure from which the linguistically creative factors coinciding with the beginnings of human life proper produced the first linguistic forms. Vocabulary and sentence structure, aided and guided by the inner form of the language, gradually became the foundation stones of a logically complete system. To express it another way, they formed the basis of ordered thinking and of logic as the theory of the art of thought.

3. THE WORD

(a) *The Priority of the Imperative*

The addressed call, characterized by imperative and locative tendencies, leads us to language. The transition from one to the other is, as we have said, unknown; we are unable to form an adequate conception of how the addressed calls were transformed into words, of how what was at first fluid became fixed. It is a question which cannot be answered without using hypotheses based purely on imagination and without any sort of empirical basis.

Language did not come about suddenly; like everything else in the world that develops and changes, it had antecedent and early forms. If we wish to form an idea of the nature of these stages we must never lose sight of the fact that the appearance of the first words and the use of them in significant combinations demand a mental world that is not comparable with that of the preceding stages. What separates language from all the non-linguistic means of communication is not basically its pragmatic significance as compared with the others, but its phonetic and structural nature, its functional richness, the scope of its activity, the autonomy of its development, and especially its intimate association with human personality and society.

One important evolutionary fact has however become clear from the preceding discussion which is of great importance for the reconstruction of the proto-history of language; namely, the causal and genetic connexion between the imperative call and the linguistic imperative.

We have seen that the categorical directed call arising out of an imperative situation has its analogue in the imperative in language. The close relationship between them naturally does not mean that the imperative call possesses or did possess the grammatical value of an imperative, much less the value of an imperative sentence. In this context the word imperative signifies only the imperative tendency, which was already the basis of the cry, but which reaches its full expression only in its verbal form. The correspondence between the two is accordingly not in their external form or definiteness of content, but in their function, intention and effect.

In the very earliest period the problem was to transform the all too limited and undifferentiated imperative calls into ever more varied linguistic imperative expressions. Man who was already capable of speech had to coin words for the purpose of inducing members of his family and clan to perform various activities; the need to tell or describe things was as yet unawakened.

The evolutionary position of the imperative and its genetic priority over other forms of linguistic expression, particularly the indicative, comes to light first of all in ontogenetic language development, both active and passive. Observation has shown that of all phonetic and gestural expressions acquired by the infant the very first is the understanding of imperative words (Take your hand away! Bring it here!) and pointing gestures. Infants begin to understand requests addressed to them as such as early as the eighth or ninth month. In the first quarter of the second year the infant reacts promptly and without hesitation to words and short sentences with imperative content, such as Jump! Give me a kiss! It is true that these infant reactions do not altogether prove the priority of the imperative, for it is mainly requests and prohibitions that the child hears from its environment in the first period of its linguistic development. Therefore nothing is more natural than that the first meaningful reactions of the child should relate to imperative expressions. On the other hand, nothing but activities or commands concerning activities (apart from calls, which produce a reflex turning toward the source of the stimulus) will claim the child's attention. Thus the true primary cause of the preference for the imperative in the first stage of linguistic development will be not the expressions used by the child's environment but its own concern with activities, and consequently its taking notice of signs and expressions for activities. It follows that the particularly early comprehension of imperative expressions can really be interpreted as indicating the chronological precedence of the imperative.

The early appearance of the imperative is displayed in a convincing way in active speech. During the first period of speech activity the language of the child is restricted almost exclusively to demanding objects and causing actions in others. Young infants demand and command, and at first do not impart information; the need to describe concrete things arises only later. Some time must elapse before the period of exclusive demanding and desiring comes to an end and makes room for the indicative and significative functions of language.

For the purpose of making its demands the infant uses words which it has heard in its surroundings and is able to imitate more or less exactly. Its first nominal, verbal and interjectional words and short sentences thus at first serve the imperative function. The fact that substantives predominate in the initial stages of infant speech is explained simply by the fact that the normal method of learning to talk starts with pointing to an object or person (motor car! apple!) (Nellie! Mamma! Daddy!) and therefore the vocabulary is composed predominantly of the names of objects and persons. In using the names of persons and objects the infant does not want to refer to the subject it is addressing nor the object of its desires, but to express the action to be performed with or upon the object. The word Mama does not indicate the presence of the mother, but is intended as a request to a familiar person to perform a certain action. The intention to name things appears later, at the age of about eighteen months. If we wish to interpret rightly the words of the first period of infant speech we must realize that what matters is not the word categories used by the child but their function in a given context. And this function is the imperative function. This proves the error of the view of Stern, who deduced the priority of object concepts (substantive stage) from the use of the noun in the earliest phase of speech development, and maintained that verb expressions appear only later in the language of the child (action stage).[1] This view, which has been generally accepted in child psychology, is therefore based on an incorrect interpretation of the facts.[2]

The delay in the use of verbs (not in their acquisition, which

[1] W. Stern, *Psychologie der frühen Kindheit* (1930).

[2] A. Sommerfelt, *Spoget som somfundorgan*, p. 75.

takes place as early as the period of merely passive comprehension of speech) therefore depends on circumstances for which not the infant but the speech of the adults who are in contact with it must be held responsible. At the beginning of speech formation verbs and nouns are in general employed together, with imperative intent. Only in a later period of speech development do the parts of speech become differentiated and assume their proper functions. We find a similar situation in primitive languages in which the boundaries between verbs, nouns and adjectives are not clearly defined: nouns are only weakly separated from verbs (both being important for imperative expression); frequently they take the same suffixes.[1]

The same considerations apply to the use of the infinitive. During the first half of the second year the grammatical form of expression of the imperative act is often rendered by the infinitive form (e.g. in German, '*Spielen!*' '*Essen!*') alongside the imperative ('*Gib!*'). Later, from eighteen months onwards, they gradually assume the proper grammatical form of the imperative. Among the moods of the verb, the child uses the infinitive first or with special predilection because adults repeat the infinitive form to the child countless times. (E.g. 'Does the child want to eat, to sleep?' 'Daddy wants to play with him.') The child is therefore virtually forced to use this word form for the imperative speech act at the beginning; as is commonly recognized, the imitative factor plays an important role.

The ontogenetic approach is most readily applicable in regard to the question of the temporal sequence of speech functions in cases where the child is forced as the result of special circumstances to find the meaning of linguistic expressions by himself. This happens with deaf mute children who grow up among normal people. The first speech gestures of these children are indeed of an imperative nature. The same can be observed in cases of hereditary mental deficiency as well as in other hereditary mental disturbances which show serious aphasia. As far as one can see

[1] A. M. Hocart, 'Mama', *Man*, 14 (1914); C. Meinhof, 'Ergebnisse der afrikanischen Sprachforschung', *Arch f. Anthropologie*, IX.

from the fragmentary evidence of the passive and active linguistic ability of idiots and imbeciles (Perez, Pinel, Seguin, Zeihen, Boulenger, Sommer, Weygandt) one can assert that young mental defectives for a long time understand only imperative actions directed to them, and can express by means of affective call sounds and primitive imitative sounds nothing but desires, with the express intent of having them immediately fulfilled.

Ontogenetic development therefore does not supply any certain evidence for the temporal priority of the verbal imperative, because the conventional nursery language of the surrounding adults avoids verbs and in particular the imperative form. For this period of linguistic development we can establish only the chronological and psychological precedence of the imperative intention and imperative activity; both normal and abnormal children apply all the means at their disposal to attain it.

For the chronological priority of the imperative in phylogenetic development we can hope for illumination only from linguistic history and comparative linguistic science. And in fact the priority of the imperative does find support in comparative linguistic science. Scaliger[1] was the first to point it out, and since then this view has been adopted by various authors, such as Wundt,[2] F. Mauthner,[3] and others. The French comparative grammarian and Sanskritist M. Bréal, who ranks the imperative as among the oldest linguistic expressions on the basis of psychological considerations and linguistic evidence, expresses it in the following manner: '*Les modes du commandement (l'imperatif et l'optatif) appartiennent donc au plus ancient fonds du langage; ils représentent une des faces essentielles, une des attitudes mâitresses du verbe.*'[4] In the Semitic language the oldest form of the verb was the monosyllabic imperative; from this earliest form arose a narrative non-temporal verbal form, the imperfect.[5] The great

---

[1] J. C. Scaliger, *De causis linguae latinae* (1540).

[2] W. Wundt, *Die Sprache*, I, p. 322, II, p. 207.

[3] F. Mauthner, *Kritik der Sprache* (1921), III, p. 53.

[4] M. Bréal, 'Les commencements du verbe', *Mem. soc. ling. de Paris*, XI (1900), p. 276.

[5] C. Brockelmann, *Semitische Sprachwissenschaft* (1916).

antiquity of the imperative is also shown by the fact that morphologically the imperative generally corresponds to the stem of the word[1] (e.g. *go, run, geh, komm, lauf, sprich, veni, scribe, cerca, paga, canta, audi, ga, kom, spreek, ἐλθέ*).[2]

I wish to call attention again in this connexion to the fact that the primacy of the imperative corresponds very well with the presumed primacy of the single-element sentence. Imperative sentences are as a rule one-word sentences, while declarative sentences can be expressed with a single word only in exceptional cases.[3] Here we are disregarding the languages of primitive peoples, in which there is no sharp boundary between word and sentence, and in which a single word can be altered and enriched by prefixes and suffixes in a way that can be expressed in our languages only by sentences consisting of several elements (see Kainz, op. cit., II, p. 146). The observed fact that in gesture language, a form of communication that must be called primitive in comparison to phonetic language, the imperative can be expressed with the greatest degree of relative adequacy, while indicative statements can be repeated by conventional (symbolic) gestural signs only with difficulty, could also be adduced in favour of the antiquity of the imperative function.

The more primitive character of the imperative as compared with the other modes of the verb is also indicated by the fact that the imperative is never absent in any verbal language, and remains in being through every stage of development; while the other modes may easily be displaced by other modal forms. (Wundt, op. cit., II, p. 205). Further, it has been shown that the

[1] It should be noted that this proposition is not true for all verb roots, for there are a number of roots that cannot be used in an imperative sense because of their meaning; such as to be born, to be dead, to resound, to dwell, etc.

[2] The fact that the imperative displays the root of the word can only be used as an argument for the primitive character of the imperative if one accepts the doctrine of the original existence of the roots as words, i.e. the assumption that the roots really existed as words at one time. If one conceives of the roots only as an 'ideal centre of meaning', as Delbrück describes them in his *Einleitung in die Sprachwissenschaft*, then they could not be regarded as supporting our genetic theory of the imperative.

[3] According to Paul the sentence always involves two elements. In his view so-called one-word sentences arise because of the psychological subject remaining unexpressed (e.g. enough, come, yes, no); in a true sense these are also two-element sentences.

imperative is not multifunctional in the sense of being able to replace other modes; while the indicative can take over the imperative function without further ado, as in 'You will do that immediately', or 'You will go and get it'. Furthermore, the imperative form of phonetic language continues to be accompanied by gestures and articulatory expressions of face and movement, a phenomenon indicative of archaic relations because they are constituent parts of the language of present-day primitive peoples. Beyond this it is only natural that a linguistic form like the imperative, expressing what is essentially an affective experience, is closer to the archetype of linguistic expression than the indicative, which presupposes an objective attitude, more dependent on the intellect.

From the point of view of phylogeny there is also the fact that commands given phonetically or by gestures are easily understood by animals. All training of both wild and domesticated animals is based on the empirical fact that animals are able to understand certain frequently repeated imperative acts. It should be remembered that animal mating calls and imperative calls represent the most primitive forms of the non-linguistic 'imperative'. To the extent that animals possess at all the capacity to enter into contact with their own kind and their human environment by means of sounds, this manifests itself exclusively or at least predominantly in the form of an imperative act. Though this cannot be compared with the linguistic or grammatical form of the imperative it is nevertheless associated with the imperative of language in its intention, expressive character and effect. Animals do not possess any other form of expression analogous to other functions of the verb.

(b) The 'Imperative Language'

If we start out with the thesis of the primitive character of the imperative act and the priority of the verbal imperative, and if we accept the evolutionary relationship between the latter and the imperative call, it then becomes possible to reconstruct a transitional form which can be fitted in between the non-verbal imperative call and language as defined by the three special functions described above. This early form of language would have the character of an imperative language.

If we assume the existence of a period when early man first began to express his desires and wishes by means of articulated and differentiated phonetic constructions—that is, words—which better served the purpose of communication and were better adapted to his mental level in his struggle for advancement than unarticulated and undifferentiated sounds and gestures; if we suppose, further, on psychological and linguistic grounds, that this instinctive tendency was first manifested in a language principally distinguished by its imperative character, we arrive at the earliest, albeit immature and incomplete, stage of language, a language possessing but *one* of the specially constitutive functions of language in its full extent, the imperative, and exhibiting only the beginnings of an indicative function.

To prevent misunderstanding we wish to emphasize that by imperative language we do not mean a language possessing only verbs, and these occurring only in imperative form. What is meant here is a language predominantly imperative in function. To-day it is, of course, no longer possible to determine whether there ever was a stage of linguistic history in which the imperative function played such a preponderant role; our languages ancient and modern have grown too far away from their early stages to be able to provide any evidence of their early forms. If, however, there actually was such a phase, it is improbable, if not unthinkable, that man in this linguistic period restricted himself exclusively to imperative expressions, much less to verbs alone. Such a conception could only be based on grammatical abstraction, not on living language or concrete speech activity. The assumed imperative language must have been richer than can be imagined on the basis of any abstract scheme, because words originally arose out of speech, and not the reverse. No matter how primitive early imperative language is conceived to have been, it must necessarily have embraced other categories of words as well as verbs; auxiliaries, and above all deictic particles, such as 'here', 'there', 'this', etc., indicating first spatial and later temporal and personal relationships.[1]

On the other hand, one must avoid starting with the developed languages in reconstructing the earliest imperative language. In the former, verbs are used only in connexion with nominal concepts, i.e. with substantive and adjectival concepts of the properties of objects. But this has no bearing on the reconstruction of early language, since sentences, word complexes, and even whole speeches can be replaced by linguistic forms of a very simple kind. Such linguistic forms, which lend themselves well to being linked with an imperative language, can be observed in various primitive languages in which quite different situations and actions can be expressed by modifying the same word, and in which a great variety of statements, reports and commands can be communicated through a relatively small number of words and grammatical forms. It is interesting, and serves as a further support for our conception of the earliest form of language, that in these languages the expression of meaning by modification relates predominantly to the verb; further, that the verbs possess an ideogrammatic significance, i.e. they represent in their variously modified forms not only a specific activity but various concrete situations which in our languages can be represented only by complex sentence constructions. Thus in the Bantu languages a number of imperative forms are constructed through auxiliaries, each of which indicates a concrete situation, e.g., 'Climb the hill!' 'Climb the hill at once!' 'Forward, climb the hill!', etc.[2] From this one could conclude that in the earliest languages as in many languages of primitive peoples the verbs and to a certain degree the imperatives too could express whole situations or

---

[1] Such words could be purely concrete at first; instead of 'here' or 'this' words could be used that expressed the concrete situation, as is seen, for example, in the Klamath language, in which the spatial relation 'this' is expressed in different ways according to whether the object has a soul or not, is very near or is far enough away so that it can just be touched or seen. See Gatschet, *The Klamath Language*, pp. 538 ff.

[2] Torrenel, *Comparative Grammar of the South African Bantu Languages*, p. 231. Cf. Lévy-Bruhl, *Fonctions mentales dans les sociétés inférieures*, 160 ff. and Malinowski, *Coral Gardens and their Magic*, II.

actions in concrete form even without other parts of speech. The so-called original language (Ursprache) which is believed to have consisted principally of 'sentence words' could communicate much that our languages cannot convey without the help of verbal and grammatical categories. If we assume that in early times the ideogrammatical significance of verbs completely governed the languages of man, we are justified in imagining the supposed imperative language as very primitive both in grammar and vocabulary.

With the imperative language we enter into the proto-historical period of language. It is a hypothetical phase, the probable starting-point of all linguistic development. As we have already mentioned above, this early phase cannot be demonstrated from historical material. On the other hand, the probability of its having really existed appears from child psychology and linguistics. One meets a kind of imperative language in children's speech, when at the end of the prelingual period the child begins to replace spontaneous cries and calls by words with an imperative content and mostly expressed in an affective state. And we have learned from linguistics that the imperative form of the verb belongs to the very earliest verbal expressions, a fact that undoubtedly speaks in favour of our assumption.

Thus in our view the earliest form of linguistic communication can hardly have been anything else than a system of one- and two-element subjectless summoning and calling sentences, i.e. activity words in connexion with gestures and words which point to persons, things and places. Schuchart argues for single-element primitive sentences, probably influenced by ontogenetic factors, in which single-element sentences formed of verbs or substantives appear first. In phylogenesis, where adult persons and not creatures immature in every respect are concerned, single-element imperative sentences could, on the grounds cited above, occur only in exceptional cases.

At a higher stage the imperative language must have been capable not only of directing commands to particular persons and of indicating the presence of the speaker and the person addressed, but also of designating by verbal symbols the most common expressions of place and time (here, there, behind, inside, now, later) and the volitional expressions 'yes' and 'no', as well as those indicating certain possessive and personal relations (my, your, I, you, me). Despite such additions and modifications the entire speech material of language in its original state must have been at the service of the imperative, i.e. words must have been nearly always used in a volitional sense. Since signs for spatial reference, thus the beginnings of the indicative, must already have been present in the imperative language, it could not have been very long until the stage was reached in which the indicative form began in its grammatical aspect.

In this connexion we must briefly discuss the vocative and optative, since both of these were probably among the components of archaic language.

The vocative belongs to the sphere of the imperative function of language. From a psychological point of view it seems a likely assumption that the vocative arose at the same time as the imperative, and consequently precedes the indicative chronologically. Vocative and imperative expressions are so closely related in their emotional content, mode of intonation and modulation and function that it seems unjustifiable in principle to separate them. Verbal forms such as Come! Go! Charles! Mother! Hello! Listen! come into being through the same situations, and represent the same intentions and the same relations among the objects of thought and volition.

Evidence supporting the link between the imperative and vocative is also to be found in linguistic history. The fact that of the eight cases of Sanskrit (nominative, genitive, dative, accusative, ablative, locative, instrumental, vocative) the vocative as an imperative in nominal form assumes a special place from the first, points to this. Brugmann and Delbrück come to no conclusive opinion on this question. On the one hand they postulate that in the Indo-Germanic languages the injunctive—which is to be regarded as the modal form corresponding to the vocative— was not originally an independent mode, but a branch of the indicative;[1] on the other, they maintain that the imperative and vocative verbal forms are very closely related to each other in character, because they have remained closer to natural sounds than other verbal forms, and at all times have retained an emphasis on concreteness. But there seems to be agreement that the imperative together with the vocative rank among the oldest of grammatical forms. This view is further supported by the fact that in most cases the vocative, like the imperative, is represented by the stem of the word.

The optative may be regarded as a weaker form of the imperative which begins ontogenetically and apparently also phylogenetically at a relatively late stage of mental development. The infant at first has demands, not wishes. To wish is to reckon with the possibility of refusal, an attitude at variance with the infant's instinctive nature. This seems to be the reason for the child's difficulty in deciding to ask for anything. To ask is to wish, and consequently to entertain the possibility of failure; which is beyond the child's mental level.

The optative is certainly distinguishable from the imperative in grammatical form and phonological character, but not in intention; and it is just this that concerns us here. There are innumerable transitions between pure imperative and optative speech, which again can be altered by intonation. Conventional forms of speech offer countless examples of imperatives expressed in optative form; for example, one could say, 'Would you be so kind as to write a letter to Mr. X' in a tone that would be peremptorily imperative in character.

We have answered the question of the genesis of language by reference to a prehistoric language, which we call the imperative language, and by pointing to the close relationship of the imperative call and the linguistic imperative. The question has been answered in the sense that we have traced an evolutionary relationship between language and primitive forms of communication having the same tendency; established the origin of the

---

[1] K. Brugmann and B. Delbrück, *Grundriss der vgl. Grammatik der indogermanischen Sprachen*, II, IV, 2, 3, p. 808.

multi-functional phonetic language as a stage-by-stage product of the evolution of non-linguistic forms of communication; and have founded these conclusions on arguments of considerable force drawn from ontogeny, phylogeny and linguistic history.

The categorical character of the imperative call and the early prehistoric origin of the imperative permit us to believe that the verbal, grammatical imperative form—probably one of the earliest linguistic utterances—not only follows the imperative call chronologically, but as it were issues from it; so that the latter may be regarded as the immediate antecedent of language, and the former as its earliest form. Thus the non-verbal imperative call forms a link between linguistic and non-linguistic communication, belonging among the prelinguistic forms of communication in respect to its wordlessness but directly associated with the linguistic forms because of its imperative character.

Outside the scope of this work are the later development of language in general and in detail; its modification, differentiation and individualization; its general and special laws of formation, its grammatical and syntactical divisions, the individual character and expression of the diverse languages, and all the other historical and psychological problems of language.

We shall, then, conclude with a brief discussion of the relationship of phonetic to gestural language.

We have restricted ourselves to phonetic language in our presentation of the forms of communication. We believe we are justified in omitting any special treatment of gesture language because phonetic language represents the medium of communication *par excellence*, while gestures can only serve to support and supplement it, occurring only exceptionally as members of an independent and more or less autonomous gestural language. We feel all the more justified in this because it must be assumed that communicative gestures have developed in a similar manner to phonetic forms. And in fact it can be shown without difficulty that the evolutionary stages of phonetic language can also be seen in gesture language.

In the field of expressive gestures the following kinesthetic manifestations correspond to phonetic expressions in their entirety. The analogue of the mere emotionally based sound is the reflex expressive facial or bodily movement. Like the sound as such, the expressive gesture as such is unrelated to language. Both of these are merely physiological preconditions of linguistic activity. To the contact sound corresponds physical or tactile contact, which is a much more general and biologically much more primitive form. Cry and call also have their analogues in gestures. The impersonal call is replaced by mimic and panto-mimic contact movements. Numerous examples of this may be found in the social intercourse of infants and animals. One may think of the spontaneous and lively arm movements of the infant, with the help of which it tries to make its wishes known. From the animal world the display of strikingly formed or coloured parts of the body by the male, the play of the features, and baring of teeth of mammals, the dancing of birds, etc., can be cited. Here too belong the clapping of hands or other noisy gestures to the extent that they are intended to reveal one's presence or make known one's will or feelings. Corresponding to the call in the gestural sphere are imperative and indicative movements of the hand and deliberate facial mimicry. Such 'gestural calls' are met with constantly in gestural language of normal people and deaf mutes. Finally, gesture language contains in place of phonetic words, symbolic gesture signs.

IX

THE IMPORTANCE OF THE
CONTACT THEORY
FOR EVOLUTION

We have distinguished three phases in the development of language: first: its prehistory, representing the preparatory stage of language; second, its proto-history, embracing the earliest beginnings of language and leading up to a hypothetical initial form; and third, linguistic history proper, representing the development of languages based on documentary records and linguistic research. These constitute in our opinion three chronologically distinct stages, in which the development of communication gradually proceeded from cries to words, each form emerging through the transformation, alteration and enrichment of a less differentiated one.[1] This genetic view is the foundation on which the *tristadial theory* rests.

The genetic connexion between the chronologically successive stages is to be seen quite clearly in the non-linguistic forms of communication. In all children in their pre-linguistic stage one can observe how the initially undifferentiated cry gradually and without a demonstrable break in continuity passes into the differentiated call, and how the diffuse character of the former acquires a significant and structured form by a process of transformation. The transition is even clearer in the case of children with poor

[1] If one is sceptical of the theory that man is derived from animals, whether because of the lack of direct proof or on other grounds, one need not regard cries and calls as stages through which human language developed, gradually or by mutation; but simply as suitable phonetic utterances occurring both in animals and in man because they are biologically related. The power of conviction of our theory is therefore independent of one's attitude to human evolution.

hearing. Delay in mental development and backwardness in linguistic motor activity retard the transformation of simple expressive sounds into the phonetic expression of needs and wishes by means of cry and call incomparably longer than in normal children, thus making the transitions more clearly perceptible. This psychological interpretation can be supported by observations in animal psychology. Although cries are used by a large number of animals for communication, calls are met with only among animals brought up in proximity to human beings and particularly adaptable because of breeding and domestication. Even among these the more intelligent ones are distinguished by the degree to which they use calls on varying occasions.

An analogous genetic connexion may also be assumed between the call and the word, even if the transformation of the sign function into a symbolic function cannot be demonstrated because of the fundamental difference between the two modes of expression and the enormous extension of aim that takes place with the coming of phonetic language. That they are nevertheless members of a single sequence of development may be inferred with some probability from the fact that human calls pass over so readily into one-element or two-element imperative sentences, and that the more or less articulated non-verbal cries and calls of infants and primitive peoples so insensibly assume the form of single-word sentences. In this connexion one may also draw attention to the close affinity between interjectional imperative calls and the verbal imperative. This appears firstly in their resemblance in respect to pitch, intonation, duration and reduplication, and secondly, in the fact that even in developed language commands are often given by non-verbal cries and calls, as in commands, messages, and warning calls produced with a loud strained voice and directed to a distance.

We have already shown that the functions of language can also be dealt with from the point of view of psychological development. This admittedly applies only to the imperative and indicative. It is beyond all doubt, as we have seen, that as a form of expression the indicative is later than the imperative. Although it is introduced during the period of imperative language, in which the deictic particle brings to light the unambiguous beginnings of indicative expression, it obtains its specific form only later. The late appearance of the interrogative function can only be demonstrated ontogenetically.

Thus the conception of psychological evolution in relation to the origin of language leads to the *stadial theory*, which, in the light of comparative psychology, reconstructs the development of communication from its first inception to its full elaboration and indicates the stages which lead, through forms progressively more differentiated and richer in content and structure, to the ultimate phase of its development, language. If, following the traditional theory of evolution, we accept that man has developed gradually out of more primitive forms of life, it follows that he must have passed through these stages before finally arriving at phonetic language. These stages correspond to the three phases of linguistic evolution in its widest sense, its prehistory, proto-history and history proper. These are the fundamentals of the *tristadial theory*.

Our theory of linguistic origins is of particular interest for evolution because it shows the antecedent stages as passing over into the earliest ones without a break, and because it interpolates before the final decisive step to full language a transitional form, the imperative language, which must have preceded true language as its first manifestation.

If we add the contact sound to the series of three stages of communication as a preparatory process, we can visualize the evolutionary sequence of phonetic means of contact as shown on Table I.

The most primitive form of contact, the contact sound, forms, with the cry and the call, the precondition and the antecedent phases of language respectively. Its true evolution begins with the spoken word. Its initial manifestation is the incomplete imperative language, which broadens out into an archaic form of language possessing all three of the basic language functions. This transitional form concludes the proto-history of language. The

TABLE I

Stages	Phases	Forms	Functions
Contact sound	Precondition of language	Antecedent form of communication	
Cry	Antecedent phases of language	Earliest form of communication	
Call		Antecedent form of language	Imperative function
Word	Initial phase of of language	Initial form of language	Imperative language
		Primitive form of language	Language with three basic functions but primitive structure
	Historical phase of language	Mature language	Lexically and grammatically developed language

same impulse that brought language into existence and made primitive men into full human beings retains its creative power throughout the entire history of language. Phonetic language gradually becomes more differentiated; vocabulary, grammar and syntax become more complex and expressive. The introduction of the subjunctive and the compound tenses and the increasing richness of nouns, adjectives, adverbs, pronouns and numbers lend language an expressive power of indescribable variety, enabling man to achieve intellectual spontaneity in all fields suited to representation, and to create systems marked by an astonishing abundance of ideas and with the finest nuances of meaning.

A remarkable evolution also takes place in the system of communicative gestures and facial expression in association with language. Along with the expressive and directly comprehensible gestures, communication becomes more intensive and extensive through the invention and application of writing. The transmission of experiences, knowledge and ideas through speech and writing exercises a powerful influence upon mankind and establishes mental contact between different generations and diverse peoples. Thus language and writing extend into the distance and into the future and in virtue of their psychic content, unite different territories and epochs. Through ceaseless activity under the pressure of expanding needs and the drive toward progress, language has become, within the framework of its phonetic and grammatical laws and in the multiplication of its lexicological material, an inexhaustible instrument of thought and communication, transmission, creation and expression.

X

THE LOGICAL STRUCTURE
OF THE CONTACT THEORY

THE structure of communicative forms described in this work is to my mind unchallengeable as a system and as a genetic sequence. As a system, because it takes into account all the main forms of phonetic and gestural communication known to have come into existence and shapes them into a natural system, and because the presence of one tendency governing all the forms of communication—namely, the contact tendency—assures the common genetic character of the stages. As a genetic sequence, because each form of its development is shown to be the continuation of a lower one. Thus as a general theory of communication our treatment permits the phenomena of animal, child and linguistic psychology, and the facts of linguistic history to be fully evaluated, combined, and arranged in a system. This applies especially to our psychological views in respect to the forms of communication and the linguistic functions. Each element in the formation of language is placed where it can function without hindrance, and then steps into the background while other elements take over the construction and development of the forms of communication. Care is taken that the gap between the individual stages be as small as possible, to avoid their having to be bridged over or eliminated by arbitrary constructions. Our three stages of communication and three phases of linguistic development pass into one another so naturally that there is no need to seek or postulate finer but at the same time less sure intermediate stages.

The general scientific importance of the contact theory consists in its being a synthesis of three doctrines that are independent and connected only by their common intention and their genetic link: the general theory of the forms of contact (Chapter VII, c), the theory of linguistic functions (Chapter VI, B), and the stadial theory (Chapter VIII, c). In the study of these fundamental problems our investigations have gone beyond the question of linguistic origins and form as it were a new foundation for linguistic psychology.

If we review the assumptions which we have employed in treating the problem of communication it will appear that the contact-theory is based on three broad concepts, each consisting of three subordinate ones. There are three contact concepts (instinctive, emotional and mental contact), three stadial concepts (cry, call and word) and three functional concepts (imperative, indicative and interrogative functions). One could also add three phase concepts: the antecedent, archaic, and developed phases of language.

These three or four triads of concepts are distinguished by the fact that each member of a triad is the subordinate member of a superordinate concept under which all the multiplicity of forms of each individual domain can be brought. If one recalls how widespread is the principle of three-fold division in all spheres of human activity and if one also bears in mind the compactness the conceptual triad affords to classifiable phenomena, acts and events; and what advantages arise out of division into three, one reaches the conclusion that what is involved is a general principle of order, classification and formation.[1] Conceivably our mental organization is so formed that we have a natural tendency to reduce the formation and subdivision of complexes to the smallest number of components. These are the numbers 2 and 3; of which the latter has a special role to play and finds its expression in

[1] Tripartite division is very commonly employed in the field of linguistic science. Thus we meet conceptual triads in the classification of the fundamental relations of language: speaker, person spoken to, and communicative subject-matter; in the classification of languages: root languages, agglutinating languages, and inflexional languages (A. Schleicher) or languages without grammatical structure, languages with affixes and languages with flexions (A. W. Schlegel), or non-flexional, flexional and analytical languages (J. Grimm). In grammar we distinguish three numbers (singular, dual, plural), three persons and three genders.

tripartite division in all spheres of thought, order and formation. The 'law of tripartite division' may be on the one hand an expression of the limitations of our intellectual powers, but at the same time a sign of mental adaptability, which turns natural limitations to advantage by converting them into methods of thought and analysis.[1]

The structure of our theory is defined by the following guiding ideas:

First, the contact principle: i.e. the tendency to simple association and co-operation underlying all forms of contact, which gives rise to communication when, at a higher level, it is joined by the impulse toward mutual comprehension.

Second, the hypothesis of a direct evolutionary sequence of development from non-verbal to linguistic forms of communication, manifested in the cry, the call and the word;

Third, the sharp distinction between purely expressive reactions and forms of contact and communication; with the consequence that the prehistory of language first begins with the intended or addressed call;

Fourth, the non-verbal command as the transition between antecedent and archaic phases of language, its imperative character providing the connexion with the earliest form of language, the so-called imperative language;

Fifth, the psychological hypothesis relative to the chronological succession of the modes of the verbs (imperative, indicative, subjunctive, etc.) which has its parallels in general linguistic history and infant speech. This hypothesis is linked with the one which follows;

---

[1] Although numerous examples can be found of the use of higher numbers than three, and especially of the number four, above all in the mystical numbers of early and primitive peoples (Lehmann, *Aberglaube und Zauberei*; M. MacGee, *Primitive Numbers*; Lévy-Bruhl, *Fonctions mentales dans les sociétés inférieurs*; Frobenius, *Kulturgeschichte Afrikas*, 1933; Jung, *Psychologie und Alchemie*; Kerény, *Einführung in das Wesen der Mythologie*), arrangement in groups of three (triad, trinity) appears to have a wholly special and unique place among principles of order because of its extraordinary distribution in religion, art, social and legal life, in science and the occult sciences, on the one hand, and because of its significance in the psychology of perception (balance, rhythm) on the other. The nature of classification by two, three and four and the advantages of the conceptual triad for theory formation is the theme of a paper in the *Acta Psychologica*, XI (1955).

Sixth, the hypothesis of an imperative language as the earliest form of linguistic communication; and

Seventh, the conception of an archaic form of language with imperative, indicative and interrogative modes of expression.

The entire structure of our theory is represented in these basic concepts and their logical implications. The first proposition provides the framework and the breadth of scope; the second, the major classification into non-verbal and linguistic forms of communication; the third establishes the starting-point, the fourth the end-point of linguistic prehistory, and simultaneously the connecting link between its prehistory and proto-history; the fifth to seventh propositions outline a picture of the development from the archaic to the fully developed form of language.

Table II sets out graphically the structure of forms and means of communication as developed in our discussion.

The tendency to simple association, to mere vital contact, which is sometimes accompanied by specific sounds, contact sounds, is only distantly related to language, forming—as repeatedly stated—merely the physiological precondition for communication in general. This form of contact is included in the table only because it expresses an intentional phonetic utterance.

The first stage of communicative contact appears phonetically in the form of cries that are intentional and related to specific needs, but not yet directed to particular individuals.

The second stage, the form of expression of which is the call based on the vocative function, represents the very earliest form of the imperative and must be regarded as the transitional form between non-verbal communicative phenomena and the earliest form of language. These two stages form the prehistory of language.

The third stage is the so-called imperative language, inserted as a hypothetical member of the evolutionary series, presumably man's oldest form of linguistic expression.

The fourth form of linguistic communication already embraces the three principal linguistic functions, but still shows a primitive structure, and does not go beyond concrete representation. The

TABLE II

The Forms of Communication and Their Position in Evolution and Linguistic History

| | FORMS OF CONTACT | FORMS OF COMMUNICATION | | | | |
| | | Non-linguistic (non-verbal) | | Linguistic | | |
		(i)	(ii)	(iii)	(iv)	(v)
Stage	Need for making contact	Intended indication of vital needs	Demands addressed to individuals	Imperative language	Language with primitive structure	Fully developed language
Medium	Contact sound	Cry	Call	Word		
Rank in Evolution	Antecedent of communication	Archaic form of communication	Primitive form of communication	Archaic form of language	Primitive form of language	Fully developed language
		Prehistory		Proto-history		Linguistic history

Occurrence:

In animals ....→

In man ....→

Schematic Diagram of

Forms of Contact	Aim of Contact or Communication (i)	Mode of Expression (ii)	Supplementary Notes to (ii) (iii)
I. Physical contact	Feeling of security; assurance of biologically important aims	Instinctive seeking of company or place of assembly	Simple need for contact and co-presence without any tendency to communicate
II. Intended indication of vital needs	1. Indication of inner excitement 2. Inducement of particular actions	Explicit desire for co-presence, assistance and co-operation, combined with feeling of expectation	Attitude and tone of the cry show that its demands are directed at the environment
III. Requests addressed to individuals	1. Indication of inner excitement 2. Demand for particular actions	Imperative expression of desires, with locative indication	Desires are expressed in categorical form. Place or aim is indicated. Onset of reciprocal communication
IV. Imperative language	1. Indication of inner excitement 2. Demand for particular actions	Imperative, vocative, locative (indications of indicative)	Appearance of symbolic mode of expression. Natural sounds continue to play a role. Bilateral communicative intent
V. Primitive language with three basic functions	1. Demand for actions and attitudes 2. Indication of subjective states and objective circumstances 3. Questions	Imperative, indicative, interrogative	Predominance of symbolic mode of expression in words and gestures
VI. Fully developed language	1. Demand for actions and attitudes 2. Indication of subjective states and objective circumstances 3. Questions	Further development of phonetic language in respect to vocabulary, grammatical categories and syntactical relations; development of gestures and mimicry; invention of writing	Mature symbolic form of communication in words, gestures and writing

the Contact Theory

Medium of Contact (iv)	Evolutionary Stage (v)	Distribution (vi)	Chief Examples (vii)
Contact sound with or without gestures	Most primitive form of contact (antecedent of communication)	Animals of all species; but especially social animals	Herds, animal societies, groups formed for the purpose of sleeping, swarming, feeding, migrating, etc., in common
Cry Natural, instinctively derived expressive phonetic and gestural utterance	Primitive form of communication	Predominantly animals and speechless infants; adults under some circumstances	Mating calls, so-called alarm signals. Infant cries without specific direction
Call Natural, instinctively derived expressive phonetic and gestural utterances, with indication of aim and sometimes of the person to whom addressed	Antecedent of language	Predominantly domestic animals, but also man	Mating calls and cries of alarm addressed to individual animals or groups; begging of domestic animals; infant calling for its mother
Call, word and gesture 1. Expressive phonetic and gestural utterance in the form of phonetic images and interjections 2. Verbs in imperative form, with nouns and deictic words in an imperative sense	Transition from prelingual to linguistic communication (archaic form of language)	Supposed earliest man	Hypothetical case
Word and gesture 1. Expressive phonetic and gestural utterances 2. Language in words and gestures, verbs, nouns, adverbs, etc. 3. Picture writing	Primitive form of language	Prehistoric man	Language of very primitive peoples. In certain respects, infant speech to about the third or fourth year
Word and gesture 1. Expressive phonetic and gestural utterances 2. Language 3. Pictorial representation 4. Writing (ideographic, phonetic)	Unlimited exchange of thoughts	Historical man	The developed languages of mankind

latter two represent the successive stages of linguistic proto-history.

Finally, after these preparatory stages, language begins as the mature symbolic form of communication. Whilst animals are limited exclusively to non-linguistic forms of communication, man makes use of linguistic forms as well.

In order to provide a clear picture of the scope, application and comprehensiveness of the contact theory, we give in Table III the principal results of our investigation within the framework of the genetic theory which we have developed.

The various forms of contact are characterized by their purpose, their medium and their manner of expression. To these are added details regarding their evolutionary rank and their distribution. Illustrative examples are also given.

Comparison of the forms of communication reveals very clearly how the purposes, media and manner of expression vary with the degree and intimacy of the contact, and how the vocative, communicative and interrogative functions gradually arise from the need for mutual relations and co-presence; how symbolic verbal language develops from instinctive phonetic and gestural expression by way of the signal function; and how the mature form of communication in words, gestures and writing develops by stages from the instinctive need for contact.

XI

THE SIGNIFICANCE OF THE CONTACT THEORY FOR LINGUISTIC HISTORY, PSYCHOLOGY AND PREHISTORY

THE significance of our theory for other sciences related to linguistics may be brought out by the following observations. If we are not mistaken, the theory is the first to go far beyond the bounds of linguistic psychology and to be developed in close relationship with linguistic history. The earlier psychologically based theories were isolated from the other sciences and their justification depended wholly on psychological considerations; with few exceptions they had no link with linguistic history. Linguists were rather free to choose among them, since these hypotheses had so little to do with the events of linguistic history that there was no danger of becoming involved in contradictions. Child psychology first acquired historical value for linguistic research because of parallels between linguistic ontogeny and phylogeny. But its subject-matter was more suited to provide material for reconstructing the proto-history of language than its prehistory. That is why the study of the so-called animal languages was taken up with such industry, in the hope of reaching a solution of the problem of origins by this approach. We have shown that this hope was vain.

The position is fundamentally altered as a result of the contact theory here developed. Our account of the genesis and earliest stages of language and the associated theory of functions may be linked without any modification with general linguistic history, and in particular with the history of the Indo-European languages. The linguistic historian will find in it the psychological basis and justification for a theory of the origins of language that is related to the history of the development of language, and he will not require any additional hypotheses. Furthermore, general linguistic history offers reliable support for the high probability of our theory, since the functions which we have defined and given an evolutionary basis appear to be in full harmony with the chronological succession of the grammatical categories. From this standpoint, the contact theory constitutes a theory of the prehistory of language, based upon psychology and linguistic history.

It is by connecting the stages of linguistic evolution with the modes of the verbs that the contact theory establishes a close relation between the prehistory and history of language. The unsuspected agreement between the evolutionary and psychological facts and the findings of linguistic history, firstly in the circumstance that the psychologically most primitive imperative form of expression has its counterpart in the most primitive and earliest grammatical form, the imperative; and secondly that the next evolutionary stage psychologically as well as historically finds expression in the indicative—all this promises new viewpoints for comparative linguistic science. It would be the task of this science to examine the primitive and early forms of the developed languages for the origin of the modes and their chronological succession in relation to our theory. Traces may perhaps still be found in them of what we have called the imperative language, and in any case there should be survivals of an archaic form of language displaying the three fundamental linguistic functions at a relatively primitive level of development. Although an imperative language is possible even without grammatical form, it may turn out that when verbs come into use the imperative forms precede the indicative.

The contact theory poses new problems and offers new interpretive viewpoints for child psychology, and especially for the study of infant speech. The so-called babbling words to which so much attention has been devoted fall into the background, since it has been shown that as purely expressive sounds they have only peripheral significance for the speech of individuals, and none at all for phylogenesis. As exercise for the speech organs and as a precondition of speech, babbling admittedly retains its value, in the same sense that spontaneous movements of the hand serve for exercising the motor apparatus. From the standpoint of psychological development it would be desirable to study the transitional forms between cry and word; our discussion of contact sounds, cries, calls and words has uncovered more trustworthy criteria than the mere phenomenal resemblance of the sounds. Further, the parallelism between ontogenetic and phylogenetic linguistic development, previously treated with so much partiality, must be given a fresh critical examination, in which the viewpoints in developmental psychology to which we have called attention, and especially the distinction between antecedent and initial stages, cannot be without influence. Our views on the imperative, optative and indicative are also suggestive for the interpretation of the earliest speech of the child. The recognition that in the development of language less depends on grammatical categories than on the functions of words and their combinations can imply considerable modification in the semasiology of child speech.

Our discussion of the contact sound and call is also of interest for animal psychology. It follows from our analysis of animal and human phonetic expressions that animal cries and the so-called animal languages, expressive as they may be, have no common basis with language, either phenomenally or functionally. On the one hand we have demonstrated the untenability of the idea of animal language; on the other, we have succeeded in tracing a relationship between animal vocative calls and the earliest form of human language, the imperative language. From this we may see the importance of the hitherto completely neglected study of the vocative function of animals. Such research will yield deeper knowledge of the social and individual contact phenomena of animals than mere observation of their cries, which has so often led to unacceptable consequences. In this way the contact theory reveals itself as a valuable working hypothesis for animal and comparative psychology.

The views presented are of interest for human prehistory because they support the thesis that man—as defined in social anthropology—was capable of speech from the very beginning. Our view of the nature of man completely precludes the assumption of a *Homo alalus*, a view which is quite groundless and arrived at only by mere abstraction. It sets in its place man endowed with speech and possessing a basic linguistic equipment despite his primitive mentality. The theory of psychological evolution here set out is incompatible with the idea that early man could have expressed his feelings and desires by unarticulated sounds. However primitive we may imagine earliest man to have been on the basis of the oldest cultural remains, we must assume that he possessed a phonetic and gestural language having the functions of commanding, informing and questioning. The discovery of fire, the manufacture of tools, rationally organized collective labour, collective defence, the transmission of individual experiences, in a word, all activities belonging to the necessary conditions of life of the simplest human societies, are unthinkable without language. Man and language must accordingly be inseparably bound together.

> C'est donc un rêve [says Renan in his fine work on the origins of language] d'imaginer un premier état où l'homme ne parla pas, suivi d'un autre état ou il conquit l'usage de la parole. L'homme est naturellement parlant, comme il est naturellement pensant, et il est aussi peu philosophique d'assurer un commencement voulu au langage qu'à la pensée.

Language as such, even in its most primitive form, must have been a creation of the human mind; man made language, and language fashioned man and made him human. This conception is an anthropological one, which receives fresh nourishment from our theory. The reciprocal relation between man and language can never be weakened by palaeontological discoveries. For even if we should eventually succeed in establishing the ancestry of man without anatomical gaps, and in extending his racial history through the missing transitional forms, the conception of the mental nature of man would not thereby be changed. If one sees in Pithecanthropus erectus or in any other species of man-like apes the ancestor of man, the question still remains open whether that transitional type was endowed with the functions of language. If this question has to be answered in the affirmative, if it should perchance be shown beyond doubt that Pithecanthropus in Java has left behind rock carvings which could not have come into being without language, we should then have to say that Pithecanthropus was human. If the answer turned out to be negative, we should have to say he was an ape and not a man.

However one may put the problem, however extend or limit it, one cannot escape conceiving of man from the very beginning as a thinking being, and therefore as one endowed with speech. No matter how primitively he may have expressed his thoughts and wishes, his form of communication can only have been language, and that language a phonetic one possessing at least imperative and vocative expressions, but more probably all three basic functions of communication.

These considerations also clearly justify the hypothesis of creative activity within the framework of evolution. If we start from the assumption of the unity of man and language, an assumption founded both on logic and evolutionary history, we reach the conclusion that our genetically oriented theory of contact is compatible with the anthropologically derived theory which asserts that language is to be conceived as the product of human activity.[1] The idea that language did not arise suddenly, but was preceded by a long period of preparation, does not contradict the view that language in all its phases, in its primitive state as well as in its full maturity, even in each individual act of speech, depends on the spontaneity and inventiveness of man. Every new word, every

[1] Nor do we come into conflict with the theological theory of the creation of language if we interpret the original creation of language in the sense of Renan and Cousins. Renan says, 'Le *véritable auteur des oeuvres spontanées de la conscience, c'est la nature humaine, ou, si l'on aime mieux, la cause supérieure de la nature. A cette limite, il devient indifférent d'attribuer la causalité à Dieu ou à l'homme*' (*De l'origine du language*, 1859, p. 94)

new concept and every new linguistic expression owes its existence to a creative human act; it must have been so essentially from
earliest times. No fundamental distinction can be made between
the original creation of language and the creative acts which
recur daily. Once man had begun to strive for linguistic expression whether for the purpose of mutual communication or from
an inner need to acquire knowledge of the objective and subjective world, the degree to which he could fashion linguistic
expressions corresponding to his thoughts depended upon his
creative capacity.

Like all genetic theories, our contact theory has to depict the
successive stages of development, and need not necessarily explore
the forces determining development and changes in function. The
hypothesis of creativity nevertheless directly relates to the effec-
tiveness of forces in linguistic origins and development. It is
their differing purposes that explains why the theory of contact
does not come into conflict with the idea of creativity.

With these remarks on the significance of the contact theory
for the various sciences we have completed the task set in our
introduction. In conclusion, we may summarize briefly as follows
the views we have advanced concerning language, its origins and
development.

Language is the most adequate means of communication for
man in his efforts towards social and mental contact. Its basic
function is to represent by phonetic symbols the contents of consciousness (sensory, ideational, emotional, volitional) in the
broadest sense.

At first language served only for mutual communication
and the influencing of one person by another, and it is to
satisfy these needs that it came into being. At a higher level of
human development it also became a means of ordered thinking, self-consciousness and self-development, entailing an enrichment of the range of speech-situation; conversation with oneself
appearing alongside dialogue.

It may be inferred from the basic uniformity of the human

race and the broad similarity of the primary needs of man that all languages, despite their diversity, probably share the same basic tendencies, which are expressed in the main in the laws of phonology, grammar, syntax, and semasiology. It follows that in theory any person is capable of learning any language in the world and using it for communicative purposes.

Language appeared at the same time as man. The existence of mankind presupposes language in its active and passive forms. It is therefore idle and pointless to draw inferences from living or dead languages, no matter how primitive, regarding the phonetic forms of communication used by any hypothetical pre-linguistic man; and even the most primitive languages of aboriginal peoples are already fully-developed languages of a rather complicated kind. What we can say definitely of the earliest spoken languages, the so-called original languages ('Ursprachen'), is that they could only have been phonetic languages, accompanied from the beginning by gestures and mimetic movements. In opposition to all other hypotheses we firmly take the view that there never was a period in which man employed for social intercourse any linguistic communicative medium other than phonetic language. Gestures served to support and extend phonetic language, and played an independent role only in exceptional circumstances. The assumption of the primacy of a gestural language like the assumption of a 'prelingual' gestural language proves to be wholly untenable from a biological and anthropological standpoint.

Language is bound together with thought, and particularly with abstract thought, and the formation of concepts and analogies. This correlation is to be seen even in the earliest stage of speech development in infancy. On this ground alone one must deny that animals have language; and the so-called animal languages do not meet a single internal or external criterion of human language. Animals certainly possess means of communication, enabling them to make their vital needs known to their fellow animals and sometimes even to their human milieu. This usually consists of voiced sounds audible at a distance, but not of verbal sounds, and does not serve to designate things, but merely to express the animals' emotional needs and the pressure to satisfy them. The absence of linguistic capacity implies the absence of the comprehension of speech. The sounds of human speech are accordingly at most signals for the animals; that is, signs of command, approval or prohibition.

From the standpoint of evolution one must, however, grant a special importance in linguistic prehistory to the unarticulated cries and particularly to the directed cries and calls. It is to be assumed that these two spontaneous media of communication were used by the hominids from which man is supposed to be derived according to traditional evolutionary theory. These cries and calls continue to be used by man, partly in their archaic form.

This last circumstance permits us to provide a place for the directed cries and calls in the prehistory of language. This view is strengthened by the consideration that the call, because of its distinct function and phonetic form, points toward the imperative function of language. It is precisely the imperative function that represents the oldest and most primitive special function, and that forms the oldest grammatical category. How the transition from call to word and from signal to symbolic sign was first effected, whether the change was sudden or gradual, and even whether it occurred at all, cannot be stated in concrete terms. In any event it was the common characteristics of the call and verbal sounds, such as in pitch, duration, accent and rhythm, that enabled the transition from call to language to take place.

The transition from signal to symbolic sign could only have come about through a functional change. A higher need, stirred perhaps by necessity and stimulated by the progressive development of intelligence, insight and the gift of inventiveness, led early man to establish mental contact with his fellows and to organize a social life. Thus man, as it were, was forced to this decisive step, by which the mental development of mankind was initiated.

The special linguistic functions, the imperative, indicative and interrogative, must have begun very early, enabling the realization of the most important aims of communication. With the introduction of the linguistic functions, which find their best expression grammatically in the modes of the verbs, the proto-history of language came to its end. All present-day languages, even the most primitive, have far outgrown these early stages. They display a greater differentiation in their phonological and linguistic structure as in their evolutionary rank, expressive capacities and lexical richness, and their study is the task of comparative linguistic science and historical grammar.

In this way, linguistic psychology and linguistic science help each other toward the goal of tracing the life of language from its origin to its full maturity, to enrich our incomplete knowledge of its growth and to identify the internal and external factors in its changes.

The informed reader will have noticed that we have taken pains to decide the conflict of opinions on the basis of well-founded arguments; to examine the early stages of linguistic development from all sides; and thereby to trace the mental evolution of man from the inception to the maturity of his linguistic forms. Our investigation found its theoretical basis in the theory of contact, the tri-functional principle, and the tri-stadial hypothesis. If we are not mistaken we have succeeded in determining the basic manifestations in the field of communication and in linking them together under a common governing principle; subordinating the stages of development to an immanent law; overcoming the difficulties of an evolutionary approach to language, and finally, establishing a system in which each of the various forms and media of communication finds its proper place.

Our main effort has been to bring back into present consciousness the age-old problem of linguistic origins and beginnings, which exists consciously or unconsciously for every epoch, and our hope is that linguists and psychologists will be aroused to further work on the basis suggested here.

XII

SUMMARY

I. INTRODUCTION

THEORIES of the evolution of language which have been previously advanced are inadequate because, lacking a consistent approach, they are unable satisfactorily to explain its origins and gradual development. In this work the attempt is made to reconstruct the evolution of the forms of communication from the simplest manifestations to the symbolic form of language on the basis of a general principle, the contact principle.

II. THE PROBLEM OF ORIGINS

If one subjects the basic concepts of evolution to critical examination it appears that the concept of 'origin' has been used in two different senses. It sometimes relates to the earliest or original form in which a phenomenon first makes its appearance: at other times, to the antecedents from which, on the basis of a specific formative event, the phenomenon or function first arises. But the prehistory of language must be clearly distinguished from its proto-history in that the archaic stage possesses certain properties associated with language which are absent in the antecedent stage. The tendency toward contact or the communicative intention provides the link between these two stages. The conditions that must be observed in reconstructing the prehistory and proto-history of language are established on grounds of logic and methodology.

III. THEORIES OF ORIGINS

(A) INTRODUCTION

Theories of the origin of language may be classified as biological and anthropological. The former lay special weight on the prehistory of language, which is said to be governed exclusively by biological principles; the latter start with a stage of development already displaying the first manifestations of language and creative linguistic activity. It is erroneous to divide linguistic development into two parts, one prelinguistic and the other linguistic. Language begins only with man, who requires language as a means of expression in consequence of his mental abilities and social nature. The idea of *Homo alalus* is self-contradictory.

(B) BIOLOGICAL THEORIES

1. All attempts to derive language from reflex and spontaneous expressive sounds or gestures are wrong in principle. Purely expressive sounds are direct indications or symptoms of a physical or emotional state, without communicative intent; consequently they have nothing to do with forms of communication, either linguistic or non-linguistic. They have a different source and pursue a different aim. Because they lack communicative intent expressive reactions are excluded from linguistic evolution. The resemblance between expressive sounds and words relates merely to their phonetic aspects, not to the form of the sounds, which is bound up with the significant content of words. Nor can the interjections have played a role in the origins of language. These attain linguistic significance only after they have been taken up into language.

2. What is true of expressive sounds also applies *a fortiori* to animal sounds. To attempt to derive elements of language from animal sounds is a vain pursuit. The phonetic contact or communicative utterances of animals grouped under the concept of 'animal languages' display neither in internal structure nor external appearance the characteristic appropriate to language.

P

There is no content of meaning in animal sounds that would justify our interpreting the so-called animal languages as antecedents of language, much less as early forms of it. In addition, animal sounds used for communication are, unlike linguistic sounds, an inherited, unalterable means of expression and incapable of development. The alleged comprehension of language by animals is illusory.

(c) ANTHROPOLOGICAL THEORIES

1. A discussion of the principles of phonetic imitation strongly indicates the untenability of theories asserting a natural connexion between the earliest words and the sensory impressions produced by the sounds of nature. Existing languages possess only a very small number of onomatopoetic words, and even these are mostly of late origin; they originate at a time when language is already functioning.

2. (*a*) The endeavour to connect babbling with the origins of language breaks down because babbling serves an entirely different function from that of language. The idea that there must have been a phase corresponding to the babbling period in the prehistory of language is nonsense.

(*b*) Infant speech owes its development not to the infant's own creative linguistic activity but to the influence of its environment; consequently it cannot provide a point of departure for the reconstruction of the archaic forms of language. Its phylogenetic significance is questionable despite certain correspondences with the languages of primitive peoples.

(*c*) To derive language from some other function of consciousness leads to contradictions. Thus, for example, to derive language from thought presupposes the priority of thought, which in turn leads to the most improbable conception of men capable of thinking but not of speaking. This functionalism leaves us exactly where we were, since it merely substitutes another problem, in our example that of the origin of thought, for the problem of the origin of language.

(*d*) There is not the slightest justification for asserting the primacy of gestural over phonetic language. Firstly, all higher animals are capable of expressive sounds as well as expressive movements, and phonetic expression is commonly of greater frequency and importance than expression by motor activity. Furthermore, neither the development of the child's speech nor the linguistic activity of primitive peoples points to a priority of gestures in psychological development. Both sounds and gestures have been and continue to be available as communicative media. From the beginning these two autonomous varieties of speech support and supplement each other, phonetic language in the end winning the upper hand. Thus language, even in its most primitive form, was phonetic though interspersed with gestures and mimic movements.

(*e*) A knowledge of the languages of primitive peoples cannot solve the problem of origins because of their great antiquity and complex structure. It may have a slight historical value for the reconstruction of language in the proto-historical stage only. Nor can an understanding of the phenomena of aphasia explain the construction of language, but only its deterioration. The linguistic material of aphasia, fragmentary as it is, belongs to the sphere of language and therefore cannot be used to reconstruct conditions existing before its origin.

(D) PHILOSOPHICAL AND THEOLOGICAL THEORIES

Philosophical accounts of language, such as naturalistic and empiristic theories on the one hand, and voluntaristic and deterministic ones on the other, are not so strongly opposed in prehistory as they are in the theory of cognition; in linguistic theory they can only be regarded as interconnected and complementary. Since philosophers who think in terms of voluntarism and determinism turn their entire attention towards the formation of language and not to its origins, they very nearly preclude themselves from a consideration of the problem of origins. The exaggerations of the voluntaristic theories and the untenability of the theories of invention should not mislead us into underestimating man's capacity for linguistic creation. Finally, theological theories are unrelated to our problem because they reject in principle any kind of genetic approach.

(E) LIMITATIONS OF THE THEORIES OF ORIGINS

All known theories of origins suffer from methodológical errors. Firstly, they fail to define the concept of language clearly, with the result that linguistic and non-linguistic forms of expression are uncritically brought into the discussion of linguistic psychology. Then, instead of emphasizing the forces that are productive and formative of language, excessive attention has been paid to the medium of language, i.e. sound and movement. This has, as it were, impeded research on linguistic origins.

(F) THE CONTACT THEORY

The contact theory provides a general account of the forms of communication and linguistic evolution, based on the results of research in animal and child psychology and on the conclusions of general and comparative linguistic science. This theory permits us to reconstruct the prehistory and proto-history of language and, thanks to its mode of construction, makes linguistic origins accessible to logical study.

IV. THE PROBLEM OF AN ORIGINAL LANGUAGE

The problem of an original language, that is, the reconstruction of the language employed by our presumed ancestors in the earliest period of human existence, is in principle insoluble. One cannot do more than indicate the factors and principles that were operative in its origin and early formation.

V. THE LANGUAGE OF EARLIEST MAN

No conclusions can be drawn regarding the linguistic activity of early man on the basis of the skeletal structure of the 'earliest men' claimed by anthropologists. It is only the cultural approach that is capable of casting light on this question. If diluvial man practised activities necessarily bound up with the existence of language, such as the production, improvement and transmission of tools, it must be presumed that he possessed language. *Homo faber* may be identified with *Homo loquens*.

VI. THE THEORY OF LINGUISTIC FUNCTIONS

(A) THE TELEOLOGICAL VIEW OF LANGUAGE

Discussion of the general nature of definition leads us to the conclusion that the essential nature of language, like that of any *organon*, is to be found chiefly in its purpose. A definition of language will be a complete one only if it takes into account all the factors constituting the speech situation: namely, its purpose, its means and its medium. Individual criteria that have been advanced, such as the symbolic function, do characterize language but do not define it fully and exactly. Although language aims primarily at communication it has other purposes and fields of application which cannot be overlooked. These are thought, imagination, self-consciousness and expression. The formulation of a new functional theory presumes a detailed treatment of the concept of function in psychology.

(B) THE TRI-FUNCTIONAL THEORY

The tri-functional theory is based on concrete speech situations. It assumes three principal functions, which embrace, and among them exhaust, all the forms of human communication. These are the imperative, indicative and interrogative. They are independent of one another and are specific criteria of language. Human intercourse can only have the intention of inducing someone to undertake an activity, of indicating something, or of asking a question. These concepts sometimes relate to psychological and sometimes to grammatical categories. Viewed psychologically, the parts of speech that give concrete linguistic form to these functions, that is in the first instance the verbs, are the most primitive elements of language. This view is in complete agreement with the conclusions of linguistic history, according to which the verb is the oldest element of language, the imperative and indicative forms being the oldest modes among the forms of the verb.

(c) THE DEFINITION OF LANGUAGE

The tri-functional theory leads to a full definition of language, embracing the purpose, the means and the concrete intentions of linguistic communication and taking account of all varieties of language. Language is the means by which, for the purpose of mutual communication and with the help of a number of articulated symbolic signs appearing in different sensory combinations, commands and wishes are expressed, objectively or subjectively perceived facts are indicated, and questions asked to provoke communication. The content of this definition remains essentially unchanged if we take into account thought, perception and self-consciousness. It is to be assumed that the earliest form of language was a phonetic language possessing these functions.

VII. HUMAN AND ANIMAL FORMS OF CONTACT

(A) INSTINCTS AND NEEDS

Biologically it is impossible to separate needs, the drive for their fulfilment, and the finding of appropriate means towards their fulfilment.

(B) THE SOCIOLOGICAL BASIS OF COMMUNICATION

There is a fundamental principle underlying all human and animal communities which is an indispensable condition for their origin, development and differentiation. This is the need for contact. This need, governing by far the greatest part of animal life, is the guiding principle here employed in determining the forms of contact and in reconstructing the course of development of all the forms of communication, including language.

(c) CONTACT AND ITS FORMS

The need for contact may be restricted to mere physical and spatial co-presence, without any tendency toward communication. Such vital contact is based purely on instinct and is at the root of all animal conglomerations or communities. In man, spatial contact is deepened into emotional contact to the degree that the emotional outgrows the purely physical. This higher form of non-linguistic contact can be characterized by a strong tendency toward forming inter-personal relationships, including emotional exchanges of a personal character.

Here again communication is not involved, but a reciprocal understanding, an emotional resonance, without the use of linguistic means. Just as a transfer of feeling is induced by emotional contact, so an exchange of thought is induced by intellectual contact. Intellectual contact has a communicative character, and employs language as its medium.

VIII. THE DEVELOPMENT OF PHONETIC FORMS OF COMMUNICATION

(A) EXPRESSION AND COMMUNICATION

The expressive sound is simply a reflex process and is to be regarded only as a symptom of inner excitement and tension. It constitutes only a material precondition of phonetic communication. The expressive sound is unrelated to the forms of communication, and therefore plays no role in linguistic prehistory.

(B) CONTACT SOUNDS

The contact sound is not produced for the purpose of communication but solely for the exchange of feeling. Since phonetic utterances of this kind convey the need for contact, the contact sound may have played a preparatory role in linguistic prehistory.

(c) THE FORMS OF COMMUNICATION

1. *The Cry.* The most primitive evolutionary form of communication is a message directed to the group, the non-linguistic cry. The cry is distinguished from the expressive sound by its communicative character, its signal function, and by a feeling of expectation, directed to the fulfilment of a desire. It is a biological inheritance, and is activated instinctively. Examples of this most primitive form of message are provided by animal sociology, child psychology and unarticulated cries directed to a distance.

2. *The Call.* The stage of linguistic prehistory following the cry reveals itself as the call directed to definite individuals. Its individual reference, its expressly imperative and locative functions and its basis in experience lend the call an entirely different character from that of the cry. Through the medium of calls satisfaction of desires is demanded from a particular individual, and with it the place, and sometimes even the object, is indicated by glance and gesture. Imperative calls are used by speechless infants and by adults. Not infrequently it has been observed that domestic animals also spontaneously express their desires to particular persons in the environment by turning toward them and perceptibly indicating the desired aim. It is clear that the animal executes this communicative act on its own impulse, on the basis of its own experience. Because of its imperative and locative character the call may be regarded as the stage directly antecedent to language.

3. *The Word.* The non-verbal imperative call seems to pass over directly into the linguistic imperative. The imperative speech act is psychologically more primitive than all other speech acts. The need of urging others of one's kind to action must have arisen earlier than the need of telling them something. The likelihood of the priority of the linguistic imperative can be shown ontogenetically and, on the basis of linguistic history, also phylogenetically. One is justified in assuming that the earliest form of language had the character of an 'imperative language'. For such an initial manifestation of language, activity words

and the most important designations of place and time would have sufficed. The imperative function finds expression not only in the grammatical imperative but also in other modes (e.g. the infinitive) and parts of speech such as nouns and adjectives. The same is true of the indicative function which comes later. The indicative, like the imperative, did not arise suddenly. It was introduced already in the period of imperative language, in which unambiguous beginnings of indicative statements appeared in the deictic particles (where, here, etc.). The growing need for communication gradually gave rise to the remaining grammatical categories and parts of speech, until finally language achieved its full range.

IX. THE IMPORTANCE OF THE CONTACT THEORY FOR EVOLUTION

Starting with the simplest forms of contact and guided by the basic principle of the need for contact, and at a higher stage by the communicative intention, it is possible to reconstruct an evolutionary sequence of forms of communication leading from the most primitive contact relations through the earlier forms of communication. The stages are indicated by three characteristic forms, cry—call—word, to which can be added as a preparatory phonetic-utterance the contact sound. The contact theory merits particular attention for the concept of evolution, because it shows each form as a development of the preceding lower one and because the stages are shown as belonging to the same order by the presence of a common tendency, the tendency to communicate. The logical order of the stages is reflected in the tristadial theory.

X. THE LOGICAL STRUCTURE OF THE CONTACT THEORY

The contact theory is characterized by four broad concepts, those of contact, phases, functions and stages, each embracing three subordinate concepts. These triads cover the entire field

Q

of language in respect to function and evolutionary development. The logical structure of the theory is based on the seven principles outlined in the tables. The first provides the framework of the theory, the second the classification of the forms of communication, the third and fourth establish the beginning and end points of linguistic proto-history, the fifth to seventh sketch the entire development from the earliest stage to fully developed language.

XI. THE SIGNIFICANCE OF THE CONTACT THEORY FOR LINGUISTIC HISTORY, PSYCHOLOGY AND PREHISTORY

The contact theory is a doctrine of the prehistory of language based on psychology and linguistic history. As the result of the many agreements in the results of the two sciences an unexpectedly close relation can be established between prehistoric development of language and linguistic history. The theory offers new prospects for research in child and animal psychology and suggests new viewpoints for interpretation. It also provides a fixed point for human prehistory in respect to the mental constitution of early man. The genetic view of linguistic origins suggested in no way diminishes the importance of the creative linguistic activity of communities and individuals during the original formation and later development of language.

BIBLIOGRAPHY

TH. ARLDT, *Die Entwicklung der Kontinente und ihrer Lebewelt*, 1907.
W. BECHTEREW, *Objektive Psychologie*, 1913.
H. BERGSON, *L'évolution créatrice*, 1910.
H. A. BERNATZIK, *Die Geister der gelben Blätter*, 1938.
L. BOUTAN, 'Le pseudo-langage', *Actes de la Société Linnéenne de Bordeaux*, 1913.
G. C. BRANDENBURG, 'The language of a three year old child', *Ped. Sem.* 22, 1915.
M. BRÉAL, 'Les commencements du verbe', *Revue de Paris du 15 décembre* 1899.
— 'Les commencements du verbe', *Mem. soc. ling. de Paris* XI, 1900.
BREHMS *Tierleben*, 4. Aufl., 1918.
A. J. P. VAN DER BROEK, *Oudste Geschiedenis van den Mensche*, 1936.
K. BRUGMANN und B. DELBRÜCK, *Grundriss der vergleichenden Grammatik der indogermanischen Sprachen*.
K. BÜCHER, *Arbeit und Rhythmus*, 1925.
CH. BÜHLER, *Kindheit und Jugend*, 1931.
K. BÜHLER, *Sprachtheorie*, Jena 1934.
— 'Die Axiomatik der Sprachwissenschaften', *Kant-Studien* 38, 1933.
E. CASSIRER, *Philosophie der symbolischen Formen*, I, Berlin 1923.
E. B. CONDILLAC, *Sur l'origine des connaissances humaines*, 1746.
B. CROCE, *Ästhetik als Wissenschaft vom Ausdruck und allgemeine Sprachwissenschaft*, 1930.
F. H. CUSHING, 'Manual Concepts', *Amer. Anthropologist*, V.
CH. DARWIN, *The Descent of Man*, London 1871.
— *The expressions of the emotions in man and animals*, 1892.
H. DELACROIX, *Psychologie du langage*, 1933.
— *L'enfant et de langage*, 1934.
— *Le langage et la pensée*, Paris 1930.
B. DELBRÜCK, *Einleitung in das Studium der indogerm, Sprachen*, 6. Aufl. 1919.
H. DEMPE, *Was ist Sprache*, Weimar 1930.
— 'Die Darstellungstheorie der Sprache', *Indogerm. Forsch.* 53, 1935.
R. DESCARTES, *Discours de la méthode*, Leyden, 1637.
O. DITTRICH, *Die Probleme der Sprachpsychologie*, 1913.
H. DRIESCH, *Der Vitalismus als Geschichte und als Lehre*, 1905.
— *Philosophie des Organischen*, 1908.
E. DUBOIS, 'De beteekenis der groote schedelcapaciteit van Pithecanthropus erectus', *Proc. Kon. Ned. Akad. v. Wetenschappen*, Amsterdam, 1920.
H. DUYKER, *Extralinguale elementen in de spraak*, Amsterdam, 1946.
K. ESCHERICH, *Die Ameise*, 1917.
R. EISLER, *Wörterbuch der philosophischen Begriffe*, 4. Aufl., 1930.

O. Funke, *Studien zur Geschichte der Sprachphilosophie,* 1927.
— *Innere Sprachform,* 1924.
K. v. Frisch, *Sprache der Bienen,* 1923.
H. Furness, 'Observations on the mentality of the Chimpanzee and Orang-Outans', *Proc. Amer. Phil. Soc.,* Philadelphia, 1916.
S. Freud, *Vorlesungen zur Einführung in die Psychoanalyse,* Ges. Schriften VII, 1924.
G. von der Gabelentz, *Chinesische Grammatik,* 1881.
A. H. Gardiner, *The Theory of Speech and Language,* Oxford 1932.
R. L. Garner, *Die Sprache der Affen,* 1900.
A. S. Gatschet, *The Klamath-Language,* 1876.
A. Gehlen, *Der Mensch,* 1940.
L. Geiger, *Der Ursprung der Sprache,* 1869.
J. v. Ginneken, *La reconstruction typologique des langues archaïques de l'humanité,* 1939.
— 'Die Erblichkeit der Lautgesetze', *Indogerm. Forsch.* 45, 1927.
Goethe, *Dichtung und Wahrheit,* Buch X.
I. Goldzieher, 'Über Gebärden- und Zeichensprache bei den Arabern', *Zeitschr. für Völkerpsychologie,* 16.
J. Grimm, *Über den Ursprung der Sprache,* 1852.
A. W. de Groot, 'Phonologie und Phonetik als Funktionswissenschaften', *Travaux du Cercle Linguistique de Prague.* IV.
— *De Nederlandsche zinsintonatie in het licht der structureele taalkunde. De Nieuwe Taalgids.*
N. Hartmann, *Das Problem des geistigen Seins,* 1933.
H. Head, *Aphasia and Kindred Disorders of Speech,* 1926.
J. G. Herder, *Der Ursprung der Sprache,* 1770.
K. Heřman, *Die Anfänge der menschlichen Sprache.* 1936.
Th. Hobbes, Elementorum philosophiae, Sectio secunda: De homine, London 1658.
A. M. Hocart, 'Mana', *Man.* 14, 1914.
H. Höffding, *Psychologie,* Leipzig, 1912.
R. Hönigswald, *Philosophie und Sprache,* 1937.
J. Huizinga, *De wetenschap der geschiedenis,* Haarlem, 1937.
W. v. Humboldt, 'Über das verg. Sprachstudium', *Abh. d. k. preuss. Akad. d. Wiss.* Berlin, 1820.
— *Über die Verschiedenheit des menschlichen Sprachbaues,* Berlin, 1836.
— *Über den Dualis,* Ges. Werke, VI.
E. Husserl, *Logische Untersuchungen* I and II, 1922.
— *Meditations Cartésiennes,* 1931.
O. Jespersen, *Language,* London, 1924.
— *Sprogets Oprindelse,* 1882.
— *Progress of Language,* 1894.
Fr. Jodl, *Lehrbuch der Psychologie,* 1903.
G. Kafka, 'Verstehende Psychologie und Psychologie des Verstehens', *Ztschr. f. Psych.* 65, 1928.
Fr. Kainz, *Psychologie der Sprache,* I and II, 1943.

G. Kautsky, *Sprachbestandsaufnahmen im Wiener psychol. Institut.*

A. Keith, *The Antiquity of Man*, 1920.

W. N. and L. A. Kellogg, *The Ape and the Child*, New York, 1933.

H. Klaatsch, Das Werden der Menschheit, 1936.

W. Köhler, *Intelligenzprüfungen an Anthropoiden*, 1918.

N. Kohts, *Untersuchung über die Erkenntnisfähigkeit des Schimpansen*, Moscow, 1923.

G. A. da Laguna, *Speech. Its Functions and Development*, New Haven, 1927.

H. Lamer, *Wörterbuch der Antike*, 1933.

J. v. Laziczius, 'Probleme der Phonologie'. *Ungarische Jahrbücher*, 15.

A. Lehmann, *Aberglaube und Zauberei*, Stuttgart, 1908.

G. W. v. Leibniz, *Nouveaux Essais sur l'entendement humain*, 1765.

H. Lévy-Bruhl, *Les fonctions mentales dans les sociétés inférieures*, Paris, 1922.

J. Locke, An Essay Concerning Human Understanding, London, 1690.

H. Lotze, *Kleine Schriften*, Bd. I, 1885.

— *Mikrokosmos*, II, Leipzig, 1869.

M. MacGee, *Primitive Numbers*, 1911.

Madvig, *Om Sprogets Väsen, Udvikling og Liv*, Copenhagen, 1842.

H. Maier, *Psychologie des emotionalen Denkens*, 1908.

A. Marty, *Untersuchungen zur Grundlegung der allgemeinen Grammatik und Sprachphilosophie*, Halle, 1908.

— *Über den Ursprung der Sprache*, 1875.

— *Gesammelte Schriften*, 1916.

Fr. Mauthner, *Kritik der Sprache*, Stuttgart, 1921.

C. Meinhof, 'Ergebnisse der afrikanischen Sprachforschung,' *Arch. f. Anthropologie*, IX.

L. Noiré, *Der Ursprung der Sprache*, 1877.

C. K. Ogden and I. A. Richards, *The Meaning of Meaning*, London, 1930.

M. Palágyi, *Naturphilosophische Vorlesungen*, 1924.

A. Pannekoek, 'Anthropogenese', *K. Ned. Akad. v. Wetensch.*, 1945.

H. Paul, *Prinzipien der Sprachgeschichte*, Halle, 1920.

W. P. Pillsbury and C. L. Meader, *The Psychology of Language*, New York, 1928.

J. Piaget, *Le langage et la pensée*, Neuchâtel, 1923.

— 'Langage et pensée', *Archives de psychologie*, 1923.

P. M. Plancquaert S. J., *Les sociétés secrètes chez les Bayaka*, 1930.

Plato, *Kratylos.*

A. Portmann, *Biologische Fragmente zu einer Lehre vom Menschen*, 1944.

H. J. Pos, *Inleiting tot de taalwetenschap*, Haarlem, 1926.

W. Preyer, *Die Seele des Kindes*, 1904.

P. Regnaud, *Origine et philosophie du langage*, 1887.

— *Origine et philosophie du langage ou principes de linguistique indoeuropéenne*, 1889.

A. Reichling, S. J., *Het woord*, Nijmegen, 1935.

E. Renan, *De l'origine du langage*, Paris, 1859.

G. Révész, *Inleiding tot de muziekpsychologie*, Amsterdam, 1944; *Einleitung in die Musikpsychologie*, Bern, 1946.

230   The Origin and Prehistory of Language

G. Révész, 'Der Ursprung der Musik', *Intern. Zeitschr. f. Ethnographie*, Bd. 40, 1941.

— 'Denken, Sprechen und Arbeiten', *Archivio di psicologia, neurologia, psichiatria*, 1940.

— *De menschelijke Hand*, Amsterdam, 1942; *Die menschliche Hand*, Basel, 1944.

— Het probleem van deb oorsprong der taal. *Nederl. Tijdschrift voor Psychologie* VIII, 1940.

— 'Das Problem des Ursprungs der Sprache', *Proc. Kon. Ned. Akademie van Wetenschappen*, Amsterdam, Vol. XLV, 1942.

— 'La fonction sociologique de la main humaine et de la main animale', *Journ. de Psychologie*, 1938.

— *Die Formenwelt des Tastsinnes*, The Hague, 1937.

— 'Die menschlichen Kommunikationsformen und die sog. Tiersprache', *Proc. Kon. Ned. Akademie van Wetenschappen*, Amsterdam. Vol. XLIII, 1940.

E. G. Sarris, 'Sind wir berechtigt, vom Wortverständnis des Hundes zu sprechen?' *Beiheft der Zeitschrift f. angew. Psychologie*, 62, 1931.

F. de Saussure, *Cours de linguistique générale*, Paris, 1922.

J. C. Scaliger, *De causis linguae latinae*, 1540.

Fr. v. Schlegel, *Philosophie der Sprache*, 1830.

Josef Schmidt, *Die Sprache und die Sprachen*, Budapest, 1923.

A. Schopenhauer, *Die Welt als Wille und Vorstellung*, 1819.

H. Schuchardt, 'Das Baskische und die Sprachwissenschaft', *Sitzungsberichte d. kaiserl. Akad. d. Wiss.* Vienna, 202-204, 1925.

Schuchardt-Brevier, *Ein Vademekum der allg. Sprachwissenschaft*. Ed. Leo Spitzer, 1928.

O. Selz, *Zur Psychologie des produktiven Denkens*, Bonn, 1922.

E. Smith, *The Search for Man's Ancestors*, 1931.

H. Spencer, *Essays*, London, 1858.

— *Principles of Psychology*, 4th Ed., 1899.

H. Steinthal, *Abriss der Sprachwissenschaft*, 1871.

— *Der Ursprung der Sprache*, 1851.

— *Grammatik, Logik und Psychologie*, 1835.

G. Stern, *Meaning of Change of Meaning*, Göteborg, 1931.

W. Stern, *Psychologie der frühen Kindheit*, Leipzig, 1930.

— *Die Kindersprache*, Leipzig, 1922.

C. Stumpf, 'Eigenartige sprachliche Entwicklung eines Kindes', *Zeitschift für pädag. Psychol.*, 3, 1901.

Süssmilch, *Beweis, dass die erste Sprache ihren Ursprung allein vom Schöpfer erhalten habe*, 1767.

E. B. Taylor, 'Origin of language', *Fortnightly Review*, 1866.

Tchang Tcheng-Ming, *L'écriture chinoise et le geste humain*, Paris, 1938.

R. Thurnwald, 'Psychologie des primitiven Menschen'. *Hand. d. vgl. Psychol.* I, 1922.

D. Tiedemann, *Kritik einer Erklärung des Ursprungs der Sprache*, 1777.

Torrenel, *Comparative grammar of the South-African Bantu-Languages*.

N. S. Trubetzkoy, *Grundzüge der Phonologie*, Prague, 1939.

H. Vaihinger, *Die Philosophie des Als Ob*, 1923.

K. Vossler, *Die Sprache als Schöpfung und Entwicklung*, 1905.

G. Vico, *Scienza nuova*, 1725.

H. de Vries, *Species and Varieties*, Chicago, 1905.

— *Die Mutationen in der Erblichkeitslehre*, Berlin, 1912.

R. Vuyk, 'Wijzen en spreken in de ontwikkeling van het kleine kind', *Ned. Tijdschrift* v. *Wijsbegeerte en Psychologie*, 1940.

E. Wasmann, S. J., *Vgl. Studien über das Seelenleben der Ameisen*, 1900.

H. Werner, *Grundfragen der Sprachphysiognomik*, 1932.

— *Einführung in die Entwicklungspsychologie*, 1933.

D. Westermann, *Festschrift für Meinhof*, 1927.

— *Grammatik der Ewe-Sprache*, 1907.

— *Die Sudansprachen*, 1911.

W. D. Whitney, *Life and Growth of Language*, 1875.

W. Wundt, *Elemente der Völkerpsychologie*, Leipzig, 1912.

— *Die Sprache*, I, II, Leipzig, 1912.

— *Sprachgeschichte und Sprachpsychologie*, Leipzig, 1901.

— *Logik*, 1922.

R. M. Yerkes, *Great Apes*, 1929.

— and B. W. Learned, *Chimpanzee Intelligence and its Vocal Expressions*, 1925.

SOME WRITINGS OF THE AUTHOR

Sense Perception

Grundlegung der Tonpsychologie, Leipzig, Veit und Comp., 1912.

Die Formenwelt des Tastsinnes, I—II, The Hague, Martinus Nijhoff, 1937.

Die menschliche Hand, eine psychologische Studie, Basel, 1944.

'Über Farbenblindheit', *Ung. Naturw. Rundschau*, 1907.

'Über Orthosymphonie' (with P. v. Liebermann), *Z. f. Psychol.* 48, 1908; 'Beiträge für Akustik und Musikwissenschaft', 4, edited by C. Stumpf; *Monatsschrift f. Ohrenheilkunde*, 10, 1908.

'Nachweis, dass in den Tonempfindungen zwei voneinander unabhängige Eigenschaften zu unterscheiden sind', *K. ges. d. Wissenschaft*, Göttingen, 1912.

'Über die beiden Arten des absoluten Gehörs', *Z. d. intern. Musikgesellschaft*, Jahrg. 14, 1912.

'Die binaurale Tonmischung' (with P. v. Lievermann). *Z. f. Psychol.* 69, 1914.

'Zur Geschichte der Zweikomponententheorie in der Tonpsychologie', *Z. f. Psychol.* 99, 1926.

'Psychologische Analyse der Störungen im taktilen Erkennen, *Z. f. d. ges. Neurol. und Psychiatrie*, 115, 1928.

'System der optischen und taktilen Raumtäuschungen, *Kon. Akad. v. Wetenschappen*, Amsterdam, Proc. Vol. XXXII, No. 8, 1929; *Zeitschr. f. Psychologie* 131, 1934.

'The problem of space with particular emphasis on specific sensory spaces', *Amer. Journ. of Psychol.*, Vol. 50, 1937.

'Gibt es einen Hörraum?' *Acta Psychologica*, III, 1937.

Optik und Haptik, Studium Generale, Springer, Heidelberg, 1956 (Posthumous).
The Human Hand, Routledge & Kegan Paul, London, 1956 (Posthumous).

Linguistic Psychology

'Die Sprache', *Kon. Akad. v. Wetenschappen*, Amsterdam, Proc. Vol. XLIII, No. 8, 1940.
'Die menschlichen Kommunikationsformen und die sog. Tiersprache, *Kon. Akad. v. Wetenschappen*, Amsterdam, Proc. Vol. XLIII, No. 9/10; XLIV, No. I, 1940/1941.
'De l'origine du langage', Centenaire de Th. Ribot, Paris, 1939. (*Journ. de Psychologie.*)
'Denken und Sprechen', *Acta Psychologica*, Vol. X, 1-2, 1954.
'The Psychogenetic Foundation of Language', *Lingua*, Vol. IV, 1954.

The Psychology of Talent

Das frühzeitige Auftreten der Begabung und ihre Erkennung, Leipzig, A. Barth, 1921.
'De ongedeeldheid der begaafdheidsvormen', *Alg. Nederl. Tijdschr. v. Wijsbeg. en Psychol.* 32, 1938.
'The indivisibility of mathematical talent', *Acta Psychologica*, V, 1940.
De creative begaafdheid, 1946.
'Beziehung zwischen musikalischer und mathematischer Begabung', Schweiz, *Zeitschr. für Psychologie*, 1946.
Talent und Genie, A. Francke, Bern, 1952.
'Age and Achievement', *The Hibbert Journal*, 1955.

Child Psychology

'Expériences sur la mémoire topographique et sur la découverte d'un système chez les enfants', *Arch. de Psychologie*, 18, 1923.
'Recherches de psychologie comparée. Reconnaissance d'un principe', *Arch. néerl. de physiol.* 8, 1923.

The Psychology of Art and Music

Die Formenwelt des Tastsinnes, Bd. II, Den Haag, Martinus Nijhoff, 1937.
The Psychology of a Musical Prodigy, London, Kegan Paul, Trench, Trubner & Co., Ltd., 1925.
Inleiding tot de Muziekpsychologie, Amsterdam, Noord-Hollandsche Uitgevers Mij, 1944 and 1946; *Einleitung in die Musikpsychologie*, Bern, A. Francke, 1946.
Kunst der blinden Bildhauer, Congrès international d'esthétique, Paris, 1937.
'Der Ursprung der Musik', *Intern. Archiv. f. Ethnologie*, 40, 1941.
'Das musikalische Wunderkind', *Zeitschr. f. pädag. Psychol.*, 1916.
'Prüfung der Musikalität', *Zeitschr. f. Psychol.* 85, 1920, und *Festschrift für G. E. Müller*, 1920.

Social Psychology

Das Schöpferisch-persönliche und das Kollektive in ihrem kulturhistorischen Zusammenhang. Tübingen, J. C. B. Mohr, 1933.
'Sozialpsychologische Beobachtungen an Affen', *Zeitschr. f. Psychol.*, 118, 1930.
Die soziobiologische Funktion der menschlichen und tierischen Hand. XI. Congrès intern. de Psychologie, Paris 1937.
'Blindenpsychologie.' (In: *Het persoonlijke en sociale leven der blinden*), Stenfert Kroese, Leiden, 1955.
Psychology and Art of the Blind, Longmans, London, 1950.

Animal Psychology

'Experimentelle Studien zur vergleichenden Psychologie', *Z. f. angew. Psychol.* 18, 1921.
'Expériences sur la mémoire topographique et sur la découverte d'un système chez des enfants et des singes inférieurs', *Arch. de Psychologie*, 18, 1923.
'Experiments on Animal Space Perception', *British Journ. of Psychology*, 14, 1924.
'Experiments on Abstraction in Monkeys', *Journ. of Comparative Psychology*, 5, 1925.
'La fonction sociologique de la main humaine et de la main animale', *Journ. de Psychologie*, 1938.
'Die sog. Tiersprache', *Kon. Ned. Akad. v. Wetenschappen*, Amsterdam, Proc. Vol. XLIII, 1940.

INDEX